for AQA 'A'

Psychology AS

The Exam Companion

Mike Cardwell • Cara Flanagan

OXFORD
UNIVERSITY PRESS

OXFORD
UNIVERSITY PRESS

Great Clarendon Street, Oxford OX2 6DP

Oxford University Press is a department of the University of Oxford.
It furthers the University's objective of excellence in research, scholarship, and
education by publishing worldwide in

Oxford   New York

Auckland   Cape Town   Dar es Salaam   Hong Kong   Karachi   Kuala Lumpur   Madrid
Melbourne   Mexico City   Nairobi   New Delhi   Shanghai   Taipei   Toronto

With offices in

Argentina   Austria   Brazil   Chile   Czech Republic   France   Greece   Guatemala
Hungary   Italy   Japan   Poland   Portugal   Singapore   South Korea   Switzerland
Thailand   Turkey   Ukraine   Vietnam

Oxford is a registered trade mark of Oxford University Press in the UK and in certain
other countries

British Library Cataloguing in Publication Data

Data available

ISBN 978 019 912982 9

10 9 8 7 6 5 4

Printed by Bell & Bain Ltd, Glasgow

Paper used in the production of this book is a natural, recyclable product made from
wood grown in sustainable forests. The manufacturing process conforms to the
environmental regulations of the country of origin.

Acknowledgements

Project development: Rick Jackman (Jackman Publishing Solutions Ltd)
Editorial management and layout: GreenGate Publishing Services, Tonbridge
Design: Nigel Harriss
Cover design: Patricia Briggs & Chris Cardwell
Cover photography: Chris Cardwell; © Zipo/Fotolia.com

Credits

Fotolia: p.12(t) © Oleg Kozlov; p.12(b) © Seb_compiegne; p.13 © Ioannis Kounadeas.

AQA examination questions are reproduced by permission of the Assessment and
Qualification Alliance.

MIX
Paper from
responsible sources
FSC® C007785
www.fsc.org

Contents

Where are the research methods questions?

You'll find them embedded in every chapter – in the same way that they are embedded throughout the AS exams.

Introduction

THIRD EDITION
for AQA 'A'

Psychology AS

*The Complete Companion
Student Book*

Matches the revised specification first examined from January 2012

Mike Cardwell • Cara Flanagan   OXFORD

This book is part of our 'Companion' series, and shares the same philosophy of providing a companion to help turn your understanding of psychology into even better exam performance.

There are three main aims of this book:

- We have tried to provide a fairly comprehensive bank of exam-style questions for students taking the AQA (A) AS level examination. The questions for this exam are intended (by the exam board) to be unpredictable, so this question bank is a selection of possible questions. On the next few pages we have described potential question styles and have represented these throughout the book.

- We have provided student answers for most of the questions, often a 'good' and a 'not so good' answer. The accompanying Examiner's comments and marks are intended to help you realise where students typically go wrong and lose unnecessary marks, and where marks could be gained. The Examiner's comments should also show you how answers can be improved. The key point is that you shouldn't try to memorise the answers – you should use the insights we have provided to enable you to tackle whatever questions come up.

- At the end of each chapter are some extra questions for you to use in preparation for your exams.

The AS exams

There are two AS exams: Unit 1 (PSYA1) and Unit 2 (PSYA2).

☆ In each exam every question will be compulsory.

☆ You will have one-and-a-half hours to complete the paper.

☆ The total score for each paper will be 72 marks.

Unit 1 PSYA1
Cognitive psychology, Developmental psychology and Research methods

The exam paper is divided into **two** sections, each worth 36 marks.

There will be **one** 12-mark extended writing question on this paper. There may be further extended writing questions worth 6, 8 or 10 marks. Quality of written communication is assessed in this question.

Section A Cognitive psychology and Research methods

In this section you will be asked questions on the topic of memory and also be given some brief descriptions of hypothetical or real studies of memory and asked research methods questions in relation to these studies.

Section B Developmental psychology and Research methods

In this section you will be asked questions on the topic of attachment and will again be asked research methods questions about hypothetical or real studies of attachment.

Unit 2 PSYA2
Biological psychology, Social psychology and Individual differences

This exam paper is divided into **three** sections, each worth 24 marks.

There will be *at least* **one** 12-mark extended writing question on this paper. There is no guarantee as to which section it will appear in. There may be further extended writing questions worth 6, 8 or 10 marks. Quality of written communication is assessed in this question.

Section A Biological psychology

Most of the questions in this section will be on the topic of stress. About 4 marks are allocated to a question or questions on 'how science works' in relation to stress research.

Section B Social psychology

This follows the same pattern as section A – mainly questions on the topic of social influence but there are also about 4 marks' worth of questions on 'how science works', this time related to social influence research.

Section C Individual differences

This also follows the same pattern as section A – mainly questions on the topic of individual differences plus there may be some questions on 'how science works', this time related to abnormality.

How science works (research methods)

The theme 'how science works' is a key feature of the psychology examination. This includes your knowledge of the methods that psychologists use when conducting research, and the strengths/limitations of these methods. It also includes the issues of reliability, validity and ethics.

In all areas of the specification you need to be prepared to answer questions related to the topic of 'how science works' but the questions will be more detailed on Unit 1. This is because, when you take Unit 1, it is expected that you will have covered the full research methods specification (see pages 126–127). If you study Unit 2 before Unit 1 you will not have covered the full research methods specification and, therefore, the exam board bears this in mind when setting 'how science works' questions on Unit 2 – see the examples on page 7.

What is examined?

There isn't a comprehensive list of all the questions that can be asked in the AS psychology exam. If questions are completely predictable then students tend to focus on memorising answers rather than getting a good understanding of the specification content. The unpredictable nature of the questions should therefore encourage you to focus on the content of the specification rather than being overly concerned with what questions might be asked.

As long as you have fully covered the specification you should be able to answer the questions – but remember that the specification doesn't just include the topic areas (which we have listed on the chapter opening page of each chapter). The specification also states the following:

Candidates will be expected to:

- Develop knowledge and understanding of **concepts, theories and studies** in relation to all areas studied.
- Develop skills of **analysis, evaluation and application** in relation to all areas studied.
- Develop knowledge and understanding of **ethical issues** associated with all areas studied.
- Develop knowledge and understanding of **research methods** in all areas studied, through:
  - Undertaking **practical research activities** involving collection, analysis and interpretation of **qualitative and quantitative data**.
  - **Analysis and evaluation of studies** relevant to all areas studied.

Kinds of AS exam questions

Having said that the exam questions are not predictable, we have in this book nevertheless tried to make them predictable! We have looked through the AS exam papers and produced a breakdown of the *kinds* of questions that you are likely to encounter. But remember this is not a definitive list and the main aim of this book is to encourage you to reflect on how to produce effective answers to whatever questions you may be asked.

Question type	Example	Advice

Recognition question	6 The following statements are all related to conformity.
	  A Doing what the group does in order to be liked by them.
	  B Doing what the group does because we don't know what else to do.
	  C Going along with the group even if we do not really agree with what they are doing.
	  D Going along with the group because we accept their beliefs and attitudes into our own cognitions.
	In the tale below, write which statement, A, B, C, or D, describes each type of conformity.
	
	Type of conformity / **Statement**
	Internalisation
	Compliance
	(2 marks)
	
	AQA, January 2009, Unit 2
		Questions like this can sometimes be quite easy and sometimes quite difficult! It is worth taking extra time to make sure you have selected the right answer rather than rushing and throwing away valuable marks.
		
		It is worth reading the question several times and making sure you follow the instructions. Candidates often lose marks because they haven't followed the instructions, for example, selecting three answers where only two were required. In such cases you will simply get 0 marks.

Short description question	What is meant by the term attachment? *(2 marks)* AQA, June 2009, Unit 1 Cognitive interviews have been developed to improve witness recall. Identify and explain **two** techniques used in the cognitive interview. *(3 marks + 3 marks)* AQA, June 2009, Unit 1 Outline the main features of the pituitary-adrenal system. *(3 marks)* AQA, January 2010, Unit 2 Outline what is involved in Cognitive Behavioural Therapy. *(3 marks)* AQA, January 2009, Unit 2	The number of marks available indicates the depth required in your answer.* The term 'identify' means 'just give a simple answer'. The term 'explain' requires further elaboration. Questions will relate to exact content in the specification, such as 'attachment' and the 'pituitary-adrenal system'. Know your specification. Always read the questions carefully – as this one did not require a definition of CBT, credit was only given for the procedures of how it is done.

CONTINUED...

* The amount of space available (lines in the answer booklet) also indicates how much to write. There may also be 'extra space' provided, but this is extra space in case you have gone wrong – don't feel you have to use it.

Question types	Example	Advice
Longer description question	Outline the main features of the multi-store model. *(6 marks)* AQA, January 2009, Unit 1 Explain how locus of control influences independent behaviour. *(4 marks)* AQA, June 2010, Unit 2 Explain how social influence research helps us to understand social change. *(6 marks)*	Again, the number of marks available gives you guidance about how much to write. You should avoid including any evaluation, which may not be creditworthy unless specifically asked for.
Research studies	Questions about research studies have a number of important features. Ignore these features at your peril because you will lose valuable marks.	
	'How' questions Outline how **one** research study investigated the accuracy of eyewitness testimony (EWT). *(4 marks)* AQA, January 2009, Unit 1 Outline **one** method that psychologists have used to study conformity. *(2 marks)* AQA, June 2009, Unit 2	Questions that say 'how' are asking for procedures only. There will be no credit for aims or findings/conclusions. Always be aware that the actual wording may be different – the second question on the left is essentially a 'how' question, worded differently.
	'Show' questions Describe what research has shown about the effect of the age of witnesses on the accuracy of eyewitness testimony. *(6 marks)* AQA, January 2010, Unit 1	Questions that say 'show' are asking for findings and/or conclusions only. Information about procedures would gain no credit.
	'Anything goes' questions Disruption of attachment can occur when children experience separation from their attachment figure during their early childhood. Outline **one** study of the effects of disruption on attachment. AQA, June 2009, Unit 1 *(4 marks)*	When questions don't say 'how' or 'show' then procedures/findings/conclusions are all creditworthy.
	'Research' questions Outline what research has shown about cultural variations in attachment *(4 marks)* AQA, June 2011, Unit 1 **'One study' questions** Describe **one** research study that has investigated stress-related illness and the immune system. In your answer you should include details of what was done and what was found. *(4 marks)*	There is an important difference between questions that say 'outline research' and those that say 'outline one study'. The difference is that in the former case you can describe several studies, whereas in the latter case you will only receive credit for the details of one study.
Applying knowledge	A student teacher finds it very difficult to remember pupils' names. She decides to look in a psychology book to find some useful strategies for improving her memory. Outline **one** strategy the student teacher could use, and explain why this might improve her memory for pupils' names. *(4 marks)* AQA, January 2009, Unit 1 In a hospital you are very likely to obey a nurse. However, if you meet her outside the hospital, for example in a shop, you are much less likely to obey. Using your knowledge of how people resist pressures to obey, explain why you are less likely to obey the nurse outside the hospital. *(4 marks)* AQA, January 2009, Unit 2 Hamish has a phobia of heights. This phobia has now become so bad that he has difficulty in going to his office on the third floor, and he cannot even sit on the top deck of a bus any more. He has decided to try systematic desensitisation to help him with his problem. Explain how the therapist might use systematic desensitisation to help Hamish to overcome his phobia. *(6 marks)* AQA, January 2010, Unit 2	In these questions you will be given an everyday situation (the question 'stem') and asked to use your psychological knowledge to provide an informed answer. You must make sure that your answer contains psychological knowledge but at the same time make sure you are answering the question. In the case of the first question on the left, many students wrote about memory techniques, but didn't explain how they would be used for remembering names. In the second example, many students just wrote about obedience research and failed to use their knowledge to explain the stem. Other students said 'you'd obey a nurse because she is in charge' but made no link to psychology. In the third example many students simply described the steps of systematic desensitisation and made no reference to using it with someone who has phobia. → You must engage with the question. → Your answer must demonstrate psychological knowledge.

Question types	Example	Advice
Evaluation, strengths and limitations	The behavioural approach assumes that abnormal behaviour is learnt through classical conditioning, operant conditioning and imitation. Evaluate the behavioural approach to psychopathology. *(4 marks)* AQA, June 2010, Unit 2 Explain **one or more** limitations of the working memory model. *(4 marks)*	Be guided by the number of marks available and be careful to answer the question. In the first example strengths and/or limitations are creditworthy. There is no requirement for a balanced answer. In the second example, strengths would not be creditworthy, and writing a second limitation would not be creditworthy.
Differences	Explain how a cognitive interview differs from a standard interview. *(4 marks)* AQA, January 2009, Unit 1 How does the behaviour of securely attached infants differ from that of insecurely attached infants? *(4 marks)* AQA, June 2009, Unit 1	You will only gain credit if you actually identify the difference rather than simply defining the two terms. You must be explicit in order to gain full marks. For full marks you can identify several differences (in limited detail) or focus on just one difference but elaborate this.
Short extended writing	Outline and evaluate Bowlby's explanation of attachment. *(10 marks)* 'Abnormality can be defined as deviation from social norms'. Outline and evaluate this definition of abnormality. *(6 marks)*	The terms 'discuss' or 'outline and evaluate' (or similar) signal that there are marks available for description (A01) **and** evaluation (A02). These marks are always equal (i.e. 3 + 3, 4 + 4 or 5 + 5).
Long extended writing	Outline and evaluate research into the effects of anxiety on the accuracy of eyewitness testimony. *(12 marks)* AQA, June 2009, Unit 1 Outline and evaluate **one or more** explanations of why people obey. *(12 marks)* AQA, June 2009, Unit 2 'Abnormality is very difficult to define. It can be hard to decide where normal behaviour ends and abnormal behaviour begins.' Discuss **two or more** definitions of abnormality. *(12 marks)* AQA, January 2010, Unit 2 'Psychologists have studied children who have lived in institutions such as orphanages.' Outline and evaluate research into the effects of institutional care. *(12 marks)* AQA, June 2010, Unit 1	The 12-mark extended writing question is worth 12 marks, divided equally into AO1 and AO2. If the word 'research' is used in a question it refers to studies and/or explanations/theories. Some questions say 'one or more', meaning that you choose either to write about one explanation or write about more explanations. If you do just write about one explanation you can still gain full marks if your answer is thorough. There is no requirement to write more. The same applies to questions that require 'two or more' – two is enough to gain full credit. The question may begin with a quotation. The quotation is intended to guide you; but make sure you answer the question, not the quotation. In the exam answer booklet there is space to plan this important answer – what you write here is also marked as long as you don't cross it out.
How science works – question type 1 *(which appear only on Unit 1)*	You will be given a description of a study and then a number of short questions such as: (a) What is the dependent variable in this study? *(2 marks)* (b) What experimental design was used in this study? *(1 mark)* (c) Explain **one** strength of this experimental design in the context of this study. *(2 marks)*	These questions only appear on Unit 1. Some of the questions require contextualisation, i.e. you only get full credit if you display your psychological knowledge and apply this to the study described in the exam question. For example, for (c) you would need to identify one strength and then say why it is a strength in this particular study.
How science works – question type 2 *(which appear on Units 1 and 2)*	How have psychologists investigated the relationship between stress and the immune system? *(4 marks)* AQA, June 2009, Unit 2 Outline **one** limitation of conducting obedience research outside a laboratory setting. *(2 marks)* AQA, January 2011, Unit 2 'Both life changes and daily hassles are often measured using questionnaires.' Give **two** limitations of using questionnaires. *(2 marks + 2 marks)* AQA, January 211, Unit 2	On both Units 1 and 2 there are questions on 'how science works', i.e. about the methods psychologists use when conducting research, the strengths/limitations of these methods as well as issues of reliability, validity and ethics. If you are asked about the strengths/limitations of a research method in the context of a topic such as stress, then you should contextualise your answer. This means making reference to stress research in your answer, e.g. considering problems faced by Holmes and Rahe (see for example page 77).

How your answers are marked

Examiners mark your answers using **mark schemes**. These mark schemes contain some guidance for examiners and information about how to award marks. Examiners only award marks, they do not grade your answers as A, B, C, etc.

The mark schemes vary slightly from question to question depending on specific demands, but on this page we have presented a sample of what they look like for the short mark questions and on the facing page we have summarised the key criteria for extended writing questions.

You can look at the mark schemes yourself on the AQA website (see http://web.aqa.org.uk/exams-office/exams-guidance/qp-ms_finder.php?id=01.

AQA mark scheme for 2 mark question

What is meant by the term *attachment*?   *(2 marks)*

AQA, January 2010, Unit 1

Mark scheme

Attachment can be defined as an emotional relationship between two people in which each seeks closeness and feels more secure when in the presence of the attachment figure.

Allocation of marks

One mark for a brief outline, such as 'an emotional bond'.
Second mark for some elaboration.

AQA mark scheme for 4-mark question

Outline how **one** research study investigated the accuracy of eyewitness testimony.   *(4 marks)*

AQA, January 2009, Unit 1

Mark scheme

Answers can refer to any research study relating to eyewitness testimony. This may be by naming a relevant study, or by identifying the study in some other way. Likely research would include a number of studies by Loftus, including those into the role of leading questions, and Yuille and Cutshall (1986) who investigated evidence from an actual crime. Studies into factors affecting the accuracy of EWT including anxiety (e.g. weapon focus) or age of witnesses would also be relevant. Flin *et al.* (1992) used a staged event and compared deterioration of children's and adults' memories over time, while Karpel *et al.* (2001) showed a video of a robbery and compared information given by young adults (17–25) with that given by older adults (65–85). Allport and Postman's (1947) study using a picture of two men arguing is relevant to EWT.

However, Bartlett's research using a story or simple drawings is not relevant.

Allocation of marks

One mark for a basic outline of the method, e.g. 'In Loftus and Palmer's study, participants were asked questions about a film'. A further 3 marks for accurate details.

AQA mark scheme for 4-mark question

QUESTION STEM Sandy and Vandita play for the same netball team. Two weeks ago, while playing in a competition, they both grazed their elbows. Vandita's wound is healing well, but Sandy's wound is taking much longer to heal. Sandy is very worried about the plans for her wedding and her forthcoming house move.

Using your knowledge of psychology, explain why Sandy's wound is taking longer to heal than Vandita's.

AQA, January 2010, Unit 2   *(4 marks)*

Mark scheme

There are a variety of different ways to answer this question: credit should be given to appropriate alternative answers.

Candidates could focus on critical life events as well as the underlying biological mechanisms. Research has shown that stress reduces the effectiveness of the immune system. People experiencing long-term stress are more likely to become ill and to take longer to heal than those who are not stressed. Sandy is experiencing two events that are on the SRRS and are known to be major stressors.

Allocation of marks

One mark for a basic statement of the relationship between stress and the immune system and a further 3 marks for elaboration of this. For full marks, the elaboration must be linked to Sandy's situation. Credit can also be given to research evidence used to support/illustrate the explanation.

4 marks Effective explanation

Effective explanation that demonstrates sound knowledge of the effects of stress and the immune system as applied to Sandy's wound healing.

3 marks Reasonable explanation

Reasonable application of knowledge to question stem.

2 marks Basic explanation

Basic explanation of the topic.

1 mark Rudimentary

Rudimentary, muddled explanation, demonstrating very little knowledge.

0 marks

No creditworthy material.

Assessment objectives AO1, AO2 and AO3

There are three assessment objectives:

Assessment objective 1 (AO1) = description, knowledge and understanding.

Assessment objective 2 (AO2) = evaluation, analysis and application of knowledge.

Assessment objective 3 (AO3) = how science works, e.g. explaining, interpreting, and evaluating research methods, ethical issues, etc.

In general you do not actually need to worry about these assessment objectives – simply answer the exam questions.

The only time you do need to think about AO1 and AO2 is for the extended writing questions.

These questions start with words such as 'Discuss' or 'Outline and evaluate'.

This means you need to provide description (AO1) and evaluation (AO2) in equal measure.

Past exam papers and mark schemes

You can study past exam questions and look how they were marked by consulting the AQA website.

However, bear in mind that from January 2012 there were some changes to the specification. This means that past exam papers contain some questions that would no longer be set. The contents of this book match the new specification.

Also remember that exams do evolve and there are often changes to the rules for marking. Use our blog to keep you up to date: www.oxfordschoolblogs.co.uk/psychcompanion/blog.

AQA mark scheme for extended writing questions

Questions worth 8, 10 or 12 marks are split into 50% AO1 and 50% AO2.
AO1 and AO2 are marked separately using the criteria given below.

Abbreviated mark scheme for extended writing questions

Marks			Description (AO1 – assessment objective 1)		
12 mark questions	10 mark questions	8 mark questions	Detail	Knowledge and understanding	Selection of appropriate material
6	5	4	Accurate and reasonably detailed	Sound	Appropriate
5–4	4–3	3	Less detailed but generally accurate	Relevant	Some evidence
3–2	2	2	Basic, lacks detail and may be muddled	Some relevant	Little evidence
1	1	1	Very brief/flawed	Very little	Largely or wholly inappropriate
0	0	0	No creditworthy material		

Marks			Evaluation (AO2 – assessment objective 2)		
12 mark questions	10 mark questions	8 mark questions	Use of material	Range of issues and/or evidence	Expression of ideas, specialist terms, spelling, etc.
6	5	4	Effective use of material to address the question and provide informed commentary and evaluation	Broad range in reasonable depth or narrower range in greater depth	Clear and good range, few errors
5–4	4–3	3	Reasonable commentary and evaluation but material not always used effectively	Range in limited depth or narrower range in greater depth	Reasonable, some errors
3–2	2	2	Basic commentary and evaluation of research	Superficial consideration of restricted range	Lacks clarity, some specialist terms, errors
1	1	1	Rudimentary commentary and evaluation	Just discernible	Poor, few specialist terms
0	0	0	No creditworthy material		

Writing good exam answers

One of the key aims of this book is to demonstrate how to produce good exam answers. It's not just about knowing which questions are likely to come up but also understanding what is required in your answers. Throughout this book we have shown a mix of good and not so good answers in order to show how marks are gained and lost.

You can see from the mark schemes on the previous spread that two key features of good exam answers are **detail** and **elaboration**.

Detail

What is detail? It is the addition of specific information. It does not mean repeating the same thing with slightly different wording. Saying the same thing over and over doesn't gain extra marks.

You need to understand what 'detail' means. Consider this question and answer:

> **Question: Outline how one research study investigated the accuracy of eyewitness testimony.** *(4 marks)*
>
> AQA, January 2009, Unit 1

Answer: In one study, participants were asked questions about a film.

This answer is accurate but lacks detail. What details could we add?

- We could say 'Loftus and Palmer' instead of 'one study'. You don't always have to write more to provide detail.
- We could give an example of the questions that were asked, 'Participants were asked questions such as "How fast were the cars going when they hit each other?"'
- We could give more precise information about the film, 'There were seven different films showing various traffic accidents'.

Elaboration

Elaboration means much the same as adding more detail. Once you have made your initial point, you need to provide further information in support. This is particularly important when making a critical point either in an essay or in answer to a question such as 'Describe **one** limitation of case studies'.

Our answer to elaboration is the **three-point rule**.

1. **Identify** your point (e.g. a strength or limitation).
2. **Justify** it (present evidence to explain why it is a strength or limitation in this particular instance).
3. **Explain** it (How does this affect the topic being evaluated? Is this good or bad for it and why?).

For example, if your criticism of a study is Loftus and Palmer's study lacked ecological validity. then you have simply identified it. You need to justify your claim in this context (e.g. They tested eyewitness testimony by showing videos of car accidents, which is not the same experience as witnessing a real car accident. In a real accident you would probably be more scared and might also be distracted by other things going on.). Finally, you need to indicate why ecological validity is a problem in this study (e.g. This means we can't reliably generalise from this study to real world EWT, which limits its explanatory usefulness.).

Contextualisation

The questions we call 'applying your knowledge' require you to contextualise your answers. Consider the question about Hamish at the bottom of page 6:

> **Explain how the therapist might use systematic desensitisation to help Hamish to overcome his phobia.** *(6 marks)*

If you simply described the use of systematic desensitisation you will only get about half marks because the question requires that you apply your knowledge to Hamish. You must contextualise by linking your answer to the context.

The same is true in some research methods questions, such as:

> **Give one** strength of using questionnaires in stress research.

You might not get full marks if you say Questionnaires enable a researcher to collect data from a large number of participants in a relatively short space of time because you have made no mention of stress research.

Depth–breadth trade-off

The AO2 mark scheme on the previous page says a 'broad range in reasonable depth or narrower range in greater depth'. What does this mean? If you cover a broad range (breadth) of points you won't have enough time to elaborate each of them and therefore the depth will only be 'reasonable'. Alternatively you could write the same amount but cover fewer points so you will have time to elaborate them each more fully.

So you can choose breadth or depth – except if you include lots of breadth but no elaboration at all, your answer would be described as 'superficial'. So always include some elaboration – get a good balance between depth and breadth.

The same principle applies to AO1. Consider this question:

> **Describe what research has shown about the effect of the age of witnesses on the accuracy of eyewitness testimony.** *(6 marks)*
>
> AQA, January 2010, Unit 1

You could describe one conclusion and provide lots of detail (little breadth, lots of depth) or describe a number of conclusions but give little detail about each. It is best to go for a balance between breadth and depth.

Difference questions

There is a bit of a knack to answering questions that ask for a 'difference'. If you simply describe the two items you will probably only receive 1 mark.

If you make an implicit contrast (i.e. describe the same aspect of each thing) you may score 2 marks. If you add some elaboration you may receive more credit. Just writing 'whereas' won't make your 'difference' explicit. Have a look at some examples on the following pages – 16, 20, 50, 56, 86, 94, 96, 112 and 121.

Our advice

In a 6-mark description question – cover three points + detail for each.

In a 6-mark evaluation question – aim to cover three or four critical points and elaborate each.

Don't panic

A moderate level of stress is good for performance but too much can impair your ability to recall information and use it effectively in the exam. A wise student learns to control their stress before the examination, and makes frequent use of stress-management techniques, even during the revision stage and especially in the exam.

One interesting fact is that physical activity (stretching your arms or feet) reduces stress because the activity tells your body that the stressor has been dealt with and the sympathetic nervous system can therefore 'stand down', putting you in a more relaxed state.

Less is more

Examiners often observe that students who write longer answers don't necessarily get the highest marks. Strange but true.

What they tend to do is write everything they know that possibly might be relevant. Examiners only credit material that is specifically relevant to the question.

Don't try to fill every line in the answer book. Just because space is available doesn't mean it has to be filled.

Answer the question

It's what everyone always says – but candidates persist in jumping in with both feet and writing a kind of 'stream of consciousness answer'. Think before you write. Often, time spent thinking and selecting exactly what is relevant to the question is very beneficial.

FAQs

Q: Do I need to include names and dates?

A: No, you won't have marks taken away if you haven't included research names and dates. However they are a good way to beef up the detail in your answer.

It is also good to include the names of researchers so that the examiner is clear about which study you are writing about. If, for example, you are describing a study on eyewitness testimony, and you write 'Participants tried to recall what they saw after watching a film', the examiner won't know which study you are writing about and will award no marks. There must be enough information in your answer for the study to be recognised, and having the researchers' names help.

Q: Can I use bullet points?

A: The only question where your expression of ideas is marked is on the 12-mark extended writing question, so you can certainly use bullet points in any other answer. BUT – some people write only a couple of words in their bullet points, which means your answer is likely to lack detail. Bullet points are OK as long as you remember to include lots of detail in them.

Q: How many words should I write when answering a 12-mark extended writing question?

A: You should aim for about 300 words *as long as it is all focused on the question that is set*. Most students include lots of material that is not relevant, such as an introduction describing what the essay will cover. When you are revising, swap essays with a friend and delete all material that is not creditworthy so you learn to write only what is necessary.

In the exam you have about 15 minutes to write the 12-mark answer and 300–350 words is about what you can produce in that time after planning and allowing time to think about what you are writing.

Q: In an extended writing question that says 'Discuss research studies', how many research studies should I include?

A: If the question asks for research studies (plural), you must include at least two. Remember the depth–breadth trade-off – you want reasonable breadth (possibly three studies) but some detail about each of them. In a 12-mark extended writing essay we have said there will be about 300 words; so 150 words will be spent describing the research studies and about 50 words for each study should give you enough to produce 'reasonably detailed' information about each study.

If a question says '**one** study' then you will only receive marks for one study.

If a question says 'research' instead of 'research studies' then credit will be awarded for studies and/or explanations (theories).

Q: Do I have to include a conclusion for my extended writing?

No, there are no special marks for this and, in fact, what students usually write is a summary of what they have already said rather than an analysis or interpretation – which is what a conclusion should be. A summary gains no marks. A genuine conclusion would gain credit, but it is not required.

Q: If a question asks for 'one limitation of xxx' do I have to start my answer saying 'One disadvantage of xxx is'?

No, just get stuck in. Don't waste time and space writing out the question.

Effective revision

Get yourself motivated

People tend to do better when they are highly motivated. We have taught many mature students who all wished they had worked harder at school the first time around. You don't owe success to your teachers or your parents (although they would be delighted), you owe it to the person you will be ten years from now. Think what you would like to be doing in ten years and what you need to get there, and let that thought prompt you into action now. It is always better to succeed at something you may not need later than to fail at something you will need.

Work *with* your memory

In an exam it is harder to access information learned by rote. When someone feels anxious it is easier for them to recall knowledge they *understand* well. Just reading or writing out notes may do little to help you create enduring memories or to understand the content. However, if you do something with your knowledge it will increase your understanding and make it more likely that material is accessible when you need it. Psychologists call this 'deep processing' as opposed to the 'shallow processing' that takes place when you read something without really thinking about it. Constructing spidergrams or mind maps of the material, or even explaining it to someone else, involves deep processing and makes material more memorable.

Become multi-sensory

Why stick to using just one of your senses when revising? Visual learners learn best by seeing what they are learning, so make the most of text, diagrams, graphs, etc. By contrast, auditory learners learn best by listening (and talking), taking in material using their sense of hearing. You may associate more with one of these styles than the other, but actually we can make use of *both* these types of learning styles. As well as *reading* your notes and *looking* at pictures and diagrams, try *listening* to your notes and *talking* about topics with other people, and even *performing* some of the material using role play.

Short bursts are best

One of the problems with revision is that you can do too much of it (at one time that is …). As you probably know all too well, your attention is prone to wander after a relatively short period of time. Research findings vary as to the optimum time to spend revising, but 30–45 minutes at a time appears to be the norm. What should you do when your attention begins to wander? As a rule, the greater the physiological change (i.e. going for a walk rather than surfing the Internet), the more refreshed you will be when you return for your next 30–45 minute stint. There is another benefit to having frequent planned breaks – it increases the probability of subsequent recall.

Revisit regularly

Have you ever noticed that if you don't use an icon on your computer for a long time, the cunning little blighter hides it? Your computer seems to take the decision that as you are not using it regularly, it can't be that important, so neatly files it away somewhere. Your brain works in a similar way; knowledge that is not used regularly becomes less immediately accessible. The trick, therefore, is to review what you have learned at regular intervals. Each time you review material, it will take less time to recall, which will surely pay dividends later on!

Work with a friend

Although friends *can* be a distraction while you are trying to study, they can also be a very useful revision aid. Working together (what psychologists call 'collaborative learning') can aid understanding and make revision more interesting and fun. Explaining something to someone else is a useful form of deep processing (see above), and by checking and discussing each other's answers to sample questions you can practise your 'examiner skills' and therefore improve your understanding of what to put into an exam answer to earn the most marks.

And finally, write your own little book of revision notes...

Why?
1. It will save you money (because you don't have to buy a revision book).
2. It will be more effective.
3. You'll have much less to memorise.

People remember more if they have processed the material they read. For example, read the text below about ECT.

An electrode is placed above the temple of the non-dominant side of the brain, and a second in the middle of the forehead (unilateral ECT). Alternatively, one electrode is placed above each temple (bilateral ECT).

The patient is first injected with a short-acting barbiturate, so they are unconscious before the electric shock is administered, and given a nerve-blocking agent, paralysing the muscles of the body to prevent them contracting during the treatment and causing fractures. Oxygen is given to the patient, to compensate for their inability to breathe.

A small amount of electric current (approximately 0.6 amps), lasting about half a second, is passed through the brain. This current produces a seizure lasting up to one minute, which affects the entire brain.

ECT is usually given three times a week, with the patient requiring between three and 15 treatments.

Now select three key pieces of information, keeping them as short as possible. For example:

- non-dominant
- barbiturate
- 0.6 amps, half a second.

It's better if you select the points because then you are processing the information and it will be more memorable for you.

In about a week's time, see if you can remember the three bullet points AND see if you can write a sentence or two about each of them.

Your little book of revision notes should be like this – just a lot of bullet lists which will act like coat pegs when you get into the exam – you think of each bullet point one at a time and write a few sentences about it. The bullet points act like prods to get information out of your brain.

You want your own little book of revision notes to be short – so you can carry it in your pocket and whip it out in any spare moment to do some quick revision. If you look at a bullet point and think 'I haven't got a clue what that refers to', then highlight it and look it up later in your textbook to remind yourself. Next time (we promise) you will remember it.

SPECIFICATION BREAKDOWN

Specification content

Comment

Models of memory

- The multi-store model, including the concepts of encoding, capacity and duration. Strengths and limitations of the model.

- The working memory model including its strengths and limitations.

In this first part of your study of memory you will look at two explanations about how your brain deals with and stores incoming information.

The first explanation or 'model' of memory is the multi-store model (MSM). This model is about 40 years old, but is important because it has influenced our understanding of memory.

A key part of the MSM is the distinction between short- and long-term memory (STM and LTM). They differ because STM lasts a short time (duration) and can only hold a limited amount of information (capacity) whereas LTM lasts a long time and holds a potentially infinite amount of information. Information is stored in a different form (encoding) in STM and LTM, as we shall see.

The second model of memory is the 'working memory model', a slightly more recent development. The working memory (WM) model focuses on one particular area of memory – immediate or working memory. This is the part of memory which is active when you are working on a problem or remembering someone's phone number.

You need to be familiar with research evidence that supports or challenges the model, as well as strengths and limitations of the model.

Memory in everyday life

- Eyewitness testimony (EWT). Factors affecting the accuracy of EWT, including misleading information, anxiety, age of witness.

- Improving accuracy of EWT, including the use of the cognitive interview.

- Strategies for memory improvement.

Memory research has many applications in everyday life. It can be used to explain your behaviour and the behaviour of people around you. One key application is in understanding our memory about events that occurred at the time a crime was committed – details of who committed the crime, what they did and events surrounding the incident. If you are asked to provide such information this is called 'eyewitness testimony' (EWT).

The big question about EWT is whether it is accurate! It's not much use if it isn't, so psychologists have conducted many studies to try to understand the factors that increase or decrease the accuracy of EWT, and then they have tried to suggest techniques (such as the cognitive interview) which police can use to improve the accuracy of eyewitnesses' recall.

Another application of memory, which is of especial interest to students, is how to improve your memory. The final part of this chapter looks at psychological research on techniques for memory improvement.

Chapter 1

COGNITIVE PSYCHOLOGY is an area of psychology that focuses on perception, thought and memory. Cognitive psychologists believe that human behaviour can be best explained if we first understand the mental processes that underlie behaviour. It is, therefore, the study of how people learn, structure, store and use knowledge – essentially how people think about the world around them.

CHAPTER CONTENTS

Cognitive psychology: memory

The nature of memory

Question 1 Below are **six** statements about memory. Place a tick in the box next to the **three** that apply to short-term memory. *(3 marks)*

- ☑ Information tends to be encoded acoustically.
- ☑ It is a limited capacity store.
- ☐ Duration and capacity are potentially unlimited.
- ☐ Information tends to be encoded in terms of meaning.
- ☑ Information is maintained through rehearsal.
- ☐ Information is held for a very brief period, e.g. milliseconds.

Question 2 Explain what is meant by encoding in memory. *(2 marks)*

Tom's answer

This is how information is stored in memory, e.g. it might be stored in the form of pictures or in sounds.

Alice's answer

Encoding refers to the way that material is changed so it can be stored in memory, e.g. information is encoded acoustically for storage in STM.

Examiner's comments

Both answers are accurate and sufficiently detailed for the **full 2 marks**. Alice has gone above and beyond what is necessary.

Question 3 Long-term memory is said to have an infinite capacity. Explain what the term 'capacity' means in this context. *(2 marks)*

This refers to how much information can be stored in memory (i.e. very little information or an infinite amount).

Capacity refers to how much material can be stored in memory, e.g. the capacity of STM is limited but LTM is potentially unlimited.

In this case Tom's answer doesn't quite hit the spot, whereas Alice has indicated which kind of memory is limited (STM). So Tom only gets **1 mark** but Alice gets the **full 2 marks**.

Question 4 Explain what is meant by the duration of short-term memory. *(2 marks)*

How long something can be stored in memory (e.g. either for just a few seconds or many years as in the case of long-term memory).

Material in STM is held there for a very limited time. Without rehearsal it becomes unavailable after just a few seconds.

Tom has foolishly ignored the demands of the question and written about LTM. He has described duration, so only gets **1 mark**. Alice receives the **full 2 marks**.

Question 5 Explain the difference between short-term memory and long-term memory. *(4 marks)*

Short-term memory has a very limited capacity, just 7±2 items, although this capacity can be increased by chunking (e.g. telephone numbers). Long-term memory has a potentially unlimited duration, with material held for many years or forever.

STM has limited capacity and duration, and material is encoded acoustically, whereas LTM has unlimited capacity and duration and is encoded semantically. Errors in STM recall tend to be a result of acoustic similarity (e.g. glass, grass), whereas errors in LTM recall tend to be a result of semantic similarity (e.g. grass, lawn).

Alice continues her perfect streak with an excellent answer that clearly contrasts features of STM and LTM, e.g. the differences in encoding. Tom has simply described STM and described LTM – which was not the question. Furthermore he has not even included an implicit contrast because he mentions capacity for STM and duration for LTM. So **full 4 marks** to Alice and **1 out of 4 marks** to Tom.

Question 6 Psychologists have investigated encoding in memory.

    (a) Describe how **one** research study has investigated encoding in memory. *(4 marks)*

    (b) Identify **one** possible ethical issue that might arise in this study and explain why it is an issue. *(3 marks)*

(a) Baddeley (1966) found that people who were given words to remember that sounded the same tended to mix them up when recalling from STM, but tended to mix up words that had a similar meaning when asked to recall from LTM. This shows that STM uses acoustic coding and LTM uses semantic coding.

(b) A possible ethical issue is deception. Baddeley would have had to deceive his participants by using a cover story (i.e. telling them that the experiment was really about something else). This is an ethical issue because it would have caused distress when the participants realised that they had been deceived by the experimenter.

(a) Baddeley (1966) carried out an experiment to test the effect of acoustic and semantic similarity on ability to recall from STM and LTM. The IV was whether the words were either acoustically similar or dissimilar and whether they were semantically similar or dissimilar. The DV was the accuracy of recalling these words from STM and LTM. The hypothesis would have been that acoustically similar words would create more difficulties when recalling from STM and semantically similar words more difficulties when recalling from LTM.

(b) A possible ethical issue is protection from psychological harm. For example, those participants who had been in the condition where they received acoustically similar words would have experienced difficulties recalling the words. This may have caused them embarrassment about their poor performance, which is an ethical issue because it might have damaged their self-esteem.

(a) Tom has again failed to read the question. He has produced accurate and detailed findings of an appropriate study – but the question asked about 'how' encoding was investigated not what it 'showed'. There is some reference to the actual techniques (e.g. 'words…that sounded the same'), so he would receive **1 mark**. At the other extreme Alice has gone over the top and written more detail than necessary, even including the aims which are not creditworthy. She gets the **full 4 marks** but may have lost valuable time writing too much.

(b) Great answers from both Tom and Alice identifying an issue, explaining the issue in the context of Baddeley's study and, for the **full 3 marks**, explaining why this is an issue.

Question 7 Chris was asked to write his new phone number down and he wrote 01 863 77 66 24. His mother wondered why he had split it into separate bits. Using your knowledge of psychology, explain why this might help someone remember his telephone number. *(4 marks)*

Chris probably split his telephone into separate bits because this made it easier to learn. It is a lot easier to learn a telephone number when it is like this than when all the numbers follow each other in one very large number. This has been supported by psychological research.

What Chris is doing is dividing a much larger number into smaller chunks. The average capacity of STM is about 7 items, and this telephone number exceeds that capacity. However, research has shown that by dividing a large number into much smaller chunks, it is possible to increase the capacity of STM beyond its usual limit of 7 (±2) digits. This technique works better when the chunks are smaller (as here) than if the number was divided into two or three larger chunks.

Tom hasn't given much more than a common sense answer; just saying it has been supported by psychological research isn't enough – the examiner wants to know what research. Just **1 out of 4 marks** for this answer which wouldn't be sufficient to get a pass on this exam. Alice has again scored a **perfect 4 marks**.

RESEARCH METHODS QUESTION

One way to study the duration of short-term memory is to show participants a consonant syllable such as TXR or GJP and then ask them to count backwards until a buzzer sounds. At this time they are asked to recall the consonant syllable. In one study the buzzer sounded either after 6 seconds or 15 seconds. Each participant was tested twice, once after 6 seconds and once after 15 seconds.

(a) Describe the operationalised independent and dependent variables in this experiment. *(4 marks)*

Tom's answer

The operationalised IV is time and the operationalised DV is the accuracy of memory.

Alice's answer

The operationalised IV is the time elapsed after presentation before recall begins (either 6 or 15 seconds). The operationalised DV is whether the nonsense syllable is correctly recalled when the buzzer sounds.

Examiner's comments

Alice has provided fully operationalised variables whereas Tom has only identified the variables. Tom gets **2 out of 4 marks** for correct identification but Alice gets the **full 4 marks**.

(b) Is the experimental design repeated measures or independent groups? *(1 mark)*

The experimental design is repeated measures because the same participants are being used for the 6 and 15 second condition.

Repeated measures.

Both Tom and Alice have got it right, but Alice has heeded the fact that only 1 mark was available and given a simple answer. **1 mark** for both Tom and Alice.

(c) Give **one** strength and **one** limitation of using this experimental design. *(4 marks)*

One strength is that it is cheaper than other designs. A limitation is that there may be order effects. These can be overcome by using counterbalancing.

A strength is that it overcomes participant variables (e.g. age or memory ability) that might affect the outcome of the DV if different participants are used in the two conditions. A limitation is the possibility of order effects, e.g. performance on later conditions could be worse because of fatigue or better because of practice.

Tom says that a strength is they are cheaper, but why? So no marks for this and only **1 out of 4 marks** for the limitation because he has identified a limitation but failed to explain what the order effects are. The final sentence is not relevant. Alice gets the **full 4 marks** for a detailed and clear response.

(d) The reason participants had to count backwards was to prevent rehearsal of the consonant syllable to be remembered. Why was this necessary? *(3 marks)*

To prevent rehearsal of the consonant syllable to be remembered. If they didn't count backwards they would be able to rehearse it.

If they hadn't counted backwards, they would have been able to keep the memory trace active through rehearsal, and therefore it would have been impossible to measure the duration of STM.

Tom has simply repeated the question – we know that counting backwards was used to prevent rehearsal, but why? So **0 marks**. Alice has explained why in sufficient detail for the **full 3 marks** (notice she has not only given an explanation but then also explained the key point that, without doing this, you could not accurately measure the duration of memory).

Extended writing question

Outline and evaluate research on encoding and/or capacity in memory. *(12 marks)*

AO1

Miller's study on capacity is very briefly outlined in the first sentence, and further findings outlined in the second sentence.

Accurate and detailed information is given of Baddeley's study of encoding. There is no requirement to include dates but these provide 'detail', an important AO1 criteria (see page 9 for the mark scheme used for extended writing questions).

Miller (1956) reviewed research on the capacity of short-term memory. He concluded that the capacity of STM is seven items. Miller also found that people could remember the same number of 'chunks' of material, for example, they could remember seven words as easily as they could remember seven letters.

However, Cowan (2001) reviewed more recent studies on the capacity of STM and concluded that it was actually limited to just four chunks. This decreased capacity of STM was further supported by research that looked at memory for visual (rather than verbal) information. These studies (e.g. Vogel et al., 2001) confirmed that the capacity of STM was limited to about four chunks of information whatever the format.

Baddeley (1966) tested the effect of acoustic and semantic similarity on the ability to recall words encoded in STM and LTM. He found that participants had more difficulty recalling acoustically similar words when using STM but not when using LTM. He also found that participants experienced more difficulty recalling semantically similar words when using LTM, but not when using STM.

The finding that STM relies on acoustic coding has been challenged by research that suggests that STM may also use visual codes (e.g. Brandimote et al., 1992). Similarly, research has also suggested that encoding in LTM may use visual codes and even acoustic encoding for some memories. This suggests that although encoding in STM is primarily acoustic, and encoding in LTM primarily semantic, it is not exclusively so.

(244 words)

AO2

The second paragraph contains further research studies but these have been used as effective evaluation and therefore count towards the AO2 mark. Each of the critical points made is elaborated.

Further AO2 material is given in the final paragraph, again using research studies as alternative, conflicting evidence.

In the final sentence further AO2 credit is gained through interpretation ('This suggests that…'). Such interpretation is important to demonstrate that you understand what the research study shows.

Examiner's comments

The description (**AO1**) content is accurate and reasonably detailed, the knowledge and understanding displayed is 'relevant' rather than 'sound' in terms of the range of research described. There is 'some evidence' of appropriate material. The **AO1** mark belongs in the second band but gains **5 out of 6 marks** as there is a greater draw towards the very top band than the basic band below.

The **AO2** content is effective and the range of material has both reasonable depth and range. Expression of ideas is clear, therefore **6 out of 6 marks** for AO2.

Total = **11 out of 12 marks**, a clear **Grade A**.

The multi-store model

Question 1 The diagram on the right represents the multi-store model of memory. Place the following terms in the appropriate place on the diagram: *Short-term memory, long-term memory, rehearsal, sensory memory* *(4 marks)*

Rehearsal

Sensory memory → Short-term memory → Long-term memory

Question 2 Outline the key features of the multi-store model. *(6 marks)*

Bill's answer

The multi-store model (Atkinson and Shiffrin, 1968) sees memory as having three separate stores, sensory memory (SM), short-term memory (STM) and long-term memory (LTM). Information coming from the senses enters SM, where it remains for only a very brief period of time. If attention is focused on any of the information in SM, then this is transferred to STM. Information held in STM decays after a few seconds unless it is rehearsed or is displaced by new information entering STM. If information in STM is subjected to elaborative rehearsal (i.e. deeper processing), then it is passed into LTM, where it can stay more or less indefinitely. Atkinson and Shiffrin believed the more information is rehearsed in this way, the better it will be remembered in LTM.

Tamara's answer

This model has three types of memory. The three types of memory are the sensory memory store, the short-term memory store and the long-term memory store. The sensory memory holds a very small amount of information, the short-term memory holds slightly more, and finally the long-term memory is like a filing cabinet and holds an unlimited amount of information. There is lots of research to support the multi-store model, for example, some research has shown that words at the start of a list and at the end of a list are more likely to be remembered than words in the middle. This is called the primary-recency effect.

Examiner's comments

Bill's answer is reasonably detailed, he has mentioned all three stores and how information is passed from one store to the next. However, he has overlooked some basic information about what each store does and therefore his answer is 'relevant' rather than 'sound'; a rather mean **4 out of 6 marks**.

Tamara's answer also covers the three stores and provides some information about each of these – although the information isn't always helpful or accurate (for example, filing cabinets don't hold an unlimited amount of information). Tamara has tried to provide some further information in the form of a research study but has not made it clear what this study tells us about the multi-store model. Therefore this information is not creditworthy. Tamara would receive **2 out of 6 marks** for a basic answer containing only some relevant material.

Question 3 Identify and explain **two** key features of the multi-store model. *(6 marks)*

The first key feature of the MSM is a distinction between different memory stores. Sensory memory receives information from the different senses and holds it for only a very brief time. STM receives information from the sensory store, where it remains for a brief period until it decays or is displaced by other information. LTM received information from STM. It is both unlimited in capacity and effectively permanent.

The second key feature is how information is passed from one part of the model to another. Information moves from sensory memory to STM if a person's attention is focused on it. Information is maintained in STM through maintenance rehearsal (verbal repetition) and is moved to LTM through elaborative rehearsal (involving deeper processing).

One key feature is short-term memory. This has a limited capacity (about 7 items) and holds information for just a limited period (a few seconds). Information is encoded in terms of what it sounds like. This is called acoustic encoding.

A second feature is long-term memory. This has unlimited capacity and holds information indefinitely. It encodes information semantically in terms of its meaning. This means that we tend to make mistakes such as misremembering words that have the same meaning (e.g. remembering the word 'lawn' rather than the word 'grass').

There is also sensory memory, which is a third feature of this model.

Bill and Tamara have interpreted this question slightly differently, which is perfectly acceptable. Bill has identified the two key features as (1) the different stores and (2) the means of information transfer. He has then provided sufficient detail about each of these for the **full 6 marks**.

Tamara has actually identified three key features (which seems strange as the question clearly says 'two'). The examiner will read all three and give credit to the best two. Thus the third feature (which is the weakest) is ignored. Time would have been better spent elsewhere.

Tamara has provided relevant, reasonably detailed information about the two stores (STM and LTM) in terms of the characteristics of each store. (One wonders why she didn't think to include this in her answer to question 2 – but candidates do sometimes fail to recognise what is required). For this answer she would receive the **full 6 marks**.

Question 4 Identify **one** strength of the multi-store model and explain in what way this is a strength. *(3 marks)*

A strength of the multi-store model is that there is lots of evidence to support its claims, for example Baddeley's research which showed how different stores used different types of coding. This is a strength, because research evidence suggests that the basis of the model is sound.

A strength of this model is that it explains how memory works, in terms of the different stores. There are three separate stores in short-term memory, and each works in a different way.

Questions about criticisms are often worth three marks, which is why we describe the 'three-point rule' (see page 10). Bill has provided three relevant points and therefore would receive **3 marks**. Tamara has tried to elaborate her answer but ends up being quite muddled (there aren't three stores in STM), and in any case explaining how memory works isn't really a strength – it would be a strength if she argued that research shows that it accurately explains how memory works. Therefore **0 marks**.

Question 5 Psychologists are interested in applying their theories to everyday life. For example, memory researchers consider how their theories might be used to improve people's ability to remember things.

Explain **one** idea for memory improvement based on the multi-store model. *(3 marks)*

The multi-store model stresses the importance of elaborative rehearsal for passing material into LTM and so creating more long-lasting memories. This has been used in the development of mnemonic techniques such as mind maps, which help to elaborate material and so make it more memorable.

A strategy for memory improvement is to organise information, e.g. having groups of words in categories. Material that is organised is more likely to be remembered than material that isn't organised (e.g. words presented in random order without categories).

Bill has correctly started by identifying a feature of the multi-store model and then explaining how this relates to a mnemonic technique. Unfortunately Tamara forgot to do this and therefore her answer gets **0 marks** – it has not been linked in any way to the multi-store model. Bill, on the other hand scores a perfect **3 marks** for making the link and explaining how the technique is related to the multi-store model and also how the technique would improve memory.

Question 6 One of the criticisms of the multi-store model is that it oversimplifies memory processes.

  (a) Explain in what way the multi-store model presents an oversimplified view of memory. Refer to psychological research in your answer. *(4 marks)*

  (b) Outline **one** other limitation of the multi-store model. *(4 marks)*

(a) Evidence suggests that STM and LTM do not operate in a uniform way. For example, there is the case study of KF, who suffered brain damage, which left him with problems dealing with verbal information in STM. However, his ability to deal with visual information was left unimpaired. Similarly, other research suggests that there are different types of LTM, including semantic, episodic and procedural memory. For example, Spiers et al. (2001) studied patients with amnesia and found that although their semantic and episodic memories were impaired, their procedural memory was unimpaired.

(b) The MSM claims that the transfer of material from STM to LTM is through rehearsal. However, in real life, material is readily transferred between the two stores without any form of active rehearsal taking place. The importance of rehearsal may well be an experimental artefact, the consequence of studying memory in artificial laboratory environments rather than the way people use memory in real life.

(a) The multi-store model is an oversimplification of memory. The working memory model offers a much better explanation of how memory works. It has different parts of short-term memory (the phonological loop and the visuo-spatial sketch pad) rather than just having the one short-term memory store as in the multi-store model. This is a much more accurate and more complicated explanation of short-term memory therefore also a better one. It is also better supported by research.

(b) Another limitation is that STM and LTM are not actually two separate stores but work together. The model says that material passes only from STM to LTM, but research has shown that for STM to work properly it needs to use LTM. Therefore they can't be completely separate.

(a) Bill has identified one deficiency in the multi-store model. In fact the question does not require just **one** criticism – you could gain full marks for more than one explanation as long as each is backed up with psychological evidence. Bill's explanation is clearly supported by two pieces of psychological research, both provided in sufficient detail for the **full 4 marks**.

Tamara has identified a different but equally acceptable explanation although it is somewhat buried in…a general criticism of the multi-store model. She didn't really think carefully about the question and has just put down a criticism of the multi-store model. The working memory model is better because a number of separate stores are identified but she needed to turn this around to say why this makes the multi-store model oversimplified. In addition, Tamara has failed to make any more than a passing reference to research – which was a requirement of the question. She would receive just **1 mark out of 4** for a very brief answer.

(b) The important thing to note here is that this question is worth 4 instead of the usual 3 marks for criticisms. Bill has made four points and would receive **4 marks** whereas Tamara's answer is less effective and would have benefitted from the addition of research evidence to explain her point. A mark of 3 seems a bit too generous, so **2 out of 4 marks.**

Question 7 Describe how psychologists have investigated the multi-store model. *(6 marks)*

Methods used to investigate the multi-store model include laboratory experiments such as Glanzer and Cunitz's study of the serial position effect, where they gave participants a list of 20 words, presented one at a time, in order to investigate whether the position of the word in the list made any difference to its recall. STM and LTM have been linked to specific areas of the brain using brain scanning techniques such as PET scans. These take images of the brain while it is performing certain tasks, and show which area of the brain is active during STM tasks and which is active during LTM tasks. Case studies have also been used to examine individuals with brain damage, and the effect on memory. For example, Scoville and Milner (1957) studied a man called HM to see the effect on memory of the removal of his hippocampus to relieve his epilepsy.

They have studied it using experiments. Experiments involve manipulating an independent variable to see what effect it has on a dependent variable. The experimenter also has to control other variables that might have an effect. Atkinson and Shiffrin carried out an experiment which told them about how the multi-store model worked. They discovered that there were three parts, sensory memory, short-term memory and long-term memory. They discovered that short-term memory uses acoustic coding and long-term memory uses semantic coding. They also found out that the capacity and duration of LTM was unlimited, but STM was limited in both of these.

Bill has provided an excellent answer, describing three different methods with examples, so the **full 6 marks.**

Tamara has gone a bit astray – it is not appropriate just to explain what an experiment is, she needed to explain it in the context of memory research. To be fair, she has tried to do this but Atkinson and Shiffrin didn't conduct an experiment, so just **1 out of 6 marks** for identifying experiments as a possible method.

Question 8 (a) Describe **one** study that supports the multi-store model. *(4 marks)*

  (b) Explain why this study supports the multi-store model. *(2 marks)*

(a) Glanzer and Cunitz (1966) gave participants a list of 20 words, presented one word at a time then asked them to recall any of the words they could remember. Two groups of participants were used in the study. Group A were tested immediately after being presented with the words. Group B had to perform a distracter task and then recall the words after 30 seconds. In Group A participants were most likely to remember words at the start of the list (the primacy effect) and the end of the list (recency effect). The recency effect disappeared in Group B participants.

(b) This supports the multi-store model because the existence of a primacy effect demonstrates that the first words in the list have been rehearsed and so transferred to long-term memory. The recency effect is evidence of short-term memory, as Group A participants were able to recall these words from their limited duration STM. However, for the Group B participants, this material had decayed and been lost, because the participants could not rehearse it.

(a) HM was the story of a man who had an operation to remove part of his brain because he had really bad epilepsy. After this part of the brain was removed he couldn't form any new long-term memories but his short-term memory was still intact. For example, he still thought that Dwight Eisenhower was the president of the United States (because he had been president when HM had his operation in the 1950s).

(b) The HM study provided evidence that the part of the brain that was removed must be something to do with long-term memory, because after it was taken out he could no longer form long-term memories. However he could still form short-term memories, so that must be separate and controlled by a different part of the brain.

(a) Bill has provided tons of detail – in fact enough for a 6 mark answer, whereas Tamara's answer is a little bit short on detail because the example doesn't really add much to her answer, so she receives **3 out of 4 marks** and the **full 4 marks** for Bill.

(b) has been answered well by both candidates – certainly more than enough for the **full 2 marks.**

A recent newspaper article reported the case of a young man injured in a car accident. He suffered damage to part of his brain and the result appears to be that he is no longer able to form long-term memories. This means that he can only remember things for about 90 seconds, the limit of short-term memory.

(a) A psychologist was interested in the case and contacted the injured man to test his abilities. He hoped to show that the man's behaviour supported the multi-store model. Outline the aims of the case study. *(2 marks)*

Bill's answer

The aims were to test the man's abilities to see if, despite losing his ability to form long-term memories, his short-term memory was still intact, which would support the multi-store model.

Tamara's answer

The aim of this study was to look at the short- and long-term memory abilities of this man after his accident, in order to see what he could still do.

Examiner's comments

Both Bill and Tamara have demonstrated understanding of what 'aims' of research means, however Tamara has not linked her aims to the predictions of the multi-store model. The **full 2 marks** for Bill and just **1 out of 2 marks** for Tamara.

(b) In what way might this case study support the multi-store model? *(3 marks)*

It supports the multi-store model because it demonstrates that damage to one type of memory (LTM) had no effect on the performance of another type (STM). Therefore it shows that there are at least two distinct stores, located in different areas of the brain (because the damage was done to just one area).

If he could still remember short-term memories but not remember things for longer than the short term, then this would support the multi-store model.

Tamara has failed to answer the question! She has simply repeated the observation that the young man no longer had LTM but did have STM. She has not explained why this supports the multi-store model, therefore **0 marks**.

Bill's answer is accurate and detailed, the **full 3 marks.**

(c) Outline **one** strength and **one** limitation of using a case study to research memory. *(3 marks + 3 marks)*

A strength of case studies in memory research is that they can be used to investigate aspects of human behaviour that are rare. For example, the study of Clive Wearing, who lost all ability to transfer memories from STM to LTM, helps psychologists to develop their understanding of how memory works.

A limitation is that it is difficult to generalise from these individual cases because they are such unusual and individual cases. For example, Wearing had been a conductor and pianist, therefore it could be argued that he had better developed procedural memory than non-musicians.

A strength of using a case study is that it enables the researcher to collect in-depth information about an individual or small group of individuals. This would not be possible with an experiment.

A limitation is that case studies often rely on a person's memory of previous events. This may not always be reliable, particularly if they are studying people with problematic memories!

Tamara's answer is unlikely to be awarded full marks because she has failed to contextualise her answers in memory research. The strength she has described is appropriate but lacks detail – simply saying 'this would not be possible with an experiment' requires more information to explain why it would not be possible in an experiment – it is always important to explain yourself fully. Tamara would receive **2 out of 3 marks** for each of her answers, whereas Bill receives the **full 3 marks** for both answers because of the detail in his answer and the reference to memory research specifically.

(d) Identify **one** ethical issue that might arise in this case study and explain how it could be dealt with. *(3 marks)*

An ethical issue is confidentiality. Case studies such as HM (Henry Molaison) can be identified even when real names are not used because of their unique characteristics. This can be considered an invasion of their privacy, which can lead to distress.

An ethical issue is lack of informed consent. The researcher might deal with it by asking for informed consent from the patient.

Bill has followed the three-point rule (see page 10) in giving his answer – he has identified the issue, he has provided evidence, and finally explained why this is an issue – BUT he has misread the question because he has not explained how the issue could be dealt with in the case study of the man injured in the car accident! So this time only **1 out of 3 marks** for Bill.

Tamara would also receive only **1 out of 3 marks** because her means of dealing with it is not realistic – how could you ask for consent from someone who has no memory?

(e) The data from a case study is usually qualitative data.
    (i) Explain the difference between qualitative data and quantitative data. *(3 marks)*
    (ii) Explain **one** strength and **one** limitation of qualitative data. *(3 marks + 3 marks)*

(i) Qualitative data includes descriptions, meanings, feelings, etc., and cannot be counted or quantified in the way that quantitative data can. In contrast, quantitative data can deal with meanings and feelings but not in the same way as qualitative data because people are not allowed to express themselves freely. They are just given a set of possible answers to select from.

(ii) A strength is that qualitative data, because it is not restricted to numerical measurements, is more likely to represent the true complexity of human behaviour and experience, for example by accessing thoughts and feelings that could not be measured by numerical values or closed questions.

A limitation is that because of the sheer variety of types of data collected and the fact that it is frequently in the form of language rather than numbers, it is often more difficult to detect patterns or to draw conclusions compared to the more simple numerical measurements involved in quantitative data.

(i) Qualitative data is in the form of words. For example, you can ask someone how they are feel about something and they tell you. Quantitative data is in the form of numbers. So, you could ask someone to say how they are feeling on a scale of 1 to 10.

(ii) A strength is that qualitative data is much richer and more detailed and so more likely to show what a person is really thinking or feeling.

A limitation is that you can't draw a graph from words so you can't represent something on a histogram or a scattergram, so you lose some informative ways of looking at the data.

(i) The temptation, in 'difference' questions, is to describe each item separately whereas what you are required to do is contrast them. Just writing 'in contrast' or 'whereas' is not enough, but Bill has said 'cannot be counted in the way that quantitative data can' which is a good contrast, and Bill also contrasts them in terms of how meanings and feelings are dealt with. Bill's answer is worth the **full 3 marks**. Tamara knows about qualitative and quantitative data but hasn't used this to answer the question effectively – she has just described both and not highlighted any difference, so just **1 out of 3 marks**.

(ii) There is no requirement to contextualise the answers here but, to get 3 marks, this is a good way to provide elaboration. Bill has managed to provide sufficient elaboration for the **full 3 marks** for both the strength and the limitation without contextualising his answers. Tamara's answers score just **2 out of 3 marks**. In the case of her strength she might have explained what 'richer and detailed' means by giving an example. In the case of her limitation her answer lacks clarity. What she is trying to say is that (1) you can't easily represent qualitative data in graphical form, (2) but if you did you'd lose some of the informative data.

Outline and evaluate the multi-store model of memory.

(12 marks)

Answer 1

AO1

The first paragraph provides a very brief description of the three stores of the multi-store model.

In the second paragraph information is given about how information is transferred between the three stores. This information is reasonably detailed and accurate.

The multi-store model (Atkinson and Shiffrin, 1968) sees memory as having three separate stores, sensory memory (SM), short-term memory (STM) and long-term memory (LTM).

Information coming from the senses enters SM, where it remains for only a very brief period of time. If attention is focused on any of the information in SM, then this is transferred to STM. Information held in STM decays after a few seconds unless it is rehearsed or is displaced by new information entering STM. If information in STM is subjected to elaborative rehearsal (i.e. deeper processing), then it is passed into LTM, where it can stay more or less indefinitely. Atkinson and Shiffrin believe the more information is rehearsed in this way, the better it will be remembered in LTM.

Evidence suggests that STM and LTM do not operate in a uniform way. For example, there is the case study of KF, who suffered brain damage, which left him with problems dealing with verbal information in STM. However, his ability to deal with visual information was left unimpaired. Similarly, other research suggests that there are different types of LTM, including semantic, episodic and procedural memory. Spiers et al. (2001) studied patients with amnesia and found that although their semantic and episodic memories were impaired, their procedural memory was unimpaired.

The MSM claims that the transfer of material from STM to LTM is through rehearsal. However, in real life, material is readily transferred between the two stores without any form of active rehearsal taking place. The importance of rehearsal may well be an experimental artefact, the consequence of studying memory in artificial laboratory environments rather than the way people use memory in real life.

(279 words)

AO2

The third paragraph identifies one limitation with the model and provides considerable explanation and support for this point.

In the final paragraph a second limitation is identified which is again well elaborated.

Examiner's comments

The description (**AO1**) is fine in terms of accuracy and detail, demonstrating relevant knowledge and understanding. However, there is no information about what each store actually does, which is fairly crucial to understanding the model. Even though the presentation of material is clear and coherent, the important omission means the **AO1** score is **4 out of 6 marks**.

The evaluation section (**AO2**) contains just two points (a very narrow range) but in considerable depth. This is going to receive **5 out of 6 marks** because, for full marks, a third criticism is probably needed.

Total = **9 out of 12 marks**, just makes a **Grade A**.

Answer 2

AO1

The description of the multi-store model does little more than identify the names of the stores, communicating little knowledge and understanding.

The multi-store model of memory has three stores. These stores are the sensory store, short-term store and long-term store. These are abbreviated as SM, STM and LTM. The SM passes information to STM and then this is passed to LTM sometimes. The three stores are different in terms of duration, capacity and encoding. You can improve how much you remember if you repeat it over and over again. Once information is in LTM it is permanent.

There have been lots of experiments that are related to the multi-store model and which show that the model is correct. One study found that short-term memory had a maximum capacity of seven items. However, other researchers have challenged this.

One of the problems with this model is that all the research has been done in laboratories so lacks ecological validity.

There have been some case studies that support the model, with people with brain damage having problems with their short-term memory and others having problems with their long-term memory, which shows they are different.

The working memory model is an alternative model. This model has lots of support and this suggests that the multi-store model may be wrong. The working memory model has several stores too. The main part is called the central executive, which controls the two other memory stores. These other stores are concerned with vision and sound. The vision part is called the visuo-spatial sketch pad and the sound part is the phonological loop, which deals with things that are presented as sounds. This is divided into the phonological store and the articulatory process.

(264 words)

AO2

This is very weak evaluation. Simply saying there is lots of research isn't of any value, and the study that has been mentioned has not been used effectively – how does this support the multi-store model (MSM)?

This is a superficial point – why do lab studies lack ecological validity?

Another superficial evaluative point, lacking specific information about such studies, and in what way this supports the MSM.

It is creditworthy to contrast the MSM with an alternative model, but any description of the second model is not creditworthy.

Examiner's comments

The description (**AO1**) is basic and closer to the band below (see mark scheme on page 9), so **2 out of 6 marks**.

The evaluation (**AO2**) might look plentiful but all of it is superficial and therefore receives **3 out of 6 marks**.

Total = **5 out of 12 marks**, a **Grade E** answer.

The working memory model

Question 1 One of the components of the working memory model is the phonological loop. From the list below, tick which two statements apply to this component. *(2 marks)*

- [ ] Deals with visual information.
- [✓] Deals with verbal information.
- [ ] Deals with spatial information.
- [✓] Preserves the order of information.
- [ ] Has unlimited capacity.
- [ ] Has no storage capacity.

Question 2 Outline key features of the working memory model. *(6 marks)*

Desmond's answer

Working memory is a type of memory that was developed by Baddeley and Hitch. It involves a central executive, which controls two other memory stores. This is the visual spatial sketch pad which deals with things a person sees in their environment, such as people in a room or when asked to count the number of windows in our house. The other is the phonological store, which deals with things that are presented as sounds. For example, when someone hears someone say something to them like 'Can I have a cheeseburger, fries and a chocolate milkshake?' they can store all the individual words in their phonological store while they try to work out what it actually means.

Ashanti's answer

Working memory is used when working on a complex task and when there is a need to temporarily store information.

The central executive directs attention towards tasks by allocating resources in the form of one of the slave systems that make up working memory. Because it has little or no capacity itself, it requires the episodic buffer, which integrates information from the central executive, the slave systems and from long-term memory.

The phonological loop deals with auditory information and is comprised of the phonological store, which deals with words that have been heard ('inner ear') and the articulatory process, which deals with words that have been seen ('inner voice').

The visuo-spatial sketch pad is used when visual or spatial information must be stored while working on a task.

Examiner's comments

If we could combine these answers, we'd end up with full marks! Ashanti has covered all the key features of the working memory model but has not always managed to convey clear understanding. By contrast, Desmond's description of the visuo-spatial sketch pad (it doesn't matter that he doesn't use quite the right term) shows better understanding through the use of appropriate examples.

However, Ashanti's answer is fairly comprehensive and close to 'sound' (see mark scheme on page 9), therefore just scrapes **5 out of 6 marks**. Desmond's answer is better described as 'basic' but closer to the top end of the range because of the degree of understanding demonstrated, therefore **3 out of 6 marks**.

Question 3 (a) Identify and explain **one** key feature of the working memory model. *(4 marks)*

(b) Describe how **one** research study has investigated the key features of the working memory model that you described above. *(4 marks)*

(a) A key feature of the working memory model is the central executive. This is the part that controls all the other parts of working memory, rather like the conductor of an orchestra. It determines which other part of working memory should be used to deal with incoming information.

(b) Research by Bunge et al. (2000) used a brain scan (fMRI) to investigate which parts of the brain were most active during working memory. They found that, when participants were doing two tasks at the same time rather than one after the other, the brain was more active. This was presumably because there were more attentional demands on the individual, and so the central executive was working harder to cope with these demands.

(a) The phonological loop deals with auditory information and is able to preserve the order in which this information is presented. Within this there are two components. The phonological store holds information that has been heard (i.e. it acts as an 'inner ear') and the articulatory process, where words are silently repeated like an 'inner voice', a form of maintenance rehearsal.

(b) Baddeley et al. (1984) carried out a lab experiment to investigate the word-length effect, i.e. people can deal with short words better than long words in working memory. This is because short words can be rehearsed in the phonological loop. They wanted to see what would happen if participants were prevented from rehearsing by having to repeat an irrelevant sound such as the word 'the' over and over again (called an articulatory suppression task). By using articulatory suppression, this prevented information being transferred to the phonological loop because it was already engaged on another task.

(a) Ashanti perhaps has wisely selected the phonological loop because there is quite a lot that can be said about this whereas the central executive is less complicated. Desmond has not mentioned that the central executive has virtually no storage space but otherwise explains the component with clarity, so **3 out of 4 marks**. Ashanti's answer is worth the **full 4 marks**.

(b) The key issue here is not just to describe a research study (which both our candidates have done) but also to make it clear how the study relates to the key feature in (a). Both our candidates have managed to do this reasonably well – although Ashanti has not used her study as effectively as Desmond. So the **full 4 marks** for Desmond and **3 out of 4 marks** for Ashanti.

Question 4 Explain **one** strength and **one** limitation of the working memory model. *(6 marks)*

The working memory model has a lot of research support. Baddeley et al. (1975) found that people were better able to remember lists of short words such as 'twice' than they were able to remember lists of longer words such as 'association'. This is known as the word-length effect.

A limitation of the working memory model is that a lot of the research evidence involves people who have suffered brain damage. This is not ideal because we don't know what their memory was like before the brain damage, so we can't make before and after comparisons.

A strength of the working memory model is that it has a great deal of research support. For example, a case study of a patient LH, who had suffered brain damage after a road accident, found that he performed better on spatial tasks than he did on visual tasks. This suggests separate visual and spatial systems within the visuo-spatial sketch pad.

A limitation of the model is that much of the evidence comes from individuals who have suffered some form of brain damage. As the process of brain damage is traumatic for the individual, it is possible that this is what caused the change in behaviour, and that perhaps the loss of certain aspects of memory is more related to losing motivation.

Desmond has given one strength – research support – but fails to explain how this study supports the model (hasn't followed the three-point rule – see page 10). For the limitation Desmond does provide the three necessary points (identify, evidence, explain). Altogether this gives him **5 out of 6 marks**.

Ashanti has provided sufficient information for both the strength and limitation to receive the **full 6 marks**.

Question 5 Research has found that people are slower when performing two visual tasks than when performing one visual and one verbal task. Explain how the working memory model can explain this finding. Refer to parts of the model in your answer. *(4 marks)*

When people have to perform two tasks at the same time, it is because there are greater demands on the central executive, and so the person finds it more difficult to perform both tasks well. This is even more difficult when both tasks are visual, for example having to count the number of people in a room and also count the number of windows in your house.

If the same component of working memory is involved in two separate tasks (e.g. two visual or two verbal), this creates difficulty because it is already engaged in one task so cannot cope with a second. For example, when the phonological loop is already dealing with one verbal task (as in articulatory suppression) and has to deal with another verbal task. This is not the case if two different components are used for the two tasks as would be the case with the visual and verbal tasks.

It appears that Desmond doesn't quite understand the working memory model as his explanation is basically wrong. There would be equal demand on the central executive if the two tasks were both visual or visual plus verbal, so **0 marks**.

Ashanti demonstrates clear understanding of the evidence and the model and gains the **full 4 marks**.

Question 6 Hassan suffered brain damage in a motorcycle accident and, after the accident, was found to perform better on spatial tasks than those involving visual imagery. Explain the implications of this research, making reference to the working memory model. *(4 marks)*

Hassan has suffered brain damage which has affected his visuo-spatial sketch pad. This is the part of the brain that deals with visual imagery, which would explain why he has difficulty remembering information that is presented visually. The other area of the working memory, the phonological loop, still works normally because this area of the brain hasn't been damaged.

The visuo-spatial sketch pad is proposed to be divided into two separate subsystems, the visual cache holds information about form and colour, and the inner scribe deals with spatial information. Hassan's problems appear to be related to those processes that are the responsibility of the visual cache. Therefore his brain damage is in the area of the brain solely associated with this area, which explains why his performance on spatial tasks is left relatively unimpaired, because the area of the brain associated with the inner scribe has not been damaged.

Both candidates have correctly referred to the visuo-spatial sketch pad (a component of the working memory model) but Ashanti has specifically linked Hassan's problems with the visual cache. Furthermore, Ashanti explains the fact that Hassan's spatial abilities are intact, a fact that Desmond hasn't mentioned. Desmond has mentioned another component of the working memory model (the phonological loop) but that isn't relevant here. So **full marks** for Ashanti and **2 out of 4 marks** for Desmond.

Question 7 (a) Describe **one** study that supports the working memory model. *(4 marks)*
(b) Explain why this study supports the working memory model. *(3 marks)*

(a) A case study of LH who had been brain damaged at the age of 18 showed that he had problems with visual tasks, for example those involving faces, but could do okay on some spatial tasks such as locating on a map where different US states (like Florida and California) should be.

(b) This suggests that there are separate systems in working memory dealing with visual and spatial tasks.

(a) Hitch and Baddeley (1976) found that when participants were asked to perform two tasks that used the same sensory modality (e.g. both involving speech input and so requiring the phonological loop) their performance slowed compared to when they performed tasks that used different sensory modalities (e.g. one involving verbal and the other visual input). In this latter case, the two different modalities would require the phonological loop and the visuo-spatial sketch pad.

(b) This supports the working memory model because it demonstrates the existence of two separate systems dealing with distinct sensory modalities, because when they are stretched by having to deal with two similar tasks at the same time, performance suffers.

(a) Both candidates have described appropriate studies and in this question both procedures and findings/conclusions are creditworthy, so all the information provided is appropriate. Desmond has not given the researcher's name but there is enough detail in his description for the study to be identifiable (it is a study by Farah *et al.* 1988), and enough for **3 out of 4 marks**. Ashanti receives the **full 4 marks** for excellent detail.

(b) Desmond's answer is appropriate but brief for **2 out of 3 marks** whereas Ashanti again receives **full marks**.

Question 8 (a) Describe **one** study that challenges the working memory model. *(4 marks)*
(b) Explain why this study challenges the working memory model. *(3 marks)*

(a) One study claims that the central executive probably has several components with different functions rather than being just one single component (Cardwell and Flanagan).

(b) This challenges the working memory model because it suggests that this part of the model (the central executive) is more complex than Baddeley originally claimed.

(a) Buchsbaum and D'Esposito carried out a review of neuroimaging studies attempting to establish the location of the phonological loop system as a distinct area of the brain. Although initial studies suggested it may be located in an area in the parietal cortex, later studies suggested different areas of the cortex were also involved. They concluded that the phonological loop does not precisely correspond to just one single brain region.

(b) This suggests that the phonological loop is not a functionally discrete system as proposed by Baddeley. This would explain why studies of phonological performance (e.g. Jones et al.) have sometimes produced results that are inconsistent with working memory predictions.

(a) Again, both procedures and findings/conclusions are creditworthy in this question so Ashanti's answer is spot on for **full marks**. Desmond's answer is very brief and this time there is not enough detail to be certain to which study he is referring – the reference 'Cardwell and Flanagan' is to the textbook but not the particular research, so just **1 out of 4 marks**.

(b) Again, Desmond's answer lacks detail – he's got the knowledge (he has explained why the study challenges the working memory model), he just hasn't got the hang of explaining his answers, so just **1 out of 3 marks**. Ashanti's answer has plenty of explanation so **3 out of 3 marks**.

RESEARCH METHODS QUESTION — Some psychology students decided to investigate the topic of memory by interviewing people of different ages about their memories. They wanted to find out early childhood memories and what kinds of things people typically remembered.

(a) **(i)** Give an example of a question that would produce qualitative data. *(2 marks)*
(ii) Explain why this question would produce qualitative data rather than quantitative data. *(2 marks)*

Desmond's answer	*Ashanti's answer*	*Examiner's comments*
(i) *'Tell me about your childhood memories.'*	(i) *'What do you remember about your first day at school?'*	(i) Both answers are fine for the **full 2 marks**.
(ii) *Because it is asking for a response in words rather than just measuring something in numbers.*	(ii) *This would produce qualitative data rather than quantitative data because it is open-ended, i.e. offers the participant the opportunity to voice their own feelings rather than offering them a closed list of alternatives.*	(ii) Ashanti has wasted time writing out the question, which makes her answer look longer than it is. Her answer is basically not much better than Desmond's and they both receive the **full 2 marks**.

(b) Give one strength of conducting an interview rather than a questionnaire. *(3 marks)*

A strength is that with an interview you are more likely to get your questions answered because people often don't return questionnaires, particularly when they are sent through the post.	*The interviewer can get information that would not be accessible with set questions, as in a questionnaire. For example, a respondent's answer to an initial question about their childhood memories can be followed up by supplementary questions as the interviewer attempts to 'dig a bit deeper'.*	Ashanti has remembered to contextualise her answer so it specifically refers to memory research whereas Desmond's answer is too general for full marks. Therefore Ashanti receives the **full 3 marks** whereas Desmond only gets **2 out of 3 marks**.

(c) Explain why it might have been preferable to use a questionnaire instead of an interview. *(3 marks)*

It would be preferable to use a questionnaire because it is cheap and easy therefore more people can be used in the study.	*Respondents might be more willing to reveal information that they believe to be confidential in a questionnaire because it is more likely to guarantee anonymity and there is no face to face interaction with an interviewer to cause embarrassment when revealing personal memories (e.g. that they found it difficult to make friends as a child).*	Desmond suggests the reason is 'cheap and easy' but hasn't explained why they are cheaper or easier, and why that enables more people to be studied, so **0 marks**. Ashanti's answer is excellent – detailed and appropriate, so **3 out of 3 marks**.

(d) Describe how the students might have conducted a pilot study. *(3 marks)*

A pilot study is a small-scale study that is carried out before the main study, and gives the researchers the opportunity to try out all the questions, instructions, etc. before carrying out the study for real.	*They could have tried out their questions on a small number of their friends prior to the main study in order to see if they understood the questions, whether they were embarrassed by any of them, etc. They could then alter the interview for the main study in the light of this.*	Oh dear, Desmond fell into the trap of saying <u>what</u> a pilot study is instead of <u>how</u> it would be done, so **0 marks**. Ashanti has focused solely on the how question and therefore receives the **full 3 marks**.

(e) Explain why it might have been a good idea to conduct a pilot study. *(3 marks)*

It would be a good idea to carry out a pilot study because once the researchers start on the main study and they discover that some things don't work (e.g. the participants don't understand some of the questions), it is too late to change things because it has to be the same for all participants.	*It would be a good idea in this study because there is the potential to cause distress by reawakening childhood memories. The pilot study would give them insights into the possibility of this happening. They may also find they have included too many questions and that respondents are likely to become bored. They can then initiate these changes in the main study.*	Desmond has provided an appropriate answer and also sufficient detail for the **full 3 marks**. He has said why, and given an example of what they might not understand and, finally, pointed out that there would be problems in making changes half way through the study. Ashanti has given two reasons – but this is fine for this question because it does not specify that only **one** reason must be given. So she also gains the **full 3 marks**.

(f) The students were concerned that some of them might have asked the questions differently when they were interviewing participants. How could the students assess the reliability of their interviews? *(3 marks)*

They could video one of them interviewing a participant and then they could use that as a model interview. This would ensure that they all asked the questions in a similar way and so increase the reliability of the interviews.	*Interviewers should be trained how to interview participants about their childhood memories and should practise using the questions (in a pilot study). They can then discuss their experiences with each other. In this way, they can check on the reliability of their interviewing and the way in which they ask, and elaborate on, the questions.*	Desmond hasn't answered the question – he has explained how reliability would be increased not how it would be assessed, so **0 marks**. Ashanti's answer is thorough and detailed, **full marks**.

(g) Explain why reliability is important when conducting interviews. *(2 marks)*

People could lie when giving their responses, so this is a way of checking their responses by asking them the same questions a week later to see if they say the same thing.	*Reliability is important because if two interviewers ask questions differently or code responses differently it would bias the results and produce conclusions that are worthless.*	Desmond's answer is muddled – he seems to be talking about validity rather than reliability because a lie would mean the data is meaningless (lacks validity). So **0 marks**. Ashanti again scores **full marks**.

Outline and evaluate the working memory model.

(12 marks)

AO1

AO2

Working memory is an explanation of short-term memory that was developed by two psychologists called Baddeley and Hitch. The main part is called the central executive, which controls the two other memory stores. These other stores are concerned with vision and sound.

The vision part is called the visuo-spatial sketch pad which deals with things a person sees in their environment, such as when trying to remember people in a room or when asked to count the number of windows in your house.

> The first four paragraphs provide a detailed and clear description of the working memory model.

The other is the phonological loop, which deals with things that are presented as sounds. There are two parts of the phonological loop. The first of these is the phonological store. This acts like an inner ear, so that when someone says something to you, you can hold the individual words in the phonological store while you work out the meaning of what they said. The other part is called the articulatory process. This operates when someone is reading, i.e. when words are written rather than spoken. It acts like an inner voice, and enables the person to silently 'speak' the words they are reading on the page.

The central executive works by directing attention towards tasks and then allocates resources in the form of one of the slave systems that make up working memory, i.e. the visuo-spatial sketch pad or the phonological loop. Because it has little or no capacity itself, it requires the episodic buffer for data storage, which integrates information from the central executive, the slave systems and from long-term memory.

A limitation of the working memory model is that a lot of the research evidence involves people who have suffered brain damage. Another problem is that other research evidence is laboratory experiments which lack ecological validity. It is a better model than the multi-store model because it isn't as simplistic.

> The final paragraph provides evaluation. The problem is the range is limited and, in particular, none of the points have been elaborated.

(307 words)

Examiner's comments

Many candidates lose marks because of insufficient evaluation (**AO2**), as is the case in this essay. The description (**AO1**) of the working memory model is excellent (detailed, sound, clear and coherent). Therefore the **AO1** mark is **6 out of 6 marks**.

The evaluation (**AO2**) is best described as a 'superficial consideration of a relatively restricted range' (see mark scheme on page 9). It would receive **2 out of 6 marks** which is perhaps a bit mean but it is very basic evaluation.

Total = **8 out of 12 marks**, so still a **Grade B** but only because of the excellent description.

Outline and evaluate **two** models of memory.

(12 marks)

AO1

AO2

> A detailed outline of the multi-store model.

The multi-store model of memory (MSM) distinguishes between different memory stores. Sensory memory receives information from the different senses and holds it for only a very brief time. STM receives information from the sensory store, where it remains for a brief period until it decays or is displaced by other information. LTM receives information from STM. It is both unlimited in capacity and effectively permanent. Information moves from sensory memory to STM if a person's attention is focused on it. Information is maintained in STM through maintenance rehearsal (verbal repetition) and is moved to LTM through elaborative rehearsal (involving deeper processing).

> A detailed outline of the working memory model.

Working memory is used when working on a complex task and when there is a need to temporarily store information. The central executive directs attention towards tasks by allocating resources in the form of one of two slave systems. The phonological loop deals with auditory information and is comprised of the phonological store, which deals with words that have been heard ('inner ear') and the articulatory process, which deals with words that have been seen ('inner voice'). The visuo-spatial sketch pad is used when visual or spatial information must be stored while working on a task.

Both models have a great deal of research support. For example the MSM is supported by a study that found that short-term memory had a maximum capacity of seven items, showing that it is a limited store. However evidence for the working memory model challenges the MSM. For example LH, who had suffered brain damage after a road accident, performed better on spatial tasks than he did on visual tasks. This suggests separate visual and spatial systems within the visuo-spatial sketch pad. However, much of the evidence comes from individuals who have suffered some form of brain damage.

> One rather superficial criticsm of the multi-store model and one elaborated criticism of the working memory model, plus a further superficial criticism.

(295 words)

Examiner's comments

A typical answer – most candidates should have a 6-mark description of each model, ready for a question on one model. In this answer the student has presented both 6-mark answers even though only 6 marks are available in total, so the **full 6 out of 6 marks** for description (**AO1**) but time was wasted.

The effect of writing so much description is that there is less time for evaluation (**AO2**). It is vital to always have equal amounts of both in an essay. Only **3 out of 6 marks** for AO2.

Total = **9 out of 12 marks**, a **Grade A**.

Accuracy of EWT: misleading information

Question 1 Explain what is meant by 'eyewitness testimony'. *(2 marks)*

Alex's answer

Eyewitness testimony is something someone can be asked in court or by police about what they remember about something.

Sadie's answer

Eyewitness testimony is the memory of an incident or event from someone who was actually there at the time.

Examiner's comments

Sadie's answer has the edge here. It is specific whereas Alex's answer is vague and sounds a bit like guesswork. The **full 2 marks** for Sadie and **1 out of 2 marks** for Alex.

Question 2 When police question eyewitnesses it is easy to unconsciously ask questions that may 'lead' the eyewitness to give predictable answers. This is described as giving misleading information.
    (a) Give an example of such 'misleading information'. *(2 marks)*
    (b) Explain why misleading information is a problem for police interviews. *(2 marks)*

(a) Misleading information can be telling someone that they were lost in a shopping mall as a child when they weren't. This is what Loftus did in one of her experiments, and 25% of the adult participants then remembered being lost in a shopping mall.

(b) This is a problem because it is wrong for the police to lie to witnesses and so would be considered unethical by the BPS.

(a) An example of misleading information would be asking witnesses if they remembered the bank robbers carrying a gun rather than asking them if they remembered them carrying anything.

(b) This is a problem because it provides post-event information that may alter the witnesses' original memory and causes them to come up with 'false' memories of the event.

(a) Again, Sadie focuses on the specific demands of the question and gives an excellent example for the **full 2 marks**. Alex has just written something that is connected with the topic. The example he has given is creditworthy but lacking clarity; his second sentence is irrelevant. **1 out of 2 marks**.

(b) Sadie is spot on again for the **full 2 marks**, but Alex has displayed no understanding – police are not necessarily acting in a deliberate manner when presenting misleading information (leading questions) and it certainly has nothing to do with the BPS (British Psychological Society). So **0 marks** for Alex.

Question 3 (a) Describe **one** study of the effects of misleading information on eyewitness testimony. *(6 marks)*
    (b) Explain **one** problem with the validity of the study you described in (a). *(3 marks)*

(a) Loftus et al. (1978) showed people a film of a car waiting at either a stop sign or a yield sign. They then asked each group questions including 'Did another car pass the Datsun when it was at the each sign?' when it was actually at a yield sign. When this happened, a lot of the participants later said that they thought it had been at a yield sign (not a each sign). This is an example of misleading information because it tells somebody something that didn't really happen and this changes their memory.

(b) A problem with validity in this experiment is that participants might be upset at being given information that wasn't true (i.e. suggesting that the Datsun was at a yield sign when it was really at a stop sign). This is unethical according to the BPS guidelines so, because deception has been used, this would make the study invalid.

(a) Loftus and Palmer (1974) showed participants films of car accidents and then asked them how fast the cars were going at the time of the accident. The researchers changed the verb used in the question to see if that had any effect on the estimates of speed. For example, 'How fast were the two cars going when they contacted each other?' or 'How fast were the two cars going when they smashed into each other?' They found that the verb used affected the estimate of speed, with 'contacted' resulting in an estimate of 31.8mph and 'smashed' resulting in an estimate of 40.8mph.

(b) This was a laboratory experiment, therefore there is a possibility that the participants did not take it as seriously or were not as emotionally aroused as people who had witnessed a real car accident. This may result in artificial distinctions between the different conditions that would not be evident in a real-life incident.

(a) Both candidates have selected an appropriate study. The question does not specify whether just procedures or just finding/conclusions are required so either or both would be creditworthy. Sadie has done both and given lots of key details about her study. However there isn't quite enough for full marks, she might have included a comment on what these results demonstrated, so **5 out of 6 marks**. Alex has selected a tricky study and got it completely muddled. There was a stop and yield sign but no questions were asked – information was presented visually. Therefore this answer is flawed and largely inappropriate, so **1 out of 6 marks**.

(b) An excellent answer from Sadie who has avoided saying 'It was a lab experiment and therefore lacked ecological validity'. Instead she has explained specifically why a lab experiment might have a negative effect on the results and has followed the three-point rule, so the **full 3 marks**. Alex is muddled again. Participants weren't given false information; they knew it was an experiment and that it was a hypothetical situation. Furthermore such deception doesn't make the data invalid. Alex get **0 marks**.

Question 4 Aside from the study described in question 3, explain another way that psychologists have investigated eyewitness testimony. *(4 marks)*

Yuille and Cutshall interviewed people who had witnessed a murder, four months after the murder had taken place. They included some leading questions to see if this would change the witnesses' memories of what they had seen four months earlier. They didn't change their memories and witnesses were still as accurate after four months as they were at the time.

Riniolo et al. used archival material of interviews with survivors from the sinking of the Titanic in 1912. They obtained transcripts of 20 survivors who had commented directly on the state of the ship as it sank (i.e. whether it was intact or breaking up). The researchers wanted to see whether the levels of anxiety and poor viewing conditions affected the accuracy of the eyewitness testimony, and whether the survivors were influenced by post-event suggestions that the Titanic sank intact. They included only those transcripts where researchers could agree on the opinion being expressed by the survivor (inter-rater reliability).

This time Alex has managed to produce some reasonably accurate details of a relevant study. However, the issue is whether there is enough detail for 4 marks – there is just about enough for **full marks** (see mark scheme on page 9).

It looks like Sadie didn't notice that there were only 4 marks available – you should always tailor how much you write to the marks available, otherwise you will be wasting valuable examination time. Sadie has provided much more information than necessary but again would receive the **full 4 marks**.

Question 5 A psychologist might be called to a trial to give expert evidence to the jury about the accuracy of eyewitness testimony. Using your knowledge of psychology, outline **one** argument that the psychologist might present to the jury about the accuracy of memory. *(4 marks)*

I would warn the jury about the accuracy of older witnesses' testimony. Older witnesses are generally less accurate than younger witnesses. Research has shown that older witnesses are more likely to have their memory of an event altered by post-event information (e.g. leading questions asked during interviewing by the police), therefore it is less reliable in court.

One argument against relying too much on eyewitness testimony in court is based on research evidence that has discovered that many convicted individuals have subsequently been shown to be innocent because of the modern availability of DNA testing. This is despite the fact that they were initially convicted on the basis of eyewitness identification alone. Wells and Olsen (2003) argue that mistaken eyewitness identification is the biggest factor contributing to the conviction of innocent people.

In this case Alex has done better than Sadie because he has answered the question. Sadie has failed to outline the argument she would present – she has gone straight to the research evidence (given in lots of detail). She has addressed one part of the question 'use your knowledge of psychology' but failed to 'outline one argument', so **2 out of 4 marks**.

By contrast, Alex has said what he would say to the jury and provided sufficiently detailed information of the psychological support so a **full 4 marks** for this answer. He has shaped his knowledge to fit this specific question.

Question 6 A doctor notices that patients tend to give predictable answers to certain questions. For example, if he is asking about headaches he finds that patients report more headaches when asked 'Do you have headaches frequently?' rather than when asked 'Do you rarely have headaches?' He thinks he should be more careful about the way he asks questions.

Use your knowledge of psychology to explain why the style of questioning is likely to affect answers obtained. *(4 marks)*

This style of questioning is likely to affect the answers because it is a doctor asking the questions. People are often intimidated by doctors so are likely to just agree with whatever they are suggesting. Here the patient may think they should be having frequent headaches otherwise they won't receive any treatment (or even be signed off work) so they are more likely, as is suggested here, to report having frequent headaches, even if they don't have them.

These are examples of leading questions, and would be suggest to the patient what is the correct or desired answer. (i.e. that they might be expected to have frequent headaches given their condition). Loftus (1975) suggested that leading questions can be coercive (e.g. 'You are taking exercise aren't you'?) or linked by association (e.g. 'Would you prefer to give up smoking or continue smoking and risk having a heart attack?'). Both types of question make one answer more likely than another.

Alex has missed the point – and forgotten to use his psychology. While his answer may be plausible, this is a psychology exam and the question required that his answer related to 'knowledge of psychology'. Alex has failed to account for why the alternative forms of the question would make a difference whereas Sadie has correctly identified this as an example of a leading question and has backed up her answer with detailed information about an appropriate piece of psychological research. So **0 marks** for Alex and the **full 4 marks** for Sadie.

RESEARCH METHODS QUESTION

A young lady was a witness to a robbery in her local shop. A police officer later interviewed her about what she saw during the robbery. The officer asked her a series of questions such as 'What did the robber look like?', 'What were you doing at the time of the robbery?', 'Was there anyone else in the shop?'.

(a) The police questions were designed so they did not contain any misleading information. Explain in what way these questions are not misleading. *(3 marks)*

Alex's answer

The questions are not misleading because they do not lead the witness into saying something that didn't really happen simply because it has been suggested in a question.

Sadie's answer

The questions are not misleading because they do not predispose witnesses to give one answer rather than another. For example, asking if the robber had any physical deformities would have suggested that he (or she) was in some way physically different to normal. By asking what they looked like removes this suggestion.

Examiner's comments

Alex's answer is fine but lacks sufficient detail for the full 3 marks, so **2 out of 3 marks**. Sadie's answer has plenty of detail for the **full 3 marks** (notice how she has followed the 'three-point rule' – described on page 10).

(b) Explain what is meant by the term 'demand characteristic'. *(2 marks)*

Something that gives participants a clue what the study is really about.

Anything in a study or in the behaviour of the person carrying out the study that makes the participants aware of the purpose of the study or how they are expected to behave.

Alex's answer is brief but appropriate, however because it lacks elaboration it receives just **1 out of 2 marks**. Sadie's answer deserves the **full 2 marks**.

(c) The police officer also asked the following question 'Did you notice anything odd about the robber's accent?'. Explain in what way this would act as a demand characteristic. *(2 marks)*

It is a demand characteristic because it demands a particular response.

By asking about the robber's accent, it suggests to the witness that the robber had a distinctive accent and they would then be more likely to remember details of someone who was not local to the area.

Sadie's answer again contains those extra details which are lacking in Alex's answers, so the **full 2 marks** to Sadie and **1 out of 2 marks** for Alex. Alex just needed to write an extra sentence explaining what response it demanded (i.e. that there was something distinctive in the robber's accent).

A group of psychology students were keen to repeat one of the lab experiments on misleading information that was in their textbook.

(a) Identify **one** lab experiment on misleading information. *(1 mark)*

Alex's answer

Loftus' car crash study.

Sadie's answer

Loftus and Palmer's study of the influence on different verbs on the estimation of car speed.

Examiner's comments

Alex could be referring to one of a number of studies by Loftus so **0 marks** here (because there is only 1 mark available), but the **full 1 mark** for Sadie.

(b) Identify the independent and dependent variables in this experiment. *(2 marks + 2 marks)*

IV = the question asked.

DV = how fast the cars were going.

The IV was the verb used when asking the question about how fast the cars were going when they crashed (e.g. 'hit', 'smashed').

The DV was the estimate of speed given by the participants after watching the film of a car crash.

Even though Alex received no marks in (a) we are going to give him the benefit of the doubt here and assume he was referring to the Loftus and Palmer study, so he receives **1 out of 2 marks** for the IV (because his answer is not operationalised) but **0 marks** for the DV because it isn't how fast the cars were going but the estimate of the speed. Sadie's answers are clearly operationalised and worth the **full 4 marks**.

(c) (i) Explain what is meant by 'operationalisation'. *(2 marks)*
(ii) Write a suitable, fully operationalised hypothesis for this study. *(3 marks)*

(i) It means making sure the variables can be measured (e.g. happiness score rather just 'happiness').

(ii) To find out whether people who are asked how fast the cars were going when they smashed into each other will say they were going faster than people who are asked how fast the cars were going when they hit each other.

(i) Stating the variables of the study in such a way that they can easily be quantified and measured.

(ii) The verb used (e.g. 'hit', 'smashed') to describe the type of contact between two cars involved in a filmed car crash when asking a question about speed, influences the estimate of speed in mph at the point of the collision.

(i) Both candidates have elaborated their answers and thus demonstrate knowledge and understanding, so the **full 2 marks**.

(ii) Alex will receive **0 marks** for this answer because he has stated it as an aim rather than a hypothesis. If he had omitted the words 'To find out whether' it would be a hypothesis and an operationalised one – although rather clumsily worded. He has also excluded three of the conditions from his hypothesis (when the words 'collided', 'bumped' or 'contacted' were used). The way Sadie has phrased her hypothesis avoids the need to state all conditions. **Full marks** for Sadie because her hypothesis meets all the requirements.

(d) Identify **one** possible extraneous variable in this study and say how you might control it. *(3 marks)*

If some of the participants have poor eyesight they may not see the film as clearly and so be more influenced by what the experimenter says in the question. I might control this by only using participants who have eyesight over a certain minimum level.

A possible extraneous variable would be the driving experience of the participants because more experienced drivers would be better able to estimate speed accurately regardless of the question. This could be controlled by giving all participants a driving experience questionnaire (e.g. whether they had passed their test, how long they had been driving etc.). Participants can then be matched in each condition on the basis of this information.

Sadie has selected an important extraneous variable and explained in detail how it might be controlled, so **3 out of 3 marks**. Alex's answer ends up worth **no marks** as eyesight is not going to be a problem – the participants don't really have to see the accident because the key issue is how the accident has been described.

(e) Briefly describe how you would conduct the study identified in (a). You could include information on a selection of participants and experimental design. *(6 marks)*

I would use a random sample of participants from the other psychology groups. They could be asked to take part in the study and if they agree an independent groups design could be used. Each group would be shown a film of a car crash and asked a question about how fast the cars were going when they crashed, but a different word could be used in each group to see if that changed their estimate of how fast the cars were going. When the participants had given their estimates, the different groups could be compared to see which word caused the highest estimate of speed. The participants could then be thanked for taking part and debriefed.

A volunteer sample could be used by putting up an invitation to take part on the school website. This would also include any exclusion criteria (e.g. people who have driving experience or knowledge of the original Loftus and Palmer study). Each volunteer would be given sufficient information about their role in the study and any risks of participation in order to obtain informed consent. There would be five conditions, with each participant being asked to estimate the speed of two cars involved in a collision, but with each condition having a different verb (e.g. 'hit', 'smashed'). A matched pairs design could be used, with participants matched across five conditions in terms of driving experience. Each participant is then shown a short film of two cars colliding and asked to estimate the speed they were going at the point of collision.

Sadie has given an extremely detailed account of how to conduct this study, beginning by stating the sampling method and how it would be done. In fact, she has written considerably more than is necessary, which makes Alex's answer look weaker than it is. Alex's answer gives information about a sampling method and includes some information about the experimental design. He then describes the procedure and finally he alludes to debriefing. So Sadie will receive the **full 6 out of 6 marks**, whereas Alex will get **5 out of 6 marks** because the answer doesn't always give details of 'how' (e.g. how random sampling would be done).

Extended writing question

Discuss the effect of misleading information on memory.

(12 marks)

AO1

This answer has slightly missed the point of the question. It begins with two research studies that show us the effects of misleading information but no attempt is made to use this material to describe the effects of misleading information, as required in the question. The material is implicitly but not explicitly relevant.

Here we have a third study, described fairly basically, and again not focused on the question.

One of the first studies of misleading information was carried out by Elizabeth Loftus. She showed different groups a short film of a car crash and then asked participants how fast the cars were going when they crashed into each other. She found that some words misled the participants into thinking they were going faster than they actually were. She then used two of the groups ('smashed' and 'hit') and asked them if they saw any broken glass. More of the 'smashed' group reported seeing broken glass than the 'hit' group. A problem with this study is that it was carried out in a laboratory. A laboratory is an artificial setting which means that the conclusions are not that relevant to real life. Also, participants are less likely to take the study as seriously as they might if it was a real-life incident.

A real-life study that tested the effect of misleading information was also carried out by Loftus and Pickrell (1995). She told adults that, when they were about seven, they had been lost in a shopping mall. She found that about 25% of the participants reported remembering the incident clearly (even though it had never happened). Studies like this are unethical because they involve deception and can cause distress in participants if they relive the experience. However, Loftus* has more recently been using this technique for more constructive means, trying to persuade people to eat more healthily by giving them misleading information about their eating habits. This is less unethical because it is trying to help people, not just using them to find out something.

(267 words)

AO2

The first criticism (about laboratory studies) is a 'knee-jerk' criticism made with no reference to this context, i.e. superficial.

The second point is reasonable but needs further elaboration.

This critical point could be more effective (by explaining why it would cause distress). However, the point is well elaborated by presenting an alternative view.

* (Bernstein, Laney, Morris and Loftus, 2005)

Examiner's comments
The descriptive content (**AO1**) is relevant but not sound, with some evidence of appropriate material. It is perhaps closer to the band below rather than the top band (see mark scheme on page 9), so **4 out of 6 marks**.

The evaluative content (**AO2**) is mixed – some superficial points and one well elaborated, therefore **4 out of 6 marks**.

Total = **8 out of 12 marks, Grade B.**

Extended writing question

Outline and evaluate research on the effect of misleading information on eyewitness testimony.

(12 marks)

AO1

A clear and detailed description of an appropriate study.

Another clear and detailed description of an appropriate (and very complicated study).

A third clear and detailed description of an appropriate study.

Loftus and Palmer (1974) showed participants films of car accidents and then asked them how fast the cars were going. They changed the verb used in the question to see if that had any effect on the estimates of speed. 'Contacted' resulted in an estimate of 31.8mph and 'smashed' in an estimate of 40.8mph. In an extension to this experiment, they took two groups (who had heard 'hit' or 'smashed' when questioned). When given misleading information 'Did you see any broken glass' (when there wasn't any), the 'smashed' group were twice as likely as the 'hit' group to report having seen broken glass.

This was a laboratory experiment, therefore there is a possibility that the participants did not take it as seriously or were not as emotionally aroused as people who had witnessed a real car accident. This may result in artificial distinctions between the different conditions that would not be evident in a real-life incident. Evidence from real life studies (e.g. Yuille and Cutshall, 1986) does not support the view that misleading information affects the accuracy of eyewitness testimony. Witnesses interviewed four months about giving testimony after a murder maintained their accuracy despite misleading questions.

Loftus et al. conducted another experiment (1978), this time presenting leading questions in the form of pictures instead of verbally. Participants were shown a set of slides depicting a car accident, and then later shown pairs of slides and asked to indicate which ones were in the original set. Participants were either in a consistent condition (they saw a red car at a stop or yield sign and were later shown the same slide) or an inconsistent condition (they originally saw the car at the stop sign and were later shown the car at the yield sign, or vice versa). Participants' answers were more likely to be correct in the consistent condition. This suggests that even when people are tested visually the accuracy of their recall is affected by misleading information. It also supports Loftus' original research that shows that misleading information alters a person's memory for an event.

Riniolo et al. (2003) used archival material of interviews with survivors from the sinking of the Titanic in 1912. They found that 75% of the witnesses maintained their view that the Titanic was breaking up as she sank, despite the widespread belief expressed at the inquiry, in the press and by naval experts at the time that this could not have happened (i.e. misleading information).

This study does have limitations, however, including eyewitnesses with different vantage points at the time of the sinking, a small sample size, and an inability to interview eyewitnesses first-hand.

(439 words)

AO2

A well elaborated point of criticism, avoiding the 'knee-jerk' comment that lab experiments lack ecological validity.

Comments that begin 'This suggests that…' form part of effective evaluation because they offer an analysis of the information presented.

Somewhat superficial evaluative points. It would have been equally effective to focus on just one point and apply the three-point rule (see page 10) to making it more effective.

Examiner's comments
The **AO1** content is clearly worth the **full 6 marks** whereas the **AO2** content doesn't quite hit the top band. There are a broad range of points but the depth is sometimes superficial, therefore **5 out of 6 marks**.

Total = **11 out of 12 marks**, a clear **Grade A** answer.

Accuracy of EWT: age and anxiety

Question 1 The graph below shows the relationship between anxiety and recall. What can you conclude from this graph? *(4 marks)*

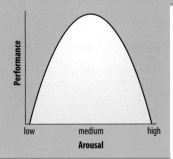

Romeo's answer

The graph shows two main things. First, it shows that recall is less accurate (operationalised as 'performance on a recall test') when anxiety (operationalised as 'arousal level') is either low or high. Second, it shows that accuracy is at its highest when anxiety levels are moderate. This represents a curvilinear relationship between anxiety and recall accuracy, with performance gradually increasing from low to moderate anxiety levels, then gradually decreasing again from moderate to high anxiety levels.

Examiner's comment

Couldn't have said it better myself! **Full 4 marks.**

Question 2 Describe **one** factor that may affect the accuracy of eyewitness testimony. *(2 marks)*

Romeo's answer

Research has shown that high levels of anxiety make eyewitness testimony less accurate, and more accurate when there are moderate levels of anxiety.

Juliet's answer

People are less likely to remember things accurately when they are drunk. People didn't see a gorilla when they were drunk but did see it when they were sober.

Examiner's comments

Both answers are fine and sufficiently detailed for the **full 2 marks.**

Question 3 Outline how **one** research study has investigated the effect of anxiety on eyewitness testimony. *(4 marks)*

One study used two experimental conditions to investigate the weapon-focus effect. Participants in both conditions heard a heated discussion in another room. In one condition, a man emerged from the room carrying a pen and with his hands covered in grease. In the second condition, a man emerged carrying a paperknife and with blood on his hands. This was designed to see whether the weapon in the second condition would distract participants and make their memory for other information less accurate.

One study wanted to know if the presence of a weapon made people more likely to remember the details of, e.g. a knife or a gun, and less likely to remember other things that were happening at the same time. An experiment was carried out to test this. They found that if people see a gun or a knife they remember details of that, but don't remember, for example, what was said, or the physical characteristics of the person carrying the gun or knife.

Neither student has included the name of the researcher but this is not a problem if there is sufficient detail in their answer to identify the study – which there is. The study was in fact conducted by Johnson and Scott (1976) and later reported by Loftus *et al.* (1978).

Romeo's answer focuses correctly on the 'how' (procedures), as required in the question, although the final sentence is concerned with aims not procedures. Therefore he gains just **3 out of 4 marks.** Juliet's answer provides information on aims and findings, but nothing on procedures – so **0 marks.**

Question 4 (a) Describe what research has shown about the effect of the age of witnesses on the accuracy of eyewitness testimony. *(6 marks)*
(b) Identify **two** ethical issues that might occur in research on the effect of age on eyewitness testimony, and explain why these issues are a problem. *(2 marks + 2 marks)*

(a) Research has shown that young children and older adults are generally less accurate in their EWT than adolescents and young adults. Parker and Carranza found that, although young children were more likely than adolescents to identify a suspect after viewing a mock crime, these identifications were frequently inaccurate. Memon et al. found that when the interval between an incident and testing was short (35 minutes), there was no difference in the accuracy of recall between adolescents and older adults. However, when this incident was longer (one week), the older adults were much less accurate in their recall. Yarmey found that although young adults were much more confident in the accuracy of their recall, when compared to older adults, there was no significant difference in the performance of the two groups.

(b) One ethical issue is deception. This is because in order to take it seriously participants might need to be told it is a real incident (i.e. a cover story). This is a problem because participants may feel angry that they have been lied to and feel used. A second ethical issue is protection from psychological harm. Witnessing a crime may be upsetting for the participants at the time and cause them some anxiety.

(a) There is a relationship between age and accuracy of EWT. Older witnesses are much less accurate than younger witnesses, but there is also something called an own-age bias. Older people are much better at identifying people from their own age group than people from other age groups. There is also an own-race bias, in that people are much better at identifying people from their own racial groups, e.g. black people are better at distinguishing other black people, and white people are much better at distinguishing other white people. Very young children also make poor witnesses although there are ways to increase their accuracy through sensitive interviewing techniques.

(b) An ethical issue is deception in that the experimenters might tell the participants that it is a real crime and it isn't. Deception is wrong according to the BPS ethical guidelines, so that makes it an ethical issue. Another ethical issue is debriefing. This is where the researchers have to tell the participants why they were deceived, answer any questions about the experiment and return them to the same state they were in when they entered the laboratory.

(a) Romeo has reported the findings from three different and appropriate studies, in plenty of detail – more than enough for the **full 6 marks.** He hasn't included the dates but there is no specific requirement to do this and the other details that have been included more than compensate for this.

Juliet's answer is a bit more difficult to assess. She has focused on own age-bias which, strictly speaking, doesn't tell us much about the effect of age on the accuracy of eyewitness testimony. It just tells us that people are likely to be more accurate when identifying people of their own age. It is peripherally relevant. However the rest of her answer goes off on a tangent and is not creditworthy at all. This answer has a 'whiff' of psychology (some relvance, basic) and therefore would receive **2 out of 6 marks.**

(b) Romeo again gains **full marks** for two ethical issues, each one explained clearly. Juliet has also identified deception as her first ethical issue, but saying that the BPS says it is wrong is not a sufficient explanation to gain credit, so **1 out of 2 marks.** Juliet's second ethical issue is debriefing which, strictly speaking is not an issue – although you might argue that lack of debriefing is an ethical issue. The bottom line is that it is best not to use debriefing as an ethical issue but include it as a means of dealing with the ethical issue of deception – so **0 marks** for the second issue.

Question 5 Danila feels extremely anxious when taking exams and feels that this affects her ability to recall important information.

(a) Explain why anxiety might affect her recall. Refer to psychological research in your answer. *(4 marks)*

(b) Explain why research into the effects of anxiety on eyewitness recall might be might be claimed to lack validity. *(3 marks)*

(a) Research by Deffenbacher et al. (2004) has shown that when people are in a heightened state of arousal this has an effect on their ability to recall information, with high levels of stress having a negative impact on recall. As Danila is extremely anxious before taking her exam, this will probably make it more difficult for her to recall information during the exam. Deffenbacher also found that moderate levels of arousal led to better performance, so if she has revised properly, her recall should be fine.

(b) Research may lack validity because much of it is carried out in an artificial environment, i.e. in a laboratory. This means that participants do not take the experiment seriously, knowing that their EWT does not really matter, and that a crime has not really been committed. This may be a reason why so many laboratory studies show relatively poor recall and why so many witnesses of real crimes show relatively good recall.

(a) Danila is anxious because exams are extremely important and she feels nervous about how she might perform. It is natural to feel like this and research has shown that many students feel anxious before taking exams and it leads to them having problems recalling important information. From my own research, I remember when I took my GCSEs, I felt very anxious, and had to learn to relax. Research has shown that if students can manage their anxiety, e.g. through stress management techniques such as meditation, they are much more likely to perform well in exams.

(b) Research in this area is often accused of lacking validity. Validity is whether something is really testing what it says it sets out to test. This can be internal validity (e.g. whether the cover story works or whether participants take the study seriously) or external validity (e.g. whether the results apply to the real world).

(a) Notice how Romeo has combined the required elements of the question into his answer – he outlines the psychological research and then applies this to Danila's problem. He could have done it the other way round (suggested what Danila should do and then linked this to a piece of research) but either way he has done what was required and gains the **full 4 marks**. Juliet has answered the question but failed to give psychological evidence as support (beyond the rather general statement that 'research has shown that many students feel anxious'). Her answer is also vague showing very little knowledge and understanding, so **1 mark out of 6.**

(b) Romeo has identified an important factor related to validity (an artificial environment) and applied the three-point rule (see page 10) in elaborating his explanation, for the **full 3 marks**. Juliet has failed to understand the question and instead has simply explained what validity is, instead of applying her knowledge to the specific situation, therefore **0 marks.**

Question 6 The police interview a number of people who witness a car accident. Some of the witnesses are residents in a nearby old people's residence. What advice would you give the police about the accuracy of the older witnesses' recall? Refer to psychological research in your answer. *(6 marks)*

I would tell them that the recall of older witnesses can be suspect, but it can still be accurate. For example, older witnesses can still be accurate provided the time interval between witnessing the accident and recalling it is quite short, but accuracy decreases the longer the interval. I would tell them that older witnesses tend to lack confidence in the accuracy of their recall compared to younger witnesses and are also less accurate (Yarmey, 1993). Finally, I would tell them that older witnesses are much more accurate at identifying people in their own age group, so that if they were asked to identify the driver (e.g. if it was a hit-and-run incident), they would be less accurate if they were from a different age group.

I would tell the police that older witnesses make more errors. One of the errors they make is called the 'source misinformation effect'. What it would mean here is that they may remember who they had seen, but mix up locations. For example, they may identify someone they had seen down at the shops earlier that day, and say he was the driver of the car. This is because they can remember people, but can't be as accurate as remembering the context of that person. When adults get older, for example, they may tell a joke back to the same person who told it to them, because they remember the joke, but not who told it to them in the first place.

Both answers here are good. Clearly Romeo has provided more specific psychological research and named some of the studies. In contrast Juliet has just focused on one piece of advice but made her understanding of this quite clear through examples that are clearly psychologically informed. Note that there was no requirement in the question to give more than one piece of advice.

Romeo's answer deserves more than 6 marks but that is all that is available, so the **full 6 marks**. Juliet's answer is better than basic but the link between the research and the advice could be clearer (she appears to have forgotten the 'advice' aspect of the question), so **4 out of 6 marks.**

Question 7 Some research has shown that anxiety leads to less accurate recall of events. Why might anxiety have this effect? Refer to psychological research in your answer. *(3 marks)*

When people are anxious, they become aroused. At low levels of arousal, people tend to perform poorly because they are poorly motivated and less alert. At moderate levels of arousal, motivation increases as does alertness, resulting in better memory. At high levels of arousal, associated with very emotional events, the high levels of cortisol circulating in the bloodstream suppress memory, resulting in poor recall (Tollenaar et al., 2008).

Research has shown that high levels of anxiety result in poor EWT and low levels of anxiety result in good EWT. One piece of research that showed this was the weapon focus study by Loftus. She found that when people see a knife covered in what appears to be blood they are distracted by it and the anxiety this creates makes them forget other aspects of the situation.

This is not an easy question and Juliet has fallen into the trap of describing a study that <u>shows</u> anxiety leads to less accurate recall but doesn't <u>explain</u> it, so **no marks**. Romeo's answer is spot on giving an explanation (high levels of arousal due to cortisol), so **full marks.**

Question 6 Some research has shown that age is associated with less accurate recall of events. Why might age have this effect? Refer to psychological research in your answer. *(3 marks)*

There are several reasons why age may be associated with less accurate recall. One of these is the own-age bias. Older adults tend to show poor performance on tests of EWT, but part of the reason for this poor performance is due to the use of younger adults as targets. Although younger participants perform better than the older adults, this is because the target subjects are of a similar age. Older adults perform better when the target subjects are also older (Anastasi and Rhodes, 2006).

As people get older, their ability to remember details gets worse. For example, Yarney (1993) found old people made worse witnesses in terms of accuracy than young people. This decline in memory is an inevitable consequence of old age. In the same way as people's physical abilities deteriorate with age, so do their mental abilities.

Romeo again has given us an answer to the question 'why', but this time Juliet has provided a better answer, giving a detailed explanation of the fact that memory deteriorates with age and linking this to poor recall in older people. **Full marks** for both Romeo and Juliet because they both have answered 'why' and referred to psychological research in their answer.

It is not required that you actually name the source of the research as long as it is identifiable as a piece of psychological research. Also remember that 'research' refers to theories/explanations as well as studies.

RESEARCH METHODS QUESTION

A researcher investigated the accuracy of the recall of real-life eyewitnesses. Each eyewitness answered a questionnaire about their experiences which included questions about how scared they were and what details they remembered. The graph on the right shows the relationship between fear (score from 1 to 10, where 10 is very scared) and amount of detail recalled. A correlation coefficient of +.55 was calculated.

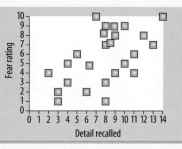

(a) (i) With reference to psychological research, explain what relationship you would expect to find between anxiety and recall. *(3 marks)*
(ii) Write a suitable directional hypothesis for this study, based on the research evidence identified in **(i)**. *(2 marks)*

Romeo's answer

(i) Based on previous research (e.g. Deffenbacher et al., 2004), I would expect to find a negative relationship between anxiety and recall, with high levels of anxiety being associated with low levels of recall, although they also suggest that there may be a curvilinear relationship between the two, with low and high levels being related to poor recall and medium levels being related to high recall.

(ii) Based on Deffenbacher et al.'s first finding, a suitable directional hypothesis would be that 'There is a negative correlation between levels of anxiety at the time of an incident and subsequent level of recall for that incident'.

Juliet's answer

(i) I would expect to find a negative correlation between anxiety and recall. The higher the anxiety, the lower the recall, and the lower the anxiety the higher the recall.

(ii) People who have high levels of anxiety when witnessing a crime will later have lower recall of it, and the lower the anxiety the higher the recall.

Examiner's comments

(i) Romeo's answer is extremely detailed so **full marks**. Juliet's answer is certainly creditworthy but fails to make an explicit link to any research so only **1 out of 3 marks**.

(ii) Both candidates have written a hypothesis which is suitably operationalised and represents a negative correlation – but Juliet has spoiled hers by adding the second ('and the lower…'). A hypothesis is an unambiguous statement of the expected relationship between variables and Juliet's ambiguity only gets **1 out of 2 marks** whereas Romeo gets **full marks**.

(b) What does the graph tell you about the relationship between fear and amount of detail recalled? *(3 marks)*

The graph shows that high levels of fear lead to better recall, and low levels of fear lead to worse recall.

The graph shows a moderate positive correlation between the level of fear and the amount of detail recalled. The higher the fear, the more detail is recalled.

Romeo's answer suggests an incomplete understanding of correlation – all that is shown is a link between fear and recall not a causal relationship as implied in his answer. Therefore **0 marks**. Juliet scores the full **3 marks** because she correctly identifies a positive correlation and notes that it is 'moderate' and, finally, interprets what this actually means.

(c) Outline **one** strength and **one** limitation of using correlational analysis to investigate eyewitness testimony. *(3 marks + 3 marks)*

A strength of correlational analysis is that it can be used in situations where it is not possible to manipulate an independent variable, e.g. where it is impractical or unethical to do so.

A limitation of correlational analysis is that it doesn't tell us anything about a causal relationship, i.e. it doesn't tell us that one variable has caused the other, just that they are co-related.

A strength is that it enables investigators to study relationships where it might be unethical to manipulate variables to look for a causal relationship. For example, it would be unethical to create fear to study its effect on recall.

A limitation is that it doesn't demonstrate a causal relationship, e.g. a correlation between fear and recall doesn't indicate that a change in recall has been caused by a change in fear level.

Both candidates have supplied appropriate and detailed strengths and limitations, but Juliet has remembered to contextualise her answer and specifically refer to research on eyewitness testimony, so Juliet would get **3 marks + 3 marks** whereas Romeo would get **2 marks + 2 marks**.

EXAM ADVICE

In some questions contextualisation is required in order to score full marks whereas in other questions you may receive full marks even though no contextualisation is included in your answer. The safest approach is to always contextualise your answers. ('Contextualise' means to place your answer in a particular context – in this case research on eyewitness testimony.) This is particularly true for questions worth more than 2 marks – the extra marks are likely to be contextualisation.

(d) Describe **one** possible factor that might lower to the validity of this study. *(3 marks)*

Participants may not be able to remember how afraid they were at the time of the incident or they may have repressed it, so the estimates may not be accurate.

A factor is whether participants would be honest about the amount of fear they experienced at the time. Because of the tendency to answer in a socially desirable way, it is possible that some participants may report experiencing less fear than they actually did, which would bias the results.

Juliet has clearly given a detailed response to this question and deserves the **full 3 marks**. Romeo's answer is also spot on but lacks the detail required for 3 marks, and would receive **2 out of 3 marks**. He could have improved his answer by explaining, for example, why the participants may have repressed their feelings of fear.

(e) How could the reliability of the questionnaire be assessed in this study? *(3 marks)*

Reliability is a measure of consistency over time. For example, if an investigator gave a test to participants and then gave them the same test a month later, the scores can then be correlated. If this produces a high positive correlation, the test has good reliability.

It can be assessed using the test–retest method. For example, participants are asked to indicate how scared they were at the time of an experience and then asked again some time later (e.g. two weeks). The answers can then be compared and should be more or less the same.

Juliet has again provided an excellent answer worth the **full 3 marks**. Romeo is on the right track, it's just a shame he used the word 'test' instead of 'questionnaire'. It shows he wasn't applying his knowledge to the actual question asked but, instead, was reeling off information he had memorised – which is also shown by the fact that he included a definition of reliability which was not required by the question. So **2 out of 3 marks** for this answer.

Extended writing question

Discuss research into the effects of age on the accuracy of eyewitness testimony.

(12 marks)

AO1

Three relevant research studies have been explained in detail.

Notice how each research study has been presented in a separate paragraph. An important AO1 criteria is the 'presentation of information' (see mark scheme on page 9). This layout ensures that the answer is clear and coherent.

There is a lot of research that shows age differences in the accuracy of eyewitness testimony. Some of the research shows that younger people are better but not always. There is also evidence that older people can be accurate in their recall.

Parker and Carranza (1989) found that when they asked young children and college students to correctly identify an individual after they had watched a mock crime, the children were more likely to wrongly identify the individual. Students also fared better when compared to older witnesses.

In another experiment, Memon et al. (2003) showed an 'incident' to people who were between 16 and 33 and to those who were between 60 and 82. They then asked the participants to identify someone who had been involved in the incident that they had witnessed. When there was about half an hour between witnessing the incident and being asked about it, the older witnesses were as accurate as the younger ones. However, when this interval was much longer, the older witnesses were much less accurate.

Anastasi and Rhodes (2006) showed photos of young, middle-aged and old adults to the same three age groups. They found that although the younger adults were better able to identify who they had already seen when later shown the same photos amongst a lot of 'distractor' photos, the older adults were better at picking out other older people than they were the other two age groups.

A lot of this research is carried out in laboratories using students rather than using real-life incidents and real people. Therefore it lacks ecological validity and can't be generalised.

(268 words)

AO2

No need for a general introduction – there are no special marks for this 'scene-setting'.

The final paragraph is a real disappointment. Where's the evaluation? Only one criticism which has been explained rather superficially.

Examiner's comments

The essay starts so well – with excellent description (**AO1**) of appropriate research. It is reasonably detailed and shows sound knowledge and understanding, so **6 out of 6 marks** for **AO1**.

The **AO2** material is marginally better than 'just discernible' (1 out of 6 marks, see mark scheme on page 9) and is rescued by the fact that the expression of ideas and spelling are good, so just **2 out of 6 marks**.

Total = **8 out of 12 marks** for a **Grade B**.

Extended writing question

Discuss research into the effects of anxiety on the accuracy of eyewitness testimony.

(12 marks)

AO1

The first paragraph contains details of an appropriate research study.

This second paragraph is not dealing with a research study but rather with an explanation – which is still 'research'. Research is both studies or theories/explanations. So either would be creditworthy in this essay.

Another study has been described in detail in the third paragraph.

This description of the study by Christiansen and Hubinette counts as AO1 material.

Research by Deffenbacher et al. (2004) has shown that when people are in a heightened state of arousal (the physiological correlate of anxiety) this has a negative impact on their ability to recall information. Low levels of arousal are also associated with low levels of accuracy, but the best performance is associated with moderate levels of arousal.

Deffenbacher's finding that there is a curvilinear relationship between anxiety and accuracy of EWT explains why some studies show a decrease in accuracy with anxiety and others show an increase in accuracy. In the case of the former, it is likely that levels of anxiety were high (leading to decreased accuracy), whereas in the latter, it is likely that levels of anxiety were moderate, leading to increased accuracy.

Johnson and Scott (1976) have investigated the weapon-focus effect. Participants heard a heated discussion in another room. In one condition, a man emerged from the room carrying a pen and with his hands covered in grease. In the second condition, a man emerged carrying a paperknife and with blood on his hands. When asked to identify the man from among 50 photos, those who had seen the pen were far more accurate than those who had seen the knife. This suggests that the anxiety created by the weapon somehow distracts witnesses' attention from other aspects of the incident.

Research such as Loftus' could lack validity because much of it is carried out in an artificial environment, i.e. in a laboratory. This means that participants do not take the experiment seriously, knowing that their EWT does not really matter, and that a crime has not really been committed. This may be a reason why so many laboratory studies show relatively poor recall and why so many witnesses of real crimes show relatively good recall. A study of real-life crime by Christiansen and Hubinette (1993) found that anxiety actually enhanced the accuracy of memory. In this study they questioned 58 people who had witnessed a bank robbery. They found that those people who had been threatened in some way remembered more details than those who had just been onlookers. Of course, because this was a natural experiment there may have been extraneous variables that also affected accuracy of recall so it may not have been anxiety.

(379 words)

AO2

The beginning of this paragraph is evaluation, starting with a well-elaborated point about validity, which then leads to a second criticism – that real-life research has shown contrasting findings.

The paragraph ends with a criticism of the real-life research. This criticism is somewhat brief. Greater elaboration could have been given by identifying a possible extraneous variable.

Examiner's comments

The description (**AO1**) of research is excellent – detailed and accurate for the **full 6 marks**.

The evaluation (**AO2**) lacks the range and/or depth for full marks. One point has been made well, and two further points have been made more briefly. This makes the answer better than a 'superficial consideration of a restricted range' (which would be a maximum of 3 out of 6 marks) but only just, so **4 out of 6 marks**.

Total = **10 out of 12**, a **Grade A** answer.

The cognitive interview

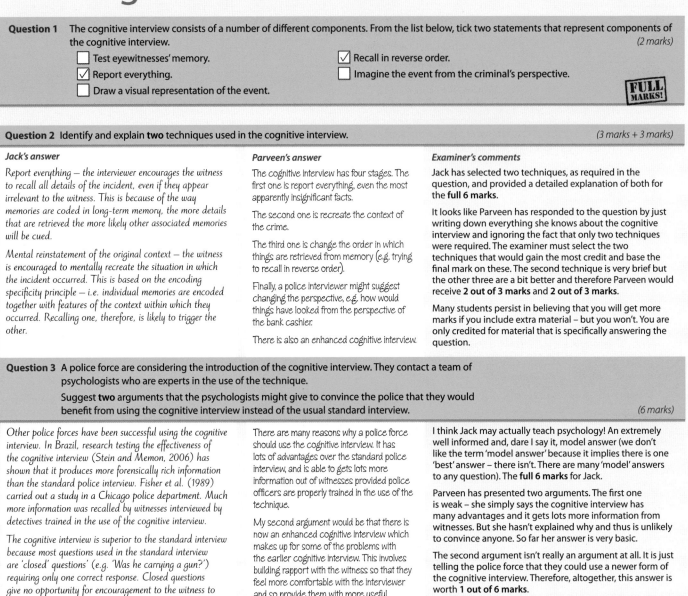

Question 1 The cognitive interview consists of a number of different components. From the list below, tick two statements that represent components of the cognitive interview.
(2 marks)

- ☐ Test eyewitnesses' memory.
- ☑ Report everything.
- ☐ Draw a visual representation of the event.
- ☑ Recall in reverse order.
- ☐ Imagine the event from the criminal's perspective.

FULL MARKS!

Question 2 Identify and explain **two** techniques used in the cognitive interview.
(3 marks + 3 marks)

Jack's answer

Report everything – the interviewer encourages the witness to recall all details of the incident, even if they appear irrelevant to the witness. This is because of the way memories are coded in long-term memory, the more details that are retrieved the more likely other associated memories will be cued.

Mental reinstatement of the original context – the witness is encouraged to mentally recreate the situation in which the incident occurred. This is based on the encoding specificity principle – i.e. individual memories are encoded together with features of the context within which they occurred. Recalling one, therefore, is likely to trigger the other.

Parveen's answer

The cognitive interview has four stages. The first one is report everything, even the most apparently insignificant facts.

The second one is recreate the context of the crime.

The third one is change the order in which things are retrieved from memory (e.g. trying to recall in reverse order).

Finally, a police interviewer might suggest changing the perspective, e.g. how would things have looked from the perspective of the bank cashier.

There is also an enhanced cognitive interview.

Examiner's comments

Jack has selected two techniques, as required in the question, and provided a detailed explanation of both for the **full 6 marks.**

It looks like Parveen has responded to the question by just writing down everything she knows about the cognitive interview and ignoring the fact that only two techniques were required. The examiner must select the two techniques that would gain the most credit and base the final mark on these. The second technique is very brief but the other three are a bit better and therefore Parveen would receive **2 out of 3 marks** and **2 out of 3 marks.**

Many students persist in believing that you will get more marks if you include extra material – but you won't. You are only credited for material that is specifically answering the question.

Question 3 A police force are considering the introduction of the cognitive interview. They contact a team of psychologists who are experts in the use of the technique.

Suggest **two** arguments that the psychologists might give to convince the police that they would benefit from using the cognitive interview instead of the usual standard interview.
(6 marks)

Other police forces have been successful using the cognitive interview. In Brazil, research testing the effectiveness of the cognitive interview (Stein and Memon, 2006) has shown that it produces more forensically rich information than the standard police interview. Fisher et al. (1989) carried out a study in a Chicago police department. Much more information was recalled by witnesses interviewed by detectives trained in the use of the cognitive interview.

The cognitive interview is superior to the standard interview because most questions used in the standard interview are 'closed' questions (e.g. 'Was he carrying a gun?') requiring only one correct response. Closed questions give no opportunity for encouragement to the witness to elaborate or extend an answer, which is what the cognitive interview does.

There are many reasons why a police force should use the cognitive interview. It has lots of advantages over the standard police interview, and is able to gets lots more information out of witnesses provided police officers are properly trained in the use of the technique.

My second argument would be that there is now an enhanced cognitive interview which makes up for some of the problems with the earlier cognitive interview. This involves building rapport with the witness so that they feel more comfortable with the interviewer and so provide them with more useful information.

I think Jack may actually teach psychology! An extremely well informed and, dare I say it, model answer (we don't like the term 'model answer' because it implies there is one 'best' answer – there isn't. There are many 'model' answers to any question). The **full 6 marks** for Jack.

Parveen has presented two arguments. The first one is weak – she simply says the cognitive interview has many advantages and it gets lots more information from witnesses. But she hasn't explained why and thus is unlikely to convince anyone. So far her answer is very basic.

The second argument isn't really an argument at all. It is just telling the police force that they could use a newer form of the cognitive interview. Therefore, altogether, this answer is worth **1 out of 6 marks.**

Question 4 A police department has been using the cognitive interview for several years. At a review meeting they conclude that its use does not appear to have improved the accuracy of eyewitness testimony.

With reference to psychological evidence, suggest **two** reasons for their lack of success when using the cognitive interview.
(6 marks)

Research by Kebbell et al. (1999) suggests that many officers trained in the use of the cognitive interview reported that they rarely had the time to conduct what they thought was a good cognitive interview, mostly because they were unable to conduct all four aspects of the cognitive interview necessary for effective witness recall.

In earlier versions of the cognitive interview, interviewers did not attempt to develop any rapport with witnesses, or make them feel at ease. Because anxiety can interfere with recall, failure to put the witness at ease may inhibit them from divulging sensitive information, which would lessen the effectiveness of the interview.

One reason why the cognitive interview may not have increased the accuracy of witnesses is that interviewers are not that good at using it. It is a bit like therapy. A therapy is only as good as the therapist that uses it, therefore if a police officer is poorly trained or cuts corners, he (or she) will not get good results.

Another reason why it may not be seen to be working very effectively is because police forces don't have enough time to use it properly. This is what Kebbell and Wagstaff (1996) discovered in their research.

This time Jack has got rather too involved with his research evidence and forgotten to answer the question. He has implicitly answered the question by describing a study that shows that police don't have time to conduct proper cognitive interviews – but he needed to state this explicitly for full marks. His second effort is slightly more explicit, so a total of **5 out of 6 marks.**

In contrast, Parveen has answered the question – but she has failed to refer to psychological evidence except in a very superficial way. This question was not marked as 3 marks + 3 marks so it is not simply a question of giving her 2 marks for each part of her answer. Altogether her answer is still basic (see mark scheme on page 9), so **3 out of 6 marks.**

Question 5 Describe what research has shown about the usefulness of the cognitive interview. *(6 marks)*

A meta-analysis of studies comparing the cognitive interview (CI) to the standard police interview found that the CI produced a significant increase in the amount of accurate information recalled (Kohnken et al., 1999). Research by Milne and Bull (2002) tested the usefulness of the different components of the CI. When compared to a control group who were just asked to 'try again', no one component on its own was superior to the control group. However, when a combination of 'report everything' and 'mental reinstatement of context' was used, recall was significantly superior. Fisher et al. (1989) carried out a study in a police department in Chicago. Much more information was recalled by witnesses interviewed by detectives trained in the use of the cognitive interview.

Kohnken et al. (1999) carried out a meta-analysis of 53 studies of the cognitive interview. They found that there was an average of 34% improvement compared to the amount of information recalled although there was also an increase in the amount of incorrect information recalled as well. One of the main problems with this meta-analysis is that most of the studies used students, so it is difficult to generalise from this to the use of the cognitive interview in more realistic settings.

There are studies of the cognitive interview used by police forces (e.g. the Thames Valley Police) and they tend to be less successful in using it. However, this might be due to the fact that many police forces don't use all the different parts of the cognitive interview.

Both students clearly know a lot about the research related to the usefulness of the cognitive interview, but how effectively have they used this? Jack has stayed focused and just given us the findings and conclusions, so a **full 6 marks**.

Parveen has strayed off the point a few times and so much of the answer is just not used effectively. Halfway through the first paragraph she raises a criticism, which is only marginally creditworthy (it does tell us how to treat the evidence itself).

In Parveen's second paragraph she describes a further finding which again is only marginally relevant – it would receive more credit if it explicitly answered the question, i.e. say 'Research shows that the cognitive interview is not that effective because many police forces do not actually use the full interview'. So Parveen's answer is closer to basic and gets **3 out of 6 marks**.

Question 6 A man walking through a train carriage notices that a woman has just got up to go to the toilet, leaving her laptop on her seat. He walks swiftly through the train carriage and grabs the laptop. The police interview the people sitting near the woman and her laptop. How could the cognitive interview be used with these eyewitnesses? *(6 marks)*

The police could start by building rapport with the witnesses. People may feel nervous about being interviewed in case the police think they have stolen the laptop themselves. They could then be asked to report everything, for example, they may feel the phone call they had overheard just before the laptop went missing is irrelevant but it might be an accomplice. The other component that has been shown to be effective is the 'mental reinstatement of context' component. The witnesses could be asked to imagine themselves back in the carriage and describe what they had seen or heard. Research has found that when doing this, witnesses remember more if they shut their eyes (Perfect et al., 2008), so witnesses could be asked to do that.

The police can ask the witnesses what they can remember about the person who stole the laptop. They can be asked to recall everything no matter how trivial or irrelevant it appears. They could then be asked to imagine themselves at the scene of the crime, or they could even be taken back physically. This helps them to remember details at the time of the crime because memories are associated together. They could then be asked to recall events in a different order, for example trying to recall events in reverse order. Finally, they could be asked to change their perspective, to imagine how somebody else who viewed the crime might have seen it.

The key difference between Jack and Parveen's answers is contextualisation. Both candidates know about how a cognitive interview is conducted but Jack has remembered to link each element to the scenario presented in the question (i.e. he has contextualised it). For example, he says 'They could then be asked to report everything' and then gives an example which is specific to this situation. Parveen fails to do this and therefore can't get full marks.

So Jack receives the **full 6 marks** whereas Parveen receives just **3 out of 6 marks** for a basic answer.

RESEARCH METHODS QUESTION

The table on the right shows the results of a content analysis. Policemen were observed while interviewing eyewitnesses and a tally was kept of the individual behaviours observed. This was done before they went on a training course and again afterwards.

Behaviour by interviewer	Before training	After training
Building rapport	22	35
Praising witness	2	44
Asking witness to elaborate what they said	17	42
Looking directly at witness	32	35

(a) Explain the processes involved in content analysis. *(3 marks)*

Jack's answer

First, the researcher chooses what they are going to analyse (e.g. we did an analysis of television adverts in class) and then they break down the adverts into different categories (e.g. expert male, female product user, etc.).

Parveen's answer

The researcher must first decide what material to sample (in this case policemen's behaviour while interviewing witnesses) and how frequently these behaviours are sampled. They must also decide on the behavioural categories to be sampled, e.g. the use of leading questions, encouragement for the witness, etc. Once they have the categories they can then count instances in each category or find examples in each category.

Examiner's comments

Parveen's answer has the edge on Jack's because of the extra detail provided. Jack has referred to an activity he did in class but has omitted to say what he did next – count frequences, so **2 out of 3 marks** for Jack and **full marks** for Parveen.

(b) State **two** conclusions that could be drawn from the content analysis above. *(4 marks)*

Before training, the policeman hardly ever praises the witness, but after training, he praises the witness a lot more.

The aspect of the policeman's behaviour that doesn't really change is looking directly at the witness. This is almost the same after training as it is before training.

The first conclusion is that the interviewer shows much more evidence of behaviours that are characteristic of the cognitive interview (e.g. asking the witness to elaborate what they said) after training than before.

The second is that whereas before training some behaviours (e.g. looking directly at the witness) were frequently used and others (e.g. praising the witness) were seldom used, after training all the target behaviours were used with similar levels of frequency.

Both candidates have reported findings rather than conclusions. Parveen does try to turn the findings into conclusions by saying 'The first conclusion…', but this isn't enough.

A conclusion should be a general statement based on the findings, for example Parveen's first conclusion would be 'Training does appear to improve the ability to use certain techniques because we can see more evidence of cognitive interview techniques (such as asking the witness to elaborate what they said) after training than before'. Both candidates would receive **2 out of 4 marks** for providing findings rather than conclusions.

RESEARCH METHODS QUESTION

A police department decided to introduce the use of the cognitive interview to its detectives. The detectives went on a training course and subsequently were asked to use cognitive interview techniques when interviewing suspects. A pair of psychologists were asked to observe the police detectives to see how effectively they were using the cognitive interview.

(a) Outline **two** behavioural categories the psychologists might use when observing the police interviewers' behaviour. *(4 marks)*

Jack's answer

They could note down whenever the interviewer interrupts the witness, as interruption is more a characteristic of the standard interview.

They could also note down anytime the interviewer makes an effort to build rapport with the witness (e.g. by smiling or thanking them for remembering).

Parveen's answer

They could use either a structured observation where the different behaviours to be observed are listed for the observer, or they could use an unstructured observation, where the observer writes down everything that they observe. Video recordings are good for this because they may miss something at the time.

Examiner's comments

The key feature of a behavioural category is that it has to be a behaviour you can observe – something you can see a person doing. Jack has identified two such behaviours and made clear how these behaviours would be linked to the cognitive interview. One behaviour would show that the person is not doing the cognitive interview, the other behaviour demonstrates that the person is using the cognitive interview technique. **Full marks** for Jack.

Parveen clearly does not know what a behavioural category is and has simply written something about conducting observations, so **0 marks**.

(b) Reliability is important when making observations.

    (i) Explain what is meant by 'reliability'. *(2 marks)*

    (ii) Outline how the reliability of the observations might be checked. *(3 marks)*

(i) Reliability refers to how consistent observations are, for example, whether each psychologist observing the cognitive interview codes behave in the same way.

(ii) To establish inter-observer reliability, it is necessary to correlate the observations of the two observers. The number of agreed observations is divided by the total number of observations. If this produces a correlation of +.8 or better, then there is high inter-observer reliability.

(i) Reliability means consistency. Consistency is very important when making observations, because without it the observations cannot really be trusted.

(ii) It is important to check the reliability of observations, whenever more than one observer is used. The reliability of the observations can be checked by correlating the two sets of data produced by the two observers together. The higher the correlation, the more reliable the observations. The lower the correlation, the less reliable the observations.

(i) Both answers are worth the **full 2 marks**. Jack has contextualised his answer even though there was no requirement for this. Of course it still gains credit.

(ii) Jack's answer is, yet again, detailed and accurate, for the **full 3 marks**. Parveen's answer contains quite a bit of irrelevant material – such as the first and last sentences. However, in the middle she does say how the reliability might be checked. She has said 'correlating' instead of just 'comparing' which makes her answer better than 'brief' and adds some further relevant information. So a solid **2 out of 3 marks**.

(c) The psychologists decided it would be best to conduct their observations using a one-way mirror so the detectives did not know they were being observed.

    (i) Explain why this would improve the validity of their observations. *(2 marks)*

    (ii) Identify **one** potential ethical issue created by this design decision and suggest how the psychologists could deal with it. *(3 marks)*

(i) If the detectives know they are being observed, this may cause them to alter their behaviour in some way. By using a covert observation method such as a one-way mirror, they may act more naturally.

(ii) By watching the detectives without their knowledge, this might be considered an invasion of privacy. This can be dealt with by informing them in advance that this would be done and only proceeding if they are okay with that.

(i) A one-way mirror would mean that the psychologists could watch the detectives without being seen.

(ii) This would create an ethical problem because it is deception. With a one-way mirror the detectives wouldn't be able to see the psychologists but the psychologists can see them. This is deception. They could deal with this by debriefing them afterwards.

(i) Jack's response is excellent as usual (**2 out of 2 marks**) but Parveen has missed the point. She hasn't explained how this would improve the validity of the observations, essentially she has just repeated the stem part of the question, **0 marks**.

(ii) Both our candidates have identified an appropriate issue and each has dealt with it differently. However, Parveen has only briefly explained how she would do this (by debriefing) whereas Jack has more fully explained what he would do. So Jack receives the **full 3 marks** and Parveen receives **2 out of 3 marks**.

(d) An alternative method of collecting data is to use a questionnaire. In this case the psychologists could have designed a questionnaire to ask the policemen what cognitive interview techniques they were using and whether they felt the cognitive interview was more effective than the methods they had previously used.

    (i) Explain why it might be better to use a questionnaire instead of observing the policemen. *(3 marks)*

    (ii) Explain why using an observation technique would be better than a questionnaire. *(3 marks)*

(i) A questionnaire could be better because the policemen may be more comfortable revealing sensitive information or how they really use the cognitive interview with the anonymity of a questionnaire rather than when being observed by a team of psychologists, when they would feel they have to do everything 'by the book'.

(ii) An observation technique might be better than a questionnaire because of the possibility of a social desirability bias. Policemen may complete the questionnaire in a way that they think it should be completed rather than how they actually use the cognitive interview. This is especially true if they feel the questionnaires might be used to determine promotion.

(i) It would be better to use a questionnaire because that would make it a lot cheaper for the police force, because they wouldn't have to employ very expensive psychologists to observe their interviewers. It would also be easier than carrying out observations (which is a specialist job).

(ii) An observation would be better because the psychologists could actually see what the detectives are doing rather than just reading their responses to questions. There is always the chance that in a questionnaire a detective may lie just to look good, but they couldn't do that in an observation, so an observation would be better.

(i) Parveen has provided two answers – which is fine because the question does not ask for only **one** benefit. However neither points are worth anything. Questionnaires are not cheap because experts have to design them. Questionnaires are also not easy because of time spent designing them – they are easier once they have been designed but this point needs to be made, so **0 marks** for Parveen. Jack receives **full marks**.

(ii) Parveen's first sentence is not creditworthy but in the second sentence she makes a valid point, albeit not as effectively as Jack, who uses the correct term 'social desirability bias'. Parveen has said more than 'they may lie to look good' (i.e. provided elaboration), therefore **2 out of 3 marks** whereas Jack receives the **full 3 marks**.

Outline and evaluate the use of the cognitive interview.

(12 marks)

Answer 1

AO1

Oh dear – how many candidates start their essay by saying what they are going to do? This gains no credit. In an exam essay you simply must get on and do it.

The main part of this answer offers a reasonably detailed account of the use of the cognitive interview.

In this essay I am going to outline the main parts of the cognitive interview, and elaborate each by giving an example of how it might be used. I am then going to move on to look at research that has been carried out on the cognitive interview, and finally I will evaluate it by looking at some of the problems with the use of the cognitive interview in the real world.

The cognitive interview has four main parts. The first is to report everything. Here the witness to a crime is encouraged to recall everything they can remember about an incident. Some things (e.g. a phone ringing) might be considered unimportant by the witness and so not mentioned, but they are encouraged to report everything they can remember, just in case it is a vital piece of evidence.

The second part is for the witness to go back (in their mind) to the scene of the crime. In this case the witness should imagine they are back in the original crime scene and try to recall everything they see. The police interviewer will encourage the witness to say anything that they see hoping that some other information might emerge.

The third part is changing the order of recall. For example, the policeman asks the witness to recall things in reverse order. Or the policeman might ask the witness to start somewhere in the middle of the event.

The fourth part is to change perspective or your viewpoint. You imagine you are one of the other people at the crime scene and imagine what they might have seen.

If I had more time I would have looked at research evidence for the cognitive interview and some of the reasons why police forces have not been as successful as they might have been with the use of this method of interviewing witnesses.

(311 words)

AO2

There is absolutely no point in stating what you might have said. Some credit might have been awarded if one piece of research evidence or one reason for lack of success had been given. As it stands a paragraph like this is simply wasting time.

Examiner's comments It might look like this answer would be worth a fair amount of marks – it's a good length and there is a lot of information. However, it is all description (**AO1**) and sometimes this is a bit repetitive, so **5 out of 6 marks** for AO1. No marks for **AO2**.

Total = **5 out of 12 marks**, equivalent to a **Grade E**.

Answer 2

AO1

In this essay the candidate has just plunged straight in and provided a detailed account of the cognitive interview.

Some of the points might be regarded as evaluation (e.g. 'This is an efficient way…') but they are credited here as AO1 as there is ample evaluation.

The cognitive interview has four main parts. The first is to report everything. Here the witness to a crime is encouraged to recall everything they can remember about an incident. Some things (e.g. a phone ringing) might be considered unimportant by the witness and so not mentioned, but they are encouraged to report everything they can remember, just in case it is a vital piece of evidence. The second part is for the witness to go back (in their mind) to the scene of the crime. This helps them to recreate the original context, which may jog their memory. The third part is changing the order of recall. For example, they may be asked to recall things in reverse order or to start in the middle. This is an efficient way of getting them to remember details because it stops them thinking in just one way (e.g. assuming that something follows something else because it usually does). The fourth part is to change perspective, trying to see things from the perspective of other witnesses.

Research evidence has generally supported the effectiveness of the cognitive interview (CI) over the standard police interview. A meta-analysis of studies comparing the CI to the standard police interview found that the CI produced a significant increase in the amount of accurate information recalled (Kohnken et al., 1999). Research with police forces has also supported the superiority of the cognitive interview. In Brazil, research testing the effectiveness of the cognitive interview (Stein and Memon, 2006) has shown that it produces more forensically rich information than the standard police interview. Fisher et al. (1989) carried out a study in a Chicago police department. Much more information was recalled by witnesses interviewed by detectives trained in the use of the cognitive interview. However, despite the advantages of the CI, its use in UK police departments is not widespread. Research by Kebbell et al. (1999) found that many officers trained in the use of the cognitive interview reported that they rarely had the time to conduct what they thought was a good cognitive interview, mostly because they were unable to conduct all four aspects of the cognitive interview necessary for effective witness recall.

(364 words)

AO2

Paragraph starts by clearly flagging this as evaluation.

The paragraph is stuffed full of research studies, perhaps lacking depth but certainly a broad range.

You are not required to present a balanced evaluation (strengths and limitations) but it does add to the effectiveness of the AO2 content.

Examiner's comments The outline (**AO1**) of the cognitive interview is excellent – accurate and detailed, so **6 out of 6 marks**.

The evaluation (**AO2**) covers a broad range of points in reasonable depth so also **6 out of 6 marks**.

12 out of 12 marks, clearly a **Grade A** answer – not perfect but sufficient for full marks.

Strategies for memory improvement

Question 1 Outline **two** strategies to improve memory. *(4 marks)*

Julio's answer

An example is to put things into a rhyme like 'twinkle twinkle little star'. Another method is putting things along a path so they can be retrieved later (method of loci).

Erica's answer

An acronym is making a word or sentence from the first letters of each word in a list, e.g. 'My Very Excellent Mother Just Made Us Nine Pizzas' for the planets. A mind map is a diagram which places the main idea at the centre and related concepts radiate out from this central point on a series of 'branches'.

Examiner's comments

Both candidates have provided two examples, although Julio's first example lacks detail so **3 out of 4 marks** for him and the **full 4 marks** for Erica.

Question 2 Student doctors have to remember a very large amount of information when they are studying for exams, such as the names of all the muscles and bones in the body and their associated functions.
  (a) Describe **one** strategy that they might use to improve their memories. *(4 marks)*
  (b) Explain **one** reason why this would be a good method to use when memorising such lists of body parts. *(3 marks)*

(a) They could put all the different parts of the body on a mind map. For example, they could create a mind map that gives them a visual representation of the different bones in the body, such as the skull, fibia and tibula, femur and collarbone. By laying it out visually like this it would make them easier to learn.

(b) By making something visual you are using more than one sense. Some people are visual learners, so find it easier to remember things that are laid out visually. This would work for body parts, particularly if there was some sort of cartoon that went with them that would help them to remember.

(a) They could use a visual mnemonic such as a mind map. This is a diagram in which the key concept (such as a particular muscle group) is in the middle and there are links with other concepts (the individual muscles), which then branch out into associated concepts such as the function of each muscle. This gives individual doctors their own unique and highly visual learning aid.

(b) It is both a visual and an active strategy for learning. Buzan (2006) claims that traditional note taking is a passive process, and therefore the brain doesn't really interact much with the material. However, by building a mind map, the brain is engaging in deeper processing, and additionally is linking muscles and their functions in a highly visual way, which is especially good for visual learners.

(a) It looks like Erica's superior knowledge has tripped her up – she is so focused on describing the mind map method in detail that she has forgotten to apply this understanding to the particular task of remembering muscles and bones, so **2 out of 4 marks** for Erica, whereas Julio gets the **full 4 marks**.

(b) The same issue continues to cause problems for Erica because she has failed to contextualise her answer, so **2 out of 3 marks** and the **full 3 marks** for Julio.

Question 3 Wendy has started a new job in a factory and she is required to follow a complex series of actions in order to produce the final product. She keeps getting confused about when to do the different activities.
Outline **one** memory strategy that would be suitable for Wendy to use to improve her recall, and explain why this might improve her memory. *(4 marks)*

One of the ways she could remember the complex series of actions that she has to perform is to write them down on post-it notes to remind her. These could be placed in lots of different places, e.g. in her bedroom, in her car and so on. By having the reminders in lots of different places, this would make it more likely that she would remember. This technique is highly effective in exam revision so would be useful here. It would improve her memory because she would be bombarded with the same information over and over again so would simply get used to it.

She could use a verbal mnemonic such as an acronym. This is a sentence in which the first letter of each word represents something in a list to be remembered. For example, if she was putting together cream teas, she could use the acronym 'Silly boys joyride cars' (scone, butter, jam, cream). This would be a good way of remembering because it organises the material by using the first letters of the words in order to create something meaningful, in this case a sentence.

It is possible that Julio's idea would help Wendy but he hasn't really tackled the issue of getting the tasks in the right order. By contrast, Erica has suggested a strategy that specifically offers help with getting things in the right order. Just **1 out of 4 marks** for Julio and the **full 4 marks** for Erica.

Question 4 Mavis is in an old people's home and her memory is starting to fade. She finds it difficult to remember the names of the other residents in the home. Suggest **one** memory strategy that would be suitable for Mavis to use to improve her recall. *(4 marks)*

The keyword system is a way of improving memory by associating a word to be remembered with a memorable image. For example, when learning Spanish, the Spanish word for cat is 'gato', so you could imagine a cat eating a gateaux and that would help you to remember how to say cat in Spanish!

Mavis could use the keyword system, which takes the words to be remembered (in this case the residents' names) and associates them with some image. For example, Cara could be imagined driving a car, Betty placing bets at a bookies, Bill as having a bird's beak and so on. In this way, every time Mavis sees a particular resident, she will remember the image, which will trigger an association with their name.

There is another good example here of no contextualisation (Julio's answer) versus contextualisation (Erica's answer). Erica has answered the question about how Mavis could use this strategy whereas Julio has only peripherally offered an answer. Julio would receive **2 out of 4 marks** whereas Erica would receive the **full 4 marks**.

Question 5 Psychologists have identified a number of successful strategies to improve memory. Outline how psychologists have investigated the benefits of these methods. *(6 marks)*

The first method is the lab experiment. This involves randomly allocating participants to the two conditions under investigation. One of these is the independent variable and the other is usually a control group, or control condition. This enables the experimenter to see whether the independent variable has an effect on the dependent variable. A second method is the observational method. This would involve observing people using strategies of improving memory in action to see if they make any difference to their memory. A third method would be the case study. This involves studying an individual who is using a particular strategy and following him over a period of time to see if his or her memory improves.

The benefits of different strategies of improving memory are usually investigated experimentally. This can be in a laboratory or in a field experiment. For example, Fontana et al. (2007) used a repeated measures experimental design to compare the relative effects of mnemonic strategies and direct instruction on academic performance in 14–16 year olds. During world history lessons, teachers alternated keywords and their illustrations with direct instruction procedures over a four-week period to teach two units of history. The independent variable was the type of instructional method and the presentation order was counterbalanced to prevent order effects, with some children receiving the keywords first then the direct instruction, and others the other way around.

Julio has approached this question by listing different research methods and, in the last two examples, has made a link between the named method and how this might be used to investigate organisation of memory. His answer contains little of real relevance, so **2 out of 6 marks**.

Erica has tried a better approach, which is to describe a relevant research study, focusing on the method that was used in this study. Her answer contains plenty of detail and deserves the **full 6 marks**.

A psychology class decides to compare the effectiveness of two methods of memory improvement, referred to as method 1 and method 2. They expect method 1 to be more effective.

(i) Write a suitable hypothesis for this study. *(3 marks)*

(ii) Is your hypothesis directional or non-directional? *(1 mark)*

Julio's answer	Erica's answer	Examiner's comments
(i) Method 1 will produce more memory improvement than method 2. (ii) A directional hypothesis because it is stating that one method (method 1) will lead to more memory improvement than the other (method 2).	(i) Students who use method 1 as a memory strategy during a psychology class subsequently are able to recall more of the content than students who use method 2. (ii) Directional.	(i) Julio's hypothesis is fine but lacks the operationalisation of Erica's. He gets **2 out of 3 marks** whereas Erica gets the **full 3 marks**. (ii) Julio has gone to town on his answer whereas all that was needed was the single word. Both students are correct for **1 mark**.

(b) Explain why it might be better to use an independent groups design rather than repeated measures in this study. *(2 marks)*

An independent groups design would be better because it would overcome order effects.	It would be better because with this way the two groups could be tested on their memory for the same material, rather than using different material, which would be an extraneous variable.	Erica gains the **full 2 marks** because she has contextualised her answer. Julio hasn't, although he has provided a brief reason, so **1 out of 2 marks**.

(i) Identify a suitable method to use in selecting participants and outline how you would do this. *(3 marks)*

(ii) Explain why this method would be best. *(2 marks)*

(i) They could use a random sample. In order to get this they could go to the refectory at lunchtime and pick (for example), the first 20 people who come into the room. (ii) This would be best because everyone has the same chance of being picked.	(i) They could use a random sample. This could be achieved by putting all the names of the members of another psychology class into a hat and drawing out the required number to make up the sample. (ii) This method would be best because it would avoid any bias in the selection of the sample, e.g. choosing the best learners or those who are more likely to try hardest.	Julio has named an appropriate method but then described a different one (picking the first 20 people is opportunity sampling), so just **1 out of 3 marks** for identifying the method. Erica's answer contains sufficient detail for the **full 3 marks** (she has given the target population and how the method would be selected from that). (ii) Both answers are correct and sufficient for **2 marks**.

(c) The students conduct their experiment in the classroom under carefully controlled conditions.

(i) Identify **one** extraneous variable that they would need to control and explain why this would be important. *(3 marks)*

(ii) Explain why this study would be considered to be a lab experiment. *(3 marks)*

(i) An extraneous variable that would need to be controlled is the sex of the participant, because males and females may learn differently so they would have to make sure that there weren't all boys in one group and girls in the other. (ii) This is a lab experiment because it is carried out in the psychology classroom (laboratory).	(i) The students would need to control the amount of distractions. This would be important because if one method was being used as the break bell went, or even as it approached, then participants would not concentrate so much and perform less well than when there were no distractions. (ii) This would be considered a lab experiment because it is being carried out in an environment (in this case a classroom) where extraneous variables can be carefully controlled.	(i) It is not really clear why there might be a gender difference so Julio's answer gets **0 marks** (just saying they learn differently doesn't make it true – this needs to be backed up). Erica has selected a much more likely issue which doesn't need research support; **full 3 marks**. (ii) Again, Julio loses marks because he has not explained his answer – saying that a classroom is a laboratory is not explaining it, so just **1 out of 3 marks** for him. Erica has explained the key issue of control over variables for the **full 3 marks**.

Extended writing question

Outline and evaluate **one or more** ways to improve memory. *(12 marks)*

AO1

The first way is to use verbal mnemonics. Mnemonics are any technique designed to help us remember. Examples of verbal mnemonics are acronyms, making up a word or a sentence by taking the first letter of each word in a list to be remembered. The effectiveness of using acronyms was demonstrated in a study by Glidden et al. (1983) who found such techniques were effective in children with learning difficulties even after 12 months.

A second technique is the method of chunking, which involves dividing a list of, for example numbers, into more memorable chunks of information. Chunking works by making more efficient use of short-term memory. Calder (2006) found that students who were encouraged to chunk information later recalled much more of it than those who were not encouraged to chunk.

A third technique is the mind map. In a mind map, the learner constructs a diagram with the key concept at the centre and associated concepts branching out from this central point. This is effective partly because it is an active technique, which aids learning, and therefore memory, and also because it helps the learner to organise the material, which makes it more memorable.

A fourth technique is the keyword system, where the individual forms a visual image to remind them of the word or name to be remembered. Because words and images are processed in different areas of the brain, any word that is turned into an image is double-encoded in memory, i.e. as a word and as an image. Because of this double encoding, the word is more likely to be recalled because there are two routes to its memory.

(274 words)

> In this essay each paragraph begins with a basic description of a method of memory improvement, sometimes extended by using an example.

AO2

> Research evidence has been used to support the effectiveness of the method, but there is little depth to this critical point.

> The same is true for this second AO2 point.

> The third paragraph contains a third AO2 point which is very superficial.

> The explanation of why the keyword system works is just about creditworthy as AO2.

Examiner's comments

The descriptive (**AO1**) element of the essay is better than basic but certainly lacks the detail necessary for the top band (see mark scheme on page 9), so **4 out of 6 marks** (perhaps a bit mean but seems closer to 'basic').

There is a range of evaluative (**AO2**) points, most of which lack depth except for the final one which is reasonably elaborated, so **4 out of 6 marks**.

Total = **8 out of 12 marks**, just missing a **Grade A**.

Extra questions for you

Some further examples of questions requiring you to apply your knowledge to novel situations.

Question 1 Eric and Ernie are standing together at the students' union bar, each waiting to order a round of drinks for themselves and their group of friends. As they stand there, each mentally rehearses the individual drinks that their friends have asked for. An old friend of Ernie's suddenly appears and briefly engages him in conversation. When Eric and Ernie are eventually served, Eric remembers all of his drinks, but Ernie appears to have forgotten his.

Using your knowledge of the multi-store model, explain why Eric has remembered his round of drinks and Ernie has forgotten his.   *(3 marks)*

Question 2 At the end of every maths lesson, the teacher gives her students a mental arithmetic test. She reads out a task such as 'What is 35 times 4 minus 43 divided by 2?' When she has finished the students have to work out the answer.

Use the components of the working memory model to explain why some students might have difficulty with this task.   *(4 marks)*

Question 3 Jasmine is employed as an advisor to her local police authority. As she is a psychology graduate, she is invited to address a class of new detectives about the dangers of misleading information when interviewing witnesses.

Explain **two** things that Jasmine can tell detectives about the dangers of misleading information when interviewing witnesses.   *(4 marks)*

Question 4 Ryan, aged 17, and his grandfather witness an armed robbery at a bank. The grandfather, aged 78, found the whole event extremely frightening, particularly having a gun waved in his face. He was subsequently very hesitant when asked to pick somebody from an identity parade. Ryan, on the other hand, was less anxious about the robbery, and when interviewed by police, was able to pick out the robber from a book of photos.

Using your knowledge of factors that influence the accuracy of eyewitness testimony, explain why Ryan's testimony might be more accurate than his grandfather's.   *(6 marks)*

Question 5 Camberwick Green Police Authority are considering introducing the cognitive interview to replace the standard police interview for witnesses to serious crimes. They are concerned, however, about whether it would significantly improve their crime detection rate and so ask you to convince senior officers about the merits of the cognitive interview.

    (a) Outline **two** reasons why you think they should introduce the cognitive interview to replace the standard police interview.   *(4 marks)*

    (b) Outline **two** reasons why senior officers might be reluctant to introduce the cognitive interview in Camberwick Green.   *(4 marks)*

Question 6 Katie is studying for her French GCSE. She loves the subject, but has problems remembering all the words and their meanings when it comes to exam time.

    (a) Explain **one** way in which Katie might improve her memory of French vocabulary.   *(3 marks)*

    (b) Using your knowledge of psychology, suggest why this method is likely to improve her memory for the exam.   *(4 marks)*

Question 7 At a holiday resort one of the competitions that is held is called 'Mr Memory' where guests compete to see who can remember the most words from a very long list. Both men and women are allowed to enter (even though it is called 'Mr Memory') so Kerry and her husband Ken decide to enter. Ken thinks he has got a very good memory but Kerry has studied psychology and knows a few tricks.

What 'tricks' might Kerry use to win the competition? Refer to psychological research in your answer.   *(4 marks)*

RESEARCH METHODS QUESTION

Question 1 Some psychology students decided they would investigate strategies for memory improvement by conducting a natural experiment. They asked everyone in their class whether they had used visual or verbal strategies when revising for GCSE exams to see which was more successful. They measured success by calculating a mean GCSE grade for each student which meant that the lower your score the better you did.

(a) Explain the difference between a natural experiment and a field experiment.	*(3 marks)*
(b) Describe the operationalised independent variable in this study.	*(2 marks)*
(c) (i) Explain what is meant by an 'extraneous variable'.	*(2 marks)*
(ii) Describe **one** potential extraneous variable in this study.	*(2 marks)*
(d) Identify **one** ethical issue that might arise in this study and suggest how they might deal with it.	*(3 marks)*
(e) (i) The students calculated a 'mean GCSE grade'. Describe how you would calculate this.	*(3 marks)*
(ii) Identify **one** other measure of central tendency and explain why the mean would be preferable to use.	*(3 marks)*
(f) The student researchers expected that students using visual techniques would do better. Write a suitable directional hypothesis for this study based on their expectations.	*(3 marks)*

RESEARCH METHODS QUESTION

Question 2 A recent study carried out a content analysis of the memories of younger and older people. Participants were asked to keep a diary of things they remembered. Every time a memory 'popped into their head' they were to answer a series of questions about the memory such as a brief description of the memory and ratings of their mood at the time. Participants carried their diaries with them for a period of seven days. The table below shows the percentage of memories in each category. Only some of the categories have been displayed.

Content of memory	People	Accidents	Stressful events	Leisure/sport	Romantic events	School	Special occasions
Younger participants	17%	13%	12%	6%	4%	5%	2%
Older participants	14%	1%	2%	12%	3%	6%	6%

(a) Explain how the researchers would have analysed the diary entries to produce the data in the table.	*(4 marks)*
(b) Give **one** strength of conducting a content analysis.	*(3 marks)*
(c) Identify **one** result from the table and suggest a conclusion that could be drawn from this.	*(2 marks)*

RESEARCH METHODS QUESTION

Question 3 Research has found that people have better short-term memories in the morning than in the afternoon. Some psychology students tested this by giving one group of participants a memory test in the morning and another group the same test in the afternoon.

(a) (i) Identify the experimental design used in this study.	*(1 mark)*
(ii) Give **one** strength of using this design in this study.	*(2 marks)*
(b) Describe how the students might have tested short-term memory.	*(3 marks)*
(c) (i) Outline **one** investigator effect that might have been a problem with the validity of this study.	*(2 marks)*
(ii) Explain how you might deal with this investigator effect.	*(2 marks)*
(d) (i) Identify **one** suitable sampling technique and explain how it could be used in this study.	*(3 marks)*
(ii) Explain **one** strength and **one** limitation of using this sampling method in this study.	*(3 marks + 3 marks)*

SPECIFICATION BREAKDOWN

Specification content	Comment

Attachment

- Explanations of attachment, including learning theory and Bowlby's theory.

- Types of attachment: secure attachment, insecure-avoidant and insecure-resistant.

- Use of the 'Strange Situation' in attachment research.

- Cultural variations in attachment.

- The effects of disruption of attachment, failure to form attachment (privation) and institutional care.

The first part of the specification is concerned with the formation of attachment between infants and their caregivers, and the importance of this relationship in early social development. Explanations of attachments offer an account of how and why children become attached to a caregiver. The best known and most developed explanation is Bowlby's theory, but there are others, such as learning theory. The specification requires that you are familiar with at least two explanations: learning theory and Bowlby's theory.

It is important to recognise that the quality of attachments varies between individuals (individual differences), for example some infants are *securely attached* whereas others are *insecurely attached*. There are two main subtypes of insecure attachment: *insecure-avoidant* and *insecure-resistant* attachment. The distinction between secure and insecure attachments stems from Ainsworth's research using the Strange Situation. You are required to study these different types of attachment as well as the method used in their investigation (the Strange Situation) as they are in the specification.

In addition to types of attachment there are variations in child rearing methods in different cultures which could, as a result, be associated with differences in attachment. Research suggests that, despite these differences, secure attachment is the most common type of attachment in all cultures.

Some children experience situations which lead to a disruption of attachment, for example when they have to spend time in hospital or when attending a day nursery. Such experiences cause separations between child and attachment figure, disrupting attachment and may have a lasting effect if substitute emotional care is not provided.

The failure to form attachments during early development may have a profound effect on emotional and social development. Such experiences of privation may occur if a child is placed in an institution (institutional care).

Attachment in everyday life

- The impact of different forms of day care on children's social development, including the effects on aggression and peer relations.

- How research into attachment and day care has influenced child care practices.

Research on attachment has led some people to believe that when a child is placed in day care the consequent separation from his/her primary attachment figure would have detrimental effects on the child's early social development. Research has found that day care experiences can have negative effects (such as increased aggression) or positive effects (such as improved abilities to cope with peer relationships).

Psychological research can be used to shape child care practices so that children can be given the best possible care in hospitals, day care centres, institutions and even at home, by their parents.

Chapter 2

DEVELOPMENTAL PSYCHOLOGY is concerned with how children and adults change as they get older. Developmental psychology looks at various influences on development, such as the influences of parents, peers and other people around you. These are all environmental influences (called *nurture*). Changes also happen as a consequence of *nature*. 'Nature' refers to biological factors, such as genes you inherit which guide your physical and psychological development.

CHAPTER CONTENTS

Explanations of attachment: learning theory

Question 1 Below are **six** statements about attachment. Place a tick in the box next to the **three** that apply to the learning theory explanation of attachment.

(3 marks)

☐ The sensitivity of the parent's responses matter more for attachment than the amount of time spent feeding a baby.

☑ Attachments are formed through conditioning.　　☑ Infants become most attached to the person who feeds them.

☑ The mother figure is initially a neutral stimulus.　　☐ Attachment is an adaptive behaviour.

☐ Attachment is an innate predisposition in an infant.

FULL MARKS!

Question 2 Briefly outline the learning theory explanation of attachment. *(3 marks)*

Wayne's answer

The learning theory of attachment states that attachment is merely the consequence of the mother's association with something that the young child needs — food. Because the mother provides food, which is reinforcing, and her presence predicts the coming of food, she becomes reinforcing in her own right and so an attachment develops between her and the child.

Colleen's answer

The learning theory of attachment comprises classical and operant conditioning. Operant conditioning states that anything that leads to a reward is more likely to be repeated. Classical conditioning states that if a neutral stimulus is presented at the same time as an unconditioned stimulus, eventually it begins to produce the same response, which is now called a conditioned response.

Examiner's comments

Colleen's answer seem better because she has described both classical and operant conditioning – but she has not applied these to attachment and therefore she would only receive **1 out of 3 marks**. Wayne's answer certainly has enough detail for the **full 3 marks**.

Question 3 Outline key features of learning theory as an explanation for attachment. *(6 marks)*

Explained from the point of view of classical conditioning, food acts as an unconditioned stimulus (UCS), which produces a feeling of pleasure (unconditioned response). The presence of a mother who provides food is a neutral stimulus (NS). The association between UCS and NS gradually leads to the mother becoming a conditioned stimulus (CS) whose presence also produces a feeling of pleasure (conditioned response). From the point of view of operant conditioning, when a child is fed, this reduces an uncomfortable hunger drive and so produces a feeling of pleasure, which is reinforcing (primary reinforcement). The person who provides food (usually the mother) becomes a secondary reinforcer, and so becomes as important to the child as food itself.

The main features of the learning theory of attachment are that infants learn who to attach to as a result of them providing something that the infant needs. The theory proposes that it is the satisfaction of hunger that leads to the infant becoming attached to the mother through association. She becomes a secondary reinforcer, with food as the primary reinforcer.

A limitation of this view is that other research doesn't support it. For example, Harlow (1959) found that rhesus monkeys would prefer to cling to a soft cuddly surrogate mother than one that provided milk. This therefore challenges the learning theory view that food is vital for the formation of attachments.

Wayne has correctly added operant conditioning this time to extend his 3 mark answer to an answer that gets the **full 6 marks**.

This time Colleen has managed to link learning theory to attachment but she has muddled classical and operant conditioning – 'association' is related to the former, whereas reinforcers are related to the latter. Colleen's second paragraph is unrelated to the question; the criticism is not one of the key features of the theory. So altogether **1 out of 6 marks** for a muddled answer.

Question 4 Evaluate the learning theory explanation of attachment. *(6 marks)*

Learning theory is an appropriate explanation of attachment, although food isn't the main reinforcer, it is responsiveness to an infant's needs that is the main reinforcer. Harlow's research challenged the importance of food as a reinforcer. He found that motherless young rhesus monkeys spent more time clinging to a surrogate monkey that provided contact comfort rather than the one that provided food. It might be argued that this study used animals, therefore would be irrelevant to human attachment. However, Harlow's conclusion was supported by a study with human infants (Schaffer and Emerson, 1964). They found that infants were more likely to attach to caregivers who were most sensitive to their needs, rather than those who provided them with food. Thus, sensitivity to needs is now accepted as the main reinforcer in the development of an attachment.

The learning theory of attachment has been proved wrong because of Harlow's research. He used rhesus monkeys and found that when they were frightened they spent most of their time clinging to a 'mother' surrogate who was covered in a soft cloth. Harlow later found that the motherless monkeys behaved in inappropriate ways when they were mothers themselves, for example they found it very difficult to mate, and were very bad mothers, with some even jamming their baby's head up against the bars of the cage. This research shows that just feeding a baby monkey (which is what the learning theory says) isn't enough to form an attachment, and without a mother it will grow up into a very disturbed adult. Other research has found the same thing as Harlow, but with human infants, so adding to claims.

Both Wayne and Colleen have covered similar ground but their answers vary in terms of the elaboration, for example Wayne has used the Schaffer and Emerson study effectively whereas Colleen just says 'Other research has found the same thing'. Colleen has included a conclusion regarding Harlow's study, 'This research shows that just feeding…' which demonstrates her understanding. Wayne has included a criticism of Harlow's research which is creditworthy as part of his evaluation. Overall Wayne has a range of points in some depth but really needs a final sentence linking the evidence back to learning theory, so **5 out of 6 marks**, whereas Colleen's answer is more superficial; **3 out of 6 marks**.

Question 5 Maria and her husband both work. They recently had a baby and Maria's mother Eva has provided a lot of help to look after the baby. Eva arrives early in the morning in time to feed the baby and bath him. In fact, Eva is probably the person who feeds and washes the child most often.

Use the learning theory of attachment to explain why the baby might form a close attachment to Maria's mother, Eva, rather than to Maria.

(4 marks)

The learning theory of attachment states that attachments form because caregivers provide reinforcement for the infant. Although Eva provides for the baby's physical needs (e.g. she is the one who feeds him), it is likely that it is his mother who is most sensitive to his emotional needs. Based on the research of Schaffer and Emerson (1964), it is sensitivity to needs rather than the provision of food that is most important in the development of an attachment, and this would explain why an attachment with the baby's mother is more likely.

The baby is more likely to form an attachment with Eva because she cares for him more of the time than Maria. Even though Maria is his real mother and she may give him a lot of affection, learning theory suggests that the baby will come to love Eva because of the association between her and being fed. The food makes him feel a sense of pleasure and this is associated more with Eva than the baby's real mother Maria.

Wayne has got totally confused – he's talking about Bowlby's attachment theory instead of learning theory and actually is explaining why the baby might be more attached to Maria (his real mother) than to Eva, so **1 out of 4 marks** for a muddled response. Colleen has managed to use her knowledge to explain why the baby might become more attached to Eva so the **full 4 marks**.

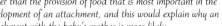

A psychologist studied the attachment relationship between infants and their parents to see which parent the infant was most strongly attached to. The psychologist was particularly interested to see if infants were most strongly attached to their mother or their father, or whether they were simply most strongly attached to the person who was the main carer (i.e. generally fed and washed the infant). Each infant was observed in the psychologist's lab by a team of two observers while playing with its mother and in a different session playing with its father. The results are shown in the table on the right.

	Percentage of infants most strongly attached
Mother main carer	37%
Father main carer	31%
Mother not main carer	22%
Father not main carer	10%

(a) This study has two hypotheses. State **two** possible hypotheses for this study. *(2 marks + 2 marks)*

Wayne's answer

Infants show more attachment behaviour towards their mother than they show towards their father.

Infants show more attachment behaviour towards the parent that is his or her main carer than the parent that is not.

Colleen's answer

An infant is more likely to be attached to its mother than its father.

Does the fact that a parent feeds and washes an infant make it more likely that they will become attached to that person?

Examiner's comments

Wayne's answers are both correct so the **full 4 marks**. Colleen's second answer is not a hypothesis so only **2 out of 4 marks**.

(b) Explain why the psychologist chose to observe the parents with their infants in a lab environment. *(2 marks)*

By studying them in a lab environment, it gives the psychologist the chance to control extraneous variables (e.g. noise) and the opportunity to use sophisticated recording equipment for later analysis.

It gives the study more ecological validity carrying it out in a lab than if they had carried out the study in the natural environment (e.g. in the infant's own home).

Excellent answer from Wayne (**full 2 marks**) but Colleen has got completely confused, a lab environment would, if anything, mean less ecological validity, so **0 marks**.

(c) Explain **one** strength of using observational techniques to study infant behaviour. *(3 marks)*

In a controlled observation, the researchers can manipulate variables to see what effect they have on an infant's behaviour. For example, in the Strange Situation, they can introduce a stranger to see how the infant will react, and relate this to attachment styles.

A strength of using observational techniques is that it gives the researcher the chance to study behaviour as it would normally happen rather than in an artificial setting.

Wayne has focused on a particular kind of observation, which is fine, and gets the **full 3 marks**. Colleen's answer is reasonable but lacks context so **2 out of 3 marks**.

(d) How might the psychologist assess the reliability of the observations recorded by the team of two observers? *(3 marks)*

They can assess reliability by correlating the observations made by the two observers. They would do this by dividing the number of times the observers agree on a particular observational category by the total number of observations.

They can assess the reliability of the observations by comparing the different observations made by the two observers. The more alike these are, the more reliable the overall observations in the study.

Colleen's answer is correct but lacks the detail provided by Wayne, so just **2 out of 3 marks** for Colleen and the **full 3 marks** for Wayne.

(e) Identify **one** possible demand characteristic and explain how it could affect the validity of the study. *(4 marks)*

A possible demand characteristic is that if the parents know they are being observed, they might be especially attentive to the infant, in an attempt to come across as a 'good parent' (social desirability bias). This would affect the validity of the study because they would not be acting naturally, and so any conclusions drawn would be invalid.

Demand characteristics are when the person being studied alters their behaviour in a way they think the researcher wants. The mother might show more 'caring' behaviour towards the infant and the father is more likely to play in a 'rough and tumble' way, because that's how they think they should be behaving.

Colleen has wasted time explaining what a demand characteristic is – but she will get credit for her second sentence. However, she has also failed to say how this might affect the validity of the study – but Wayne has, so the **full 4 marks** for Wayne and just **2 out of 4 marks** for Colleen.

Extended writing question

Outline and evaluate the learning theory explanation of attachment. *(12 marks)*

AO1

The first paragraph is identical to the answer on the facing page to the 6 mark question 'Outline key features of learning theory as an explanation for attachment'. This is fine to construct your essay from separate components – in fact it is an excellent idea because it makes an essay seem less daunting.

Explained from the point of view of classical conditioning, food acts as an unconditioned stimulus (UCS), which produces a feeling of pleasure (unconditioned response). The presence of the mother who provides food is a neutral stimulus (NS). The association between UCS and NS gradually leads to the mother becoming a conditioned stimulus (CS) whose presence also produces a feeling of pleasure (conditioned response). From the point of view of operant conditioning, when a child is fed, this reduces an uncomfortable hunger drive and so produces a feeling of pleasure, which is reinforcing (primary reinforcement). The person who provides the food (usually the mother) becomes a secondary reinforcer, and so becomes as important to the child as food itself.

Learning theory is an appropriate explanation of attachment, although food isn't the main reinforcer, it is responsiveness to an infant's needs that is the main reinforcer. Harlow's research (Harlow, 1959) challenged the importance of food as a reinforcer. He found that motherless young rhesus monkeys spent more time clinging to a surrogate monkey that provided contact comfort rather than the one that provided food. It might be argued that this study used animals, therefore would be irrelevant to human attachment. However, Harlow's conclusion was supported by a study with human infants (Schaffer and Emerson, 1964). They found that infants were more likely to attach to caregivers who were most sensitive to their needs, rather than those who provided them with food. Thus, sensitivity to needs is now accepted as the main reinforcer in the development of an attachment.

(255 words)

AO2

The evaluation part of this essay is also taken from the answer to a 6-mark question on the facing page 'Evaluate the learning theory explanation of attachment'.

Examiner's comments

The two paragraphs above were marked on the facing page and received **6 out of 6 marks** for the description (AO1) element and **5 out of 6 marks** for the evaluation (AO2). This illustrates the extent to which extended writing questions can be constructed from shorter answer questions.

Total = **11 out of 12 marks**, a **Grade A**.

Explanations of attachment: Bowlby's theory

Question 1 Outline Bowlby's theory of attachment. *(6 marks)*

Greg's answer

Bowlby claimed that human infants have an innate drive to attach themselves to their mother. He believed this from observations of ducks who imprinted at a very early age on the mother duck and followed her wherever she went. This meant they were likely to be safe from predators. Bowlby believed that human infants also attached because it kept them safe. He claimed that infants who did not attach were more likely to die by being attacked or die through exposure and that attachment behaviour became widespread simply because it was the infants who were attached who survived (and passed on their genes to the next generation), and those who didn't attach missed the opportunity to pass on their genes because they didn't survive until sexual maturity.

Sue's answer

Bowlby believed that attachment served an important adaptive function in humans, in that it promotes survival. Attachment develops during a sensitive period, which is between three and six months. Outside this period attachments are more difficult to form. The attachment process is a reciprocal one, as adults have an innate tendency to become attached to their young, something that is made more likely by social releasers such as the baby smiling. Bowlby also believed that the infant would develop one special bond with their primary caregiver (monotropy) although they may also form secondary attachments with other important figures in their life. This attachment relationship sets up an internal working model of what they might expect from other loving relationships in their life, with securely attached individuals continuing to be emotionally competent whereas insecurely attached individuals are more likely to experience social and emotional difficulties throughout life.

Examiner's comments

Greg's answer outlines one aspect of Bowlby's theory – that it is adaptive – but doesn't move on to any other key features. Therefore this would be described as basic and worth **3 out of 6 marks** as it is closer to the top rather than the bottom of the band (see mark scheme on page 9). Greg has covered two features – the innate and adaptive nature of attachment.

By contrast, Sue has covered a number of key features (adaptiveness, sensitive period, reciprocity, social releasers, monotropy, secondary attachments, internal working model, continuity), all in reasonable detail. Therefore she receives the **full 6 marks**.

Question 2 Briefly outline the Bowlby's theory of attachment. *(3 marks)*

Bowlby claimed that if children were deprived of mother love, they would experience emotional difficulties later on. He claimed that mother love in infancy was as important for emotional development as vitamins were for physical deprivation. He showed this to be the case in a study of 44 juvenile thieves who had suffered maternal deprivation in childhood and grew up to be delinquents.

Bowlby believed that infants form an attachment with their primary caregiver during a sensitive period (between three and six months). He believed that infants form one special bond with their primary attachment figure (monotropy) although they may also form secondary attachments with other important figures in their life. This attachment relationship sets up an internal working model of what they might expect from other loving relationships in their life.

It is possible that you could be asked for a 3-mark version instead of a 6-mark version of Bowlby's theory as here. Both candidates have produced a reduced version but Greg's version relates to Bowlby's maternal deprivation hypothesis (Bowlby, 1951) rather than his theory of attachment, and would only receive **1 out of 3 marks** for peripheral relevance. Sue gains the **full 3 marks**.

Question 3 Outline what research has shown about Bowlby's theory of attachment. *(4 marks)*

Bowlby studied 44 juvenile thieves who were guilty of being persistent delinquents. He found that many of them had been deprived of mother love in infancy and quite a few of them had developed affectionless psychopathy. Another study is Lorenz's study of imprinting in geese. He found that young geese followed the first moving thing that they saw, and as a result were more likely to survive. Lorenz found that if he was the first thing the young geese saw, they would follow him.

Tronick et al. (1992) provided support for Bowlby's claim that attachment is an innate process. They found evidence of infants in Zaire still having one primary attachment figure despite being looked after by multiple caregivers. Sroufe et al. (2005) studied infants through to adolescence and found that, consistent with Bowlby's theory, those who were securely attached in infancy were rated highest for social competence.

Sue's answer is exactly what was required – a report of appropriate findings – so the **full 4 marks**. Greg has described two research studies and correctly focused on the findings rather than the methods. However there is no explicit link made between these studies and Bowlby's theory. In fact, Bowlby's 44 thieves study is not relevant to his theory of attachment. Lorenz's research is relevant, so **1 out of 4 marks** for Greg.

Question 4 Explain one criticism of Bowlby's theory of attachment. *(3 marks)*

There are a number of criticisms of Bowlby's theory. One is that he claimed that infants would form one main attachment (monotropy), but research has shown that children often form attachments to many people (e.g. mother and father and grandmother). Another criticism is to do with the claim that whatever type of attachment the infant formed when young, this would determine how they would develop later on and how easy they would find it to develop adult relationships.

Bowlby argued for continuity between early attachment styles and social and emotional development in adulthood. However, there is an alternative explanation for this relationship. The temperament hypothesis proposes that an innately trusting and friendly personality could be the main reason why an infant becomes securely attached and also why they form close adult relationships more easily. This is supported by the finding (Belsky and Rovine, 1987) that babies between one and three days old who were calmer and less anxious were more likely to go on to become securely attached.

Sue has presented an extensive explanation of her one criticism, enough elaboration for the **full 3 marks**. Greg has explained two criticisms despite the question only asking for one, and therefore the examiner selects the better of the two and awards marks for this. Greg's first criticism is not accurate – monotropy doesn't mean that children only have one attachment but just that they only have one special attachment. Greg's second criticism hasn't been fully explained so either of these would receive only **1 out of 3 marks**.

Question 5 In some cultures children are raised collectively by the community. The infants spend quality time with their mothers but during the day are looked after by whichever adults are around.
Use Bowlby's theory of attachment to explain why such children still remain most attached to their biological mothers. *(3 marks)*

These children are most likely to remain more attached to their biological mothers because she probably spends more time with her child than any single other adult who looks after the child during the day. There may also be a rapid turnover in the other adults who care for the child.

Bowlby argued that infants might form a number of attachments, but their primary attachment figure is the person who is most sensitive to the infant's needs. In the community, although many different adults cater for the infant's needs, the fact that it is the mother who spends quality time with her child means that the primary attachment would form with her.

Sue's answer is detailed and well informed for the **full 3 marks**. Greg's answer is flawed. He is wrong to suppose that the children spend more time with their mother and wrong to suppose a rapid turnover of adults (this might be true in a day care centre but not a community), so **0 marks**.

Question 6 Attachment has been explained in terms of learning theory and Bowlby's theory. Explain how these two theories are different. *(4 marks)*

The learning theory claims that attachment is a result of the mother's association with food (classical conditioning). Bowlby's theory claims that attachment develops during a sensitive period of development during the first year. Learning theory also suggests that mothers feed the child, which gets rid of their unpleasant hunger drive, which is reinforcing. Bowlby's theory claims that the attachment bond is more likely to form with the person who is most sensitive to the infant's needs.

The learning theory view of attachment claims that the mother is important only because she is associated with the provision of food, whereas in Bowlby's theory she is important because she responds sensitively to all the infant's needs. The two theories are also different because in the learning theory view, the attachment bond is learned (either by classical or operant conditioning), whereas in Bowlby's theory attachment is an innate predisposition, the result of natural selection.

Sue has answered the question appropriately because she has contrasted the two theories explicitly by saying 'whereas' and has, more importantly, compared them on the same dimension. So the **full 4 marks**.

Greg has described the two theories but made no attempt to say how they are different (as required in the question). There isn't even an implicit comparison so only **1 out of 4 marks**.

RESEARCH METHODS QUESTION

Bowlby's theory predicts that mothers who respond more sensitively to their infants will have infants who are more securely attached. This was tested in a study which scored mothers in terms of sensitivity on a scale of 1 to 10, where 10 is very sensitive. Infants were rated in terms of secure attachment, again on a scale of 1 to 10 where 10 is high in terms of secure attachment. The results are shown in the scattergram on the right.

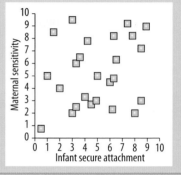

(a) Describe the results of the study shown in the scattergram. *(3 marks)*

Greg's answer

The scattergram shows a very low correlation between maternal sensitivity and an infant's secure attachment.

Sue's answer

The scattergram shows zero or close to zero relationship between the maternal sensitivity score and the level of secure attachment in the infants. This therefore shows that mothers who respond sensitively to their infants do not have infants who are more securely attached.

Examiner's comments

There is no relationship shown in the scattergram, so Sue gets it right and has also provided an explanation of what this means for the **full 3 marks**. Greg gains **no marks**.

(b) (i) State a directional hypothesis for this study. *(2 marks)*
 (ii) State whether the scattergram supports your hypothesis. *(1 mark)*

(i) Maternal sensitivity in the mother leads to secure attachment in children.

(ii) The results don't support it because the correlation shown in the scattergram is very low, and it would have to be significant to prove the hypothesis correct.

(i) Maternal sensitivity scores are positively correlated with levels of secure attachment in the infant.

(ii) The scattergram does not support this hypothesis.

(i) Sue is right again because she has written a correlational hypothesis whereas Greg's hypothesis suggests that the sensitivity is causing the secure attachment, whereas there was no such suggestion in the stem to the question. The **full 2 marks** for Sue but **0 marks** for Greg.

(ii) Both candidates would gain **1 mark** here – Sue's brief answer is sufficient for 1 mark.

(c) Give **one** strength and **one** limitation of using a correlational analysis to study infant–mother behaviour as in this study. *(3 marks + 3 marks)*

A strength is that it is easy to carry out and can tell the researcher a great deal about any relationship between the variables. It can show whether there is a positive or negative relationship and how strong it is.

A limitation is that it can't show if there is a causal relationship between the variables, the researchers would have to carry out an experiment to show that.

A strength is that a correlation can be used when it isn't possible to manipulate variables. This is particularly the case where it would be unpractical or unethical as here. It would not be appropriate to manipulate maternal sensitivity because of its potential impact on the attachment bond that forms as a result.

A limitation is that there may be other unknown variables that might explain the relationship such as the child's temperament. A happy and friendly infant may be more likely to form a secure attachment, and make it easier for the mother to be sensitive towards him or her.

An excellent answer for both parts of the question from Sue, so the **full 6 marks**. Most importantly she has placed both answers in context, as required in the question.

In Greg's first part he has actually given two answers. In the case of some questions (such as those relating to research methods) your first answer only will receive credit – not the best of the two, so **0 out of 3 marks**. Greg's answer to the second part is appropriate but not sufficiently elaborated for the full marks because there is no context, so **2 out of 3 marks**.

Answer 1

AO1

The first paragraph provides a brief outline of learning theory.

The third paragraph attempts to offer a brief outline of Bowlby's theory but this is muddled. The points about imprinting, a sensitive period and privation are appropriate but haven't been clearly applied to attachment theory.

There are two main theories of attachment. The first of these is the learning theory one. This says that children just attach to their mothers because the mother is the person that feeds them. She isn't important for any other reason apart from the fact that she provides food. This is why this theory is also called the cupboard love theory.

This theory has been shown not to be accurate because Harlow found that if you put motherless monkeys in a cage and give them the chance to cling to either a wire surrogate from which they can get food or a surrogate covered in soft cloth but which doesn't give food, they will prefer the one that is soft and cuddly. There is also evidence from studies in different countries that supports the learning theory view of attachment.

The second theory is Bowlby's theory. He thought that human infants imprinted upon their mother in more or less the same way that baby ducks imprinted on their mothers when they were very young. It is important for this to happen during a sensitive period, which is in the first year of life. If the infant doesn't imprint during this time it won't be able to later on. They then suffer from what is called privation and are likely to have all sorts of problems forming relationships later on.

This theory has been challenged by Freud who said that children are most influenced by their parents at about six years of age rather than in the first year of life and this leads to the development of the superego, which is important for the sort of person that they grow into. There is also evidence from studies in different countries that supports Bowlby's theory.

(293 words)

AO2

Two critical points are made and the first one shows some depth but there is no explanation of what this research shows us about learning theory. The second point is very superficial.

This final point is simply wrong. Freud was dead by the time Bowlby produced his theory and Freud's theory did not suggest that children were most influenced at age six.

Examiner's comments

The question allows for an answer looking at more than one theory, as here, or looking at just one theory. Either approach is equally creditworthy. However, neither of the theories selected in this essay have been described in detail, so the description (**AO1**) would receive a generous **3 out of 6 marks** because we are not tempted by the band below (see mark scheme on page 9) that says 'very brief/flawed' – otherwise we would award 2 out of 6 marks.

The **AO2** is a superficial consideration of a restricted range so **2 out of 6 marks**, which is perhaps slightly on the mean side.

Total = **5 out of 12 marks**, equivalent to about a **Grade E**.

Answer 2

AO1

This answer illustrates the modular approach again (as explained on page 45). The first paragraph is the same as an answer to the 6-mark question 'Outline key features of the evolutionary explanation for attachment'.

There is some AO1 credit for the description of this explanation of attachment.

Bowlby believed that infants form an attachment with their primary caregiver during a sensitive period (between three and six months) and that outside this period attachments would be more difficult to form. He believed that attachment was an innate process that served an important adaptive function in humans, in that it promotes survival. Bowlby believed that infants form one special bond with their primary attachment figure (monotropy) although they may also form secondary attachments with other important figures in their life. This attachment relationship sets up an internal working model of what they might expect from other loving relationships in their life, with securely attached individuals continuing to be emotionally competent, whereas insecurely attached individuals are more likely to experience social and emotional difficulties throughout life. The attachment process is a reciprocal one, as adults have an innate tendency to become attached to their young, something that is made more likely by social releasers such as the baby smiling.

Tronick et al. (1992) provided support for Bowlby's claim that attachment is an innate process. They found evidence of infants in Zaire still having one primary attachment figure despite being looked after by multiple caregivers. This also supports Bowlby's notion of monotropy. Hodges and Tizard (1989) provided evidence for the importance of the sensitive period, showing that infants who failed to form an attachment during this period had greater difficulties with peers later on. This suggests that attachments are important for later happy relationships.

However, there is an alternative explanation for this relationship between early experience and later relationships. The temperament hypothesis proposes that an innately trusting and friendly personality could be the main reason why an infant becomes securely attached and also why they form close adult relationships more easily. These characteristics of the infant in turn shape the mother's responsiveness to the child, making it more likely that an attachment will develop. This is supported by the finding (Belsky and Rovine, 1987) that babies between one and three days old who were calmer and less anxious were more likely to go on to become securely attached. Therefore, it is possible that the early attachment type does not have a causal influence on later relationships, but that both are caused by temperament differences.

(373 words)

AO2

The second paragraph is all AO2. Two studies have been used, each of them clearly linked to Bowlby's theory and each of them provided in depth.

The final paragraph presents an alternative explanation. AO2 credit is given for the introductory sentence and the study used as support.

Examiner's comments

A clear **Grade A** essay, with accurate and detailed description (**AO1**) demonstrating sound knowledge and understanding, **6 out of 6 marks**.

The evaluation presents a broad range of critical points in reasonable depth. The range could have been broader but the depth makes up for this (narrow range in greater depth), **6 out of 6 marks**.

Total = **12 out of 12 marks, Grade A.**

EXAM ADVICE

The first thing to notice is that this extended essay is worth 8 instead of 12 marks. An equal amount of AO1 and AO2 is still required, i.e. 4 marks' worth of each.

Extended writing question

Outline and evaluate Bowlby's theory of attachment.

(8 marks)

Answer 1

AO1

> Two aspects of Bowlby's theory are covered here, but in a somewhat limited fashion.

AO2

> The first criticism is not completely accurate – monotropy doesn't mean that children have only one attachment but just that they have only one *special* attachment. The second criticism is only just discernible.

Bowlby claims that human infants have an innate drive to attach themselves to their mother. He believed this from observations of ducks who imprinted at a very early age on the mother duck and followed her wherever she went. This meant they were likely to be safe from predators. Bowlby believed that human infants also attached because it kept them safe. He claimed that infants who did not attach were more likely to suffer when they grew up and said in one book that 'mother love in infancy was as important for mental health as vitamins and nutrients were for physical health'.

There are a number of criticisms of Bowlby's theory. He claimed that infants would form one main attachment (monotropy), but research has shown that children often form attachments to many people (e.g. mother and father and grandmother). Another criticism is to do with the claim that whatever type of attachment the infant formed when young, this would determine how they would develop later on and how easy they would find it to develop adult relationships. This has been found not to be the case.

(186 words)

Examiner's comments

The description (**AO1**) would receive **3 out of 4 marks** because somewhat limited.

The evaluation (**AO2**) is worth only **2 out of 4 marks** because the material is basic (superficial consideration and lacking clarity).

Total = **5 out of 8 marks, Grade B** or **C**.

Answer 2

AO1

> Again, in this essay two features of Bowlby's theory are described (an innate process and the internal working model). Both are given detailed explanation.

AO2

Infants form an attachment with their primary caregiver during a sensitive period (three to six months). Outside this period attachments are more difficult to form. Bowlby believed that attachment was an innate process that promotes survival in humans. Bowlby believed that infants form one special bond with their primary attachment figure although they may also form secondary attachments with other important figures. This attachment relationship sets up an internal working model of what they might expect from other loving relationships in their life, with securely attached individuals continuing to be emotionally competent whereas insecurely attached individuals experience social and emotional difficulties throughout life.

Tronick et al. (1992) provided cross-cultural support for Bowlby's claim that attachment is an innate process. Infants in Zaire still had one primary attachment figure despite being looked after by multiple caregivers. This also supports Bowlby's notion of monotropy. Hodges and Tizard (1989) provided evidence for the importance of the sensitive period, showing that infants who failed to form an attachment during this period had greater difficulties with peers later on. This demonstrates the effect of the internal working model.

(183 words)

> The evaluative content here is a reduced version of the answer on the facing page, as appropriate for an 8 mark question.

Examiner's comments

The description (**AO1**) is reasonably detailed and accurate, therefore **4 out of 4 marks**.

The evaluation (**AO2**) covers a range of criticisms in some depth, enough for **4 out of 4 marks**.

Total = **8 out of 8 marks, Grade A.**

A question for the next topic (types of attachment)

Question 1 The following statements all relate to types of attachment.

A An infant greets his mother enthusiastically on reunion.
B An infant is only mildly upset when his mother leaves him with a stranger and is easy to soothe.
C An infant both seeks and rejects his mother's attention.
D An infant is indifferent or very distressed when his mother leaves him with a stranger.

In the table below write which statement applies to which type of attachment.

(4 marks)

Secure attachment	A, B
Insecure attachment	C, D

Types of attachment and the Strange Situation

Question 1 See previous page.

Question 2 Explain what is meant by insecure-avoidant attachment and by insecure-resistant attachment. *(2 marks + 2 marks)*

Leonard's answer	Mary's answer	Examiner's comments
Insecure attachment can be insecure-avoidant, where the child shows avoidant behaviour upon reunion with the mother and also is indifferent when separated. Insecure-resistant is where the child shows distress when reunited after a period of separation and is distressed on separation.	There are two main types of attachment – secure and insecure. Insecure attachment is subdivided into insecure-avoidant where an infant avoids contact, and insecure-resistant, where an infant is resistant.	Leonard's answer has some detail for each attachment type for the full **2 marks + 2 marks**. Mary has written lots but the first sentence is not relevant and the second sentence states the obvious. The key question is 'Avoids contact with whom?' so **0 marks** for each.

Question 3 Explain the difference between a child who is securely attached and a child who is insecurely attached. *(4 marks)*

Children who are securely attached show some distress when separated from their mother, whereas children who are insecurely attached tend to be relatively indifferent when parted from their mother. A securely attached child is willing to explore their environment, using their mother as a safe base, whereas insecurely attached children are less willing to explore.	A child who is securely attached has a very loving and close emotional bond with their mother and is capable of developing close emotional relationships later in life. A child who is insecurely attached lacks close emotional relationships and is more likely to experience emotional problems in their later relationships.	Leonard has compared how two different aspects of attachment differ – so the **full 4 marks** for two explicit comparisons. Mary's answer might appear to be two stand-alone descriptions of each attachment type with no attempt to juxtapose the different aspects – but comparisons are implicitly there. Therefore **3 out of 4 marks** for an implicit comparison plus some elaboration.

Question 4 Outline how psychologists investigate attachment using the Strange Situation. *(6 marks)*

Ainsworth developed the Strange Situation. This is a controlled laboratory observation used to assess the type of attachment shown by an infant. It is conducted in a novel environment and tests an infant's reaction to mild anxiety, e.g. the mother leaves the room and later returns, and when the infant is confronted with a stranger. These situations assess separation anxiety and stranger anxiety. Ainsworth also used the naturalistic observation method to study interactions between mother and infant, to see if maternal responsiveness led to the development of secure attachment.	The Strange Situation is used by psychologists to investigate attachment between an adult and their child. It was first used by Mary Ainsworth to study middle-class children in America. Three people are involved – the mother, her child and a stranger. The steps are: (1) Mother and child are playing. (2) A stranger comes in and the mother leaves. (3) The mother comes back and the stranger leaves. (4) The mother and stranger both leave.	Mary starts with unnecessary details as the question simply requires a description of the Strange Situation, not the background to its development. She does outline the stages but this is muddled and incomplete. Furthermore she doesn't include the broader details of how the technique is used. Her answer is basic, so **2 out of 6 marks**. Leonard has wisely steered away from just listing the stages of the Strange Situation, instead giving an overview of the technique and also mentioning Ainsworth's other research, so the **full 6 marks**.

Question 5 Outline what research has shown about secure attachment. *(5 marks)*

Ainsworth (1978) studied children using the Strange Situation. She found that infants showed consistent patterns of responding, with 66% being securely attached and the remainder insecurely attached. In a Ugandan study, Ainsworth (1967) found that mothers who were more sensitive to their infants' needs tended to have securely attached children. Securely attached children cried less and explored their environment more. Ainsworth later carried out a similar study in the USA and discovered the same relationships between maternal sensitivity and secure attachment. Mothers who were responsive to their children's crying had children who cried less and were more likely to be securely attached. Both these studies supported the role of maternal sensitivity in attachment.	Ainsworth carried out the Strange Situation (SS) to investigate different types of attachment. This has eight stages. The main part is where the mother leaves and later returns, and when the infant is left alone with a stranger. The SS tests the attachment type the infant has and also whether they suffer from stranger anxiety. Ainsworth found that about one third of the infants were securely attached. They were distressed when their mother left but were able to be comforted by her when she returned. About one-third were insecure-anxious and they were also distressed when their mother left but couldn't be calmed down when she returned. The last third were also insecure attached. The two insecure types showed stranger anxiety but not the secure infants.	Many candidates fail to notice the difference between this question and the previous one – question 4 says 'how' whereas question 5 says 'show'. Mary has made just that mistake and described how, and therefore receives **0 marks**. Leonard has provided lots of detailed information from various studies for the **full 6 marks**. He could have just focused on one study and still received full marks, the key factor is the number of findings/ conclusions included in the answer.

Question 6 Sophia has two children. The older child Thomas was always easy to look after and never minded if she left him with her husband or her own mother. However, Sophia's younger son Edgar gets very agitated when left with anyone else and ignores his mother when she comes back.

(a) What types of attachment are shown by Sophia's two sons? *(2 marks)*
(b) Using your knowledge of psychology, explain what may have caused the difference between the two boys. *(4 marks)*

(a) Thomas is showing secure attachment. Edgar is showing insecure-avoidant attachment. (b) Thomas might have become securely attached because as the first child it is possible that his mother was more responsive to his needs but when Edgar was born it was less of a novelty having children therefore she was less responsive to him. Another reason is that there are temperamental differences between the two boys. Thomas might have been a more friendly baby therefore his parents found it easier to bond with him. Edgar might have been a difficult baby and this made it more difficult for his parents to bond with him.	(a) Thomas is securely attached and Edgar is insecurely attached. (b) Sometimes when parents have two children they have a favourite. This seems to be what has happened here. Thomas is securely attached because his parents have shown him more love. Edgar is insecurely attached because his parents have shown him less attention and love, and that is the result. It is also possible that there are genetic differences and Thomas has inherited whatever makes him securely attached and Edgar has different genes so is insecurely attached.	(a) Both answers are sufficient for the **full 2 marks**. (b) Both candidates have managed to engage with the question and, importantly, demonstrated knowledge of psychology in their answer. Mary has said 'less attention and love' which lacks the preciseness of Leonard's answer, so **3 out of 4 marks** for Mary (2 out of 4 would be harsh as she has engaged well with the stem) and the **full 4 marks** for Leonard.

Ainsworth developed a technique called the Strange Situation to observe types of attachment. This technique consists of a number of different episodes involving a mother, an infant and a stranger.

(a) Identify the research method used in this study and explain the reason for your answer. *(4 marks)*

Leonard's answer

This is a controlled laboratory observation. This type of research study involves a researcher observing behaviour in conditions over which they have some control. In this study the researchers can change aspects of the situation (e.g. the mother leaving, a stranger entering the room and the mother returning). The child's behaviour can then be recorded in response to each of these different episodes.

Mary's answer

This is an observational study because the researchers are observing how a mother and her baby interact together, and how the baby responds if they meet a stranger. This can be carried out in a laboratory but this could be criticised as being artificial.

Examiner's comments

Leonard has given a detailed and accurate answer for the **full 4 marks**. Mary's answer is also appropriate but lacks the detail, although she has identified an appropriate method and pointed out it can be conducted in a laboratory. Her justification ('it was an observation because they were observing') is a bit circular, so **2 out of 4 marks**.

(b) Identify **one** ethical issue in this study and explain how a researcher might deal with it. *(1 mark + 3 marks)*

A possible ethical issue is distress to the infant. Because the infant is not old enough to give informed consent, the researchers must explain to the parents all the possible risks of participation, then it is up to them to agree (or not) to allow their child to take part. If they agree then it is the responsibility of the researchers to minimise any anxiety in the infants during the study (e.g. stopping it if the child becomes too distressed).

An ethical issue in this study is lack of informed consent. The infant cannot give their informed consent so should not be involved. The researchers cannot really deal with this ethical issue, therefore the best way to deal with it is for the study not to take place in the first place.

Both candidates have identified appropriate issues, so **1 mark each**. Leonard has provided a detailed explanation of how it could be dealt with – notice how he has managed to link in protection of harm because if there is an issue with informed consent then protection from harm is even more important. The **full 3 marks** for Leonard but **0 marks** for Mary because she hasn't dealt with the issue – she should know that in situations like this a parent is asked for consent.

(c) The infant's behaviour was recorded using behavioural categories.
Suggest **two** behavioural categories that could be used in this study. *(2 marks)*

Willingness to explore and behaviour towards the mother at reunion.

Separation anxiety and stranger anxiety.

Mary's answers are not behaviours that can be 'seen' (observed) and therefore she gains **0 marks**. Leonard receives the **full 2 marks**.

(d) A team of three observers recorded the behaviour of each infant.
Explain why this would increase the reliability of the observations. *(2 marks)*

It is possible that just one observer might classify the behaviour of the infant in a biased way. However, if there is agreement between the three observers, this means that the observations are more consistent and therefore more objective.

Having three observers increases the likelihood that they may disagree in their observations. This is why it is important to check the inter-observer reliability.

Not an easy question to answer but Leonard has managed it, for the **full 2 marks**. Mary's answer is wrong – it does increase the likelihood of disagreements but that does not explain how this would benefit reliability, so **0 marks**.

Extended writing question

'Psychologists have investigated secure and insecure attachment in young children.'
Outline and evaluate research studies related to types of attachment. *(12 marks)*

AO1

The method and findings of Ainsworth's baseline study are described in detail.

A second study is described briefly, but it is used as support for a point and therefore potentially evaluation rather than AO1 description.

Further research studies are described in detail.

Ainsworth developed the Strange Situation. This is a controlled laboratory observation used to assess the type of attachment shown by an infant. It is a novel environment and tests an infant's reaction to situations of mild anxiety, i.e. when the mother leaves the room and then later returns, and when the infant is confronted with a stranger. Ainsworth found that infants showed consistent patterns of responding, with three main attachment types emerging. Of these infants, 66% were securely attached and the remainder were insecurely attached, 22% were insecure-avoidant and 12% were insecure-resistant.

The predictive validity of this classification has been demonstrated in a number of studies, a longitudinal study by Prior and Glaser (2006) provided support for the continuity between early attachment types and later psychological outcomes. For example, secure attachment was associated with positive outcomes such as less emotional dependence, and insecure-resistant attachment was more associated with withdrawn behaviour. However, this study does raise important ethical issues, including whether it is acceptable to place young infants it situations that cause them distress. Ainsworth defended this by claiming that the Strange Situation was not intended to be any more stressful that ordinary life situations. Despite this claim, in episode 6, 20% of the infants cried desperately, which suggests that the costs of the study outweigh the possible benefits.

Van Ijzendoorn et al. (1999) carried out a meta-analysis of 80 studies across the USA, covering 6,000 infants. They found 62% of the infants were securely attached with the remainder being insecurely attached. Their results differed from Ainsworth in that 15% of the infants showed characteristics of an insecure-disorganised type of insecure attachment. Insights such as this have been applied in projects that have attempted to alter caregiver–infant interactions. For example, the 'Circle of Security' project (Cooper et al., 2005) resulted in a decrease in the number of caregivers classed as disordered and an increase in the number of infants classed as securely attached after participation in the project.

(328 words)

AO2

The second half of this paragraph offers evaluative comments on the original study regarding the ethics. Ainsworth's defence counts as further AO2 (evaluation). Altogether this adds up to as considerable 'depth'.

A small amount of credit can be awarded for the comment on how these results differ from Ainsworth's, and also to the application of research findings, but this hasn't been done very effectively – the material is more descriptive than analytical.

Examiner's comments

The description (**AO1**) focuses on research studies, as required, and is detailed and accurate, and the information is presented in a clear and coherent manner, so **6 out of 6 marks**.

The evaluation is excellent in the second paragraph but in the third paragraph it is more like a 'superficial consideration', therefore, on balance, **4 out of 6 marks** for a reasonable range but lacking depth in places.

Total = **10 out of 12 marks**, equivalent to a **Grade A**.

Cultural variations in attachment

Question 1 Explain what is meant by 'cultural variations in attachment'. *(3 marks)*

Olek's answer

This refers to the fact that attachment may be different in different cultures. For example, in one culture most infants might be securely attached while in another most might be insecurely attached.

Cassidy's answer

This refers to the ways that different groups of people vary in terms of child rearing practices and favoured forms of infant behaviour that could, in turn, give rise to different forms of attachment being widespread in those cultures.

Examiner's comments

Both candidates have provided decent answers, covering both cultural variation and attachment, so the **full 3 marks**.

Question 2 Psychologists have used the Strange Situation technique in many different countries around the world, even though it was developed in America and based on American child rearing ideas.

> **(a)** Explain **one** or more difficulties encountered by psychologists when using this method in different countries. *(4 marks)*
> **(b)** Outline **one** way that attachment varies from one culture to another. *(4 marks)*

(a) One of the difficulties that psychologists have when carrying out research in other cultures is that they don't speak the language. Language difficulties can create problems because the participants may not really understand any instructions and the researchers may not really understand what the participants are saying.

(b) One study in Germany found that most German infants were insecurely attached rather than securely attached. In Ainsworth's study in the USA, most of the infants were securely attached.

(a) It is an assumption of the Strange Situation that 'willingness to explore' is a sign of secure attachment in infants as it indicates independence in the infant. However, in Japanese culture, dependence rather than independence is seen as an indication of secure attachment, therefore the Strange Situation classification of attachment would not be appropriate in Japan. This is an example of an imposed etic in psychology, i.e. developing a technique in one culture and then using it in another culture where it might not be appropriate.

(b) Takahashi (1990) used the Strange Situation to study Japanese infants and their mothers. Although they found similar levels of secure attachment as in American infants, they found no evidence of insecure-avoidant attachment but high levels of insecure-resistant attachment. Even the most securely attached infants in the Japanese sample showed extreme levels of distress when they were left alone.

(a) Olek has selected communication difficulties which, unfortunately, are not wholly appropriate here. This would affect some aspects of the research but it is likely that the researchers would be from the respondents' own culture so it shouldn't be too much of a problem. Also, data is collected non-verbally so the main part of the study would not be affected. Therefore this answer receives **0 out of 4 marks**. Cassidy's answer is spot on for the **full 4 marks**.

(b) Olek has provided two answers, and will only get credit for one. Neither is worth more than **1 out of 4 marks**. Another excellent answer from Cassidy, the **full 4 marks**.

Question 3 Outline how psychologists have investigated cultural variations in attachment. *(6 marks)*

Ainsworth used the naturalistic method to study attachment in Uganda and in the USA. She found that levels of secure attachment were more or less the same in both. She also found that in both cultures mothers who were more responsive to their children were more likely to have securely attached children. Another study was carried out in Japan. This used the Strange Situation. This study found that a lot more Japanese infants were insecurely attached compared to infants in the West.

Psychologists have used a range of techniques to investigate cultural variations in attachment. Ainsworth (1967) used naturalistic observation to study mothers and infants in Ugandan villages. Van Uzendoorn and Kroonenberg (1988) carried out a meta-analysis of 32 studies over eight different countries. A meta-analysis allows the researchers to assess overall trends in the different cultures, e.g. whether culturally specific child rearing practices have any influence on the development of attachment. Takahashi (1990) used the Strange Situation with Japanese mothers and their infants in order to see whether the priority placed on dependence rather than independence in Japanese families affected the different types of attachment found.

Olek has not read the question carefully and, even though he has presented lots of different research in detail, he has focused on the findings rather than the procedures. Therefore he receives only **2 out of 6 marks** for brief mention of the two different methods used, which is a generous mark.

Cassidy has described a range of methods and receives the **full 6 marks**.

Question 4 Explain what research has shown about cultural variations in attachment. *(6 marks)*

Ainsworth studied attachment in two cultures, Uganda and USA. This was a cross-cultural study and showed that in both cultures most infants were securely attached. In Uganda the children were looked after by lots of different women, but still had one main attachment with their mother. In the USA they tended to be looked after by just the one mother. Another study was carried out in Japan and studied Japanese children. They found that the most common form of attachment was insecure-resistant attachment.

Van Uzendoorn and Kroonenberg (1988) carried out a meta-analysis of 32 studies in eight different countries. They found that variations within cultures were greater than differences between cultures. Secure attachment was the most common form of attachment in all the cultures studied. Grossmann and Grossmann (1991) studied attachment in German mothers and infants. They found that insecure attachment was more common in German infants, which is probably a consequence of German culture's desire to keep some interpersonal distance between parents and their children. Takahashi (1990) studied Japanese infants and their mothers. They found similar levels of secure attachment as in American infants, but found high levels of insecure-resistant attachment.

Cassidy has again focused on the exact demands of the question and provided findings and conclusions in sufficient detail for the **full 6 marks**.

Olek's answer is a bit harder to disentangle. The first sentence is scene-setting, the second sentence provides creditworthy conclusions which could be more effectively linked to the observations of the third sentence. The final sentence provides another finding. Overall this answer gains **3 out of 6 marks**.

Question 5 Rachel lives in a community farm in Israel. When she had a baby, she continued to work on the farm and the baby spent most of its day in a community nursery. In the evenings Rachel and her husband looked forward to being with their baby and playing games.
Using your knowledge of psychology, explain how such child rearing practices may have affected the attachment relationship between Rachel and her baby. *(4 marks)*

Bowlby suggested that children who are separated from their mother are more likely to show disturbed behaviour later on. It also depends whether the infant is securely or insecurely attached. If the child is insecurely attached they will suffer more during the separation. However, it is possible that the infant will attach to the other children on the community farm.

Research on attachment where children are looked after in communal children's homes like this has shown that despite spending the daytime hours in the community nursery in the company of adults other than the mother, an infant still shows more attachment to his or her mother in the evenings. This is most likely because the mother shows greater sensitivity towards her own child's needs, and it is this greater sensitivity that leads to the development of an attachment.

Olek has tried hard to combine his knowledge of psychology with an answer to the question, drawing on lots of information but not quite saying how this will affect the attachment relationship, thus his answer lacks engagement with the stem and gets just **1 out of 4 marks**. Cassidy's answer is excellent and again she would receive the **full 4 marks**.

Students in a sixth-form college decide to investigate cultural variations in attachment because the students in the college come from diverse cultural backgrounds. They plan to develop a questionnaire to find out about different child rearing practices and expectations about mother–infant attachment.

(a) Write **one** question that would produce quantitative data and **one** question that would produce qualitative data. *(2 marks + 2 marks)*

Olek's answer

Quantitative: 'Does your child get distressed when left with a babysitter?' YES/NO

Qualitative: 'What do you think about mothers who ignore their children when they are distressed?'

Cassidy's answer

Quantitative: If your child cries, does your mother: (1) 'Respond immediately? (2) Leave him/her for a few minutes to see if he/she settles? (3) Ignore him/her?'

Qualitative: 'Some child care experts believe that by responding immediately to a crying child we are making them too dependent'. What is your view on this?'

Examiner's comments

Both candidates have produced appropriate questions, so the **full 2 marks** for both questions. Cassidy gains no extra marks for a more elaborate answer and has wasted important exam time.

(b) Explain **one** issue that might affect the validity of their questionnaire and suggest how this could be dealt with. *(3 marks + 3 marks)*

The external validity of the questionnaire might be affected if the researchers only ask parents of the children at their school. This gives them a very small sample and doesn't tell them much about families whose children are at different schools.

They can overcome this by advertising in a national paper like the Daily Mail or maybe putting a questionnaire on a website (or creating a Facebook group) and simply asking people from other cultural groups to fill it in.

Their questionnaire might be affected by social desirability bias, the tendency to answer questions in a way that shows the person in a good light. For example, a question about responding to a crying infant might be more likely to produce answer (1) simply because that is perceived as the 'proper' thing to do.

This could be dealt with by making the questionnaire completely anonymous and allowing respondents to post back their questionnaires in a pre-paid envelope so that there is no personal information given that might lead the researchers to guess who had completed the questionnaire, and thus the people who fill them in would be more honest in their responses.

Both candidates have identified an issue that would affect the validity of their questionnaire. Cassidy has provided a more detailed explanation of the issue so the **full 3 marks**, whereas Olek gains **2 out of 3 marks** as his answer is slightly muddled (he is confusing the size of the sample and its representativeness).

Olek has made a good suggestion about how to improve his sample, so the **full 3 marks**, whereas Cassidy's solution is not wholly appropriate. People may still display a social desirability bias even when the answers are anonymous, so **2 out of 3 marks**.

(c) Explain **one** strength of using a questionnaire to find out about cultural variations in attachment. *(3 marks)*

A strength is that questionnaires take less time than interviews so lots of people can be used. Interviews take a lot longer and are more expensive so are less suitable.

A strength is that respondents may be more willing to answer sensitive questions about maternal behaviour in a questionnaire than in a face-to-face interview. This is particularly the case when the interviewer might be of a different cultural group to the person being interviewed. This is less of a problem in questionnaires, where respondents will not feel they are being evaluated.

Notice how both candidates compare questionnaires with an alternative method – an excellent strategy when trying to write about a strength (or limitation). Cassidy has provided sufficient detail for the **full 3 marks**. Olek's answer is only partially correct as some questionnaires might actually take longer, so **1 out of 3 marks** for a flawed answer.

(d) (i) Identify a suitable method that could be used to select participants and explain how it would be done. *(3 marks)*
(ii) Give **one** limitation with the method you identified in **(i)**. *(2 marks)*

(i) They could use a stratified sample, taking a certain proportion of parents in each cultural group represented at the school.

(ii) A limitation is that there may be very few people in some cultural groups so it would be difficult to get enough people.

(i) They could use a volunteer sample by advertising on the college website for volunteers. All parents could receive an email asking them if they would like to take part, and directing them to the website for more details.

(ii) A limitation of this method is that the researchers would end up with a biased sample of respondents, for example, the sample would be only those sufficiently motivated to volunteer for such studies.

(i) Olek's answer lacks details of how this would be done, so **2 out of 3 marks**, whereas Cassidy receives the **full 3 marks**.

(ii) Good limitations from both candidates. Cassidy's answer is not contextualised but that was not required in this question. So the **full 2 marks** for both of them.

Extended writing question

Outline and evaluate research related to cultural variations in attachment. *(12 marks)*

AO1

Three research studies each described in reasonable detail.

Van IJzendoorn and Kroonenberg (1988) carried out a meta-analysis of 32 studies in eight different countries. They found that variations within cultures were greater than differences between cultures. Secure attachment was the most common form of attachment in all the cultures studied. Grossmann and Grossmann (1991) studied attachment in German mothers and infants. They found that insecure attachment was more common in German infants, a consequence of German culture's desire to keep some interpersonal distance between parents and their children. Takahashi (1990) studied Japanese infants and their mothers. They found similar levels of secure attachment as in American infants, but found no evidence of insecure-avoidant attachment and high levels of insecure-resistant attachment. Even the most securely attached infants in the Japanese sample showed extreme levels of distress when they were left alone.

Van IJzendoorn and Kroonenberg claimed that many of the cultural similarities they observed in their research could be explained by the widely available Western child rearing ideas that appear in the mass media. Because many of the samples studied in non-Western cultures are from urban centres they are more likely to have been exposed to Western television, books and the Internet, which has defined the way mothers interact with their children.

An additional problem arises in research that has used the Strange Situation to measure secure attachment. It is an assumption of the Strange Situation that 'willingness to explore' is a sign of secure attachment in infants as it indicates independence in the infant. However, in Japanese culture, dependence rather than independence is seen as an indication of secure attachment, therefore the Strange Situation classification of attachment would not be appropriate in Japan. This is an example of an imposed etic in psychology, i.e. developing technique in one culture and then using it in another culture where it might not be appropriate.

(303 words)

AO2

The interpretation and explanation of the findings count as evaluation and analysis.

The final paragraph deals with one critical point in considerable depth.

Examiner's comments

The description (AO1) is clearly worth **6 out of 6 marks**. For the evaluation (AO2), a very narrow range of points has been covered but in considerable depth so not really enough for full marks, therefore **5 out of 6 marks**.

Total = **11 out of 12 marks, a Grade A.**

Disruption of attachment

Question 1 Psychologists have investigated the attachments that form between a mother and her child. In some cases children may experience disruption of attachment.

(a) Explain what is meant by 'disruption of attachment'. *(2 marks)*

(b) Outline how **one** research study investigated disruption of attachment. *(4 marks)*

Craig's answer

(a) Disruption of attachment refers to any prolonged physical separation from the primary caregiver, which is out of the ordinary, e.g. hospitalisation.

(b) James and Joyce Robertson carried out a series of case studies on children whose attachment bond had been disrupted. James Robertson used a non-participant observation method, filming John, a 17-month-old boy who had to attend a residential nursery for nine days. Joyce recorded how John's behaviour changed over the nine days, and how he behaved towards his mother when they were reunited.

Charlotte's answer

(a) It means being separated from the mother. Another word for this is broken, as in when the bond between mother and child is broken.

(b) One study was by the Robertsons, where they recorded the lives of various children when they were briefly separated from their families. This study was meant to show how substitute emotional care made a difference to the effects of disruption. Afterwards the children seemed unharmed by their experience.

Examiner's comments

(a) Charlotte has tried to explain disruption but she hasn't got it quite right so only **1 out of 2 marks**, whereas Craig's answer is worth the **full 2 marks**.

(b) Charlotte has described the study rather than focusing solely on the methods, as required by the question. 'There is some mention of the method, but nothing else, so **1 out of 4 marks**. Craig's answer contains plenty of procedural detail for the **full 4 marks**.

Question 2 (a) Describe what research has shown about the effects of disruption of attachment. *(4 marks)*

(b) Identify **one** ethical issue that has arisen in such research and explain why it is an issue. *(3 marks)*

(a) The Robertsons carried out a study of John, a 17-month-old boy, sent to a residential nursery. John displayed a set of behaviours starting with protest at being separated from his parents, moving to despair as the nurses failed to provide him with replacement emotional care, and finally detachment, where he rejects his mother upon reunion. They also studied a child called Kate, who they looked after while her mother was in hospital. They provided replacement emotional care and Kate adjusted well to her separation and didn't reject her mother upon reunion.

(b) An ethical issue in the study of John is protection from psychological harm as John was clearly distressed during this study and it could be argued that the Robsertsons should have abandoned their 'fly on the wall' role and tried to reduce his distress.

(a) There was a very early study by Spitz and Wolf during the Second World War. They observed that 'normal' children became depressed after having to spend time away from their parents. The Robertson studies also found that children who have to go into hospital often become so distressed because they are separated from their mother that they become emotionally detached from her.

(b) Confidentiality is an ethical issue in the Robertson studies. The Robertsons filmed these children and made no attempt to hide their identity. Nowadays the film makers might make their faces fuzzy so they couldn't be recognised.

(a) Notice that both candidates have provided results from more than one study – which is fine. Craig has not focused entirely on findings but it is difficult to avoid some mention of aims/procedures. His findings are sufficiently detailed for the **full 4 marks**. Charlotte's answer is less precise, especially regarding the Robertson's research, so **3 out of 4 marks**.

(b) Charlotte has identified and explained an ethical issue, so the **full 3 marks**. Craig has made a classic mistake – John's situation was not engineered by the researchers and therefore any psychological harm was not an ethical issue for the researchers. So **no marks** for Craig.

Question 3 Tracey and Darren are planning to go on holiday for two weeks and leave their baby with Tracey's parents. Tracey studied psychology at school and is worried about the negative effects this may have on her baby.

(a) Outline such possible effects. *(4 marks)*

(b) What advice might Tracey give to her mother, based on her knowledge of psychology, in order to avoid the negative effects? *(4 marks)*

(a) Such separation could lead to distress and emotional detachment which might be shown when the baby is reunited with its mother. It is also possible that any negative effects of this disruption may not surface until later in life when there are other triggers (significant stressors) that affect the individual. Early disruption of attachment, therefore, may make a child more vulnerable to mental disorders such as depression or anxiety disorders.

(b) The grandmother should try to give the baby a high level of substitute emotional care during the separation, as the Robertsons found in their study. This could involve lots of contact comfort, which was what Harlow found was important in determining attachment. They should also try to maintain emotional links with Tracey and Darren. This could be by phone calls if the baby is old enough to recognise their voices. This was also shown in the Robertson's study.

(a) The most obvious effect is that the baby will be really upset because it is being split from its parents. If the baby is not looked after properly there is a chance that it will develop abnormally as a result. It might grow up with all sorts of mental disorders such as depression. The baby may also reject the mother when they come back from holiday. This could threaten the attachment bond or at least make the child less secure in its attachment.

(b) Tracey could advise her mother that they could stay in touch through Facebook. The baby could then see its parents everyday and they could send it messages. Her parents could be told not to ignore the baby and to try and provide lots of love to temporarily replace the parents while they are away. Her parents could also try to distract the baby from worrying too much about being split from its parents.

(a) Both candidates have mentioned a number of short- and long-term effects although Craig's answer is a little bit more detailed and better organised so **3 out of 4 marks** for Charlotte and the **full 4 marks** for Craig.

(b) Craig's answer is clearly well informed by psychology and provides appropriate, psychologically based advice for the **full 4 marks**. Charlotte's advice isn't always appropriate (a baby couldn't use Facebook), nor is there any link to psychological research, so **1 out of 4 marks**.

Question 4 Kylie's parents have separated and her father no longer lives at home. She was very attached to her father and now only sees him every Sunday for a few hours. She is not close to her mother. Using your knowledge of psychology, explain what effect this separation may have on Kylie. *(4 marks)*

Bowlby proposed that contact with a primary attachment figure is very important for emotional development. Kylie may become withdrawn and unhappy. The separation may also make her more vulnerable to depression later in life because her working model of relationships means she expects to lose close relationships.

Kylie would become distressed and if the separation lasts long enough she may become emotionally detached from her father. This might also be the case if Kylie's mother introduces a new 'father' figure into her life. He may take the place of Kylie's real father and so gradually she will miss him less and so there will be no more negative effects.

Charlotte has provided some appropriate comment but her answer mainly goes off on a tangent (discussing the effect of a new father) and doesn't answer the question, so **1 out of 4 marks**. Craig has looked at two possible effects, each clearly linked to Bowlby's theory, so the **full 4 marks**.

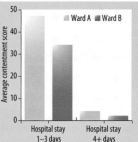

RESEARCH METHODS QUESTION

Many years ago people did not believe that separation between parents and their children would have serious emotional consequences. One hospital decided to conduct their own research to see if parental contact would improve the recovery rates of children in their hospital. Each child who arrived at the hospital for treatment was assigned to one of two wards – Ward A and Ward B. In Ward A parents were allowed and even encouraged to visit as often as possible. In Ward B visiting time was restricted to two hours per day. When each child was due to go home, a psychologist interviewed the child and assessed their behaviour, producing a 'contentment score'. The results are shown in the bar chart.

(a) Describe how the independent and dependent variables were operationalised in this study. *(4 marks)*

Craig's answer

Independent variable – the amount of parental visiting time during the child's recovery whilst in hospital.

Dependent variable – the children's contentment score following the psychologist's interview.

Charlotte's answer

The IV is the visiting time in the two wards (Ward A and Ward B).

The DV is how well they recover after they leave hospital.

Examiner's comments

Craig's answer is excellent, for the **full 4 marks**. Charlotte's description of the IV is fine but the DV isn't recovery as that was not measured, so **2 out of 4 marks**.

(b) The bar chart shows the findings from this study. What does it show about the effects of disruption of attachment? *(4 marks)*

You can see two things. First the children on both wards were less contented if their stay was four days or longer, second that the children in Ward A were generally more contented.

The bar chart shows that the children were less contented if they had to stay in hospital longer (4+ days).

Charlotte has managed one conclusion only, so **2 out of 4 marks**, whereas Craig receives the **full 4 marks**.

(c) Explain how investigator effects may have reduced the validity of this study. *(3 marks)*

It is possible that if the psychologist knows which ward the child has been in, this might influence their judgement of their 'contentment score' following the interview. If, for example, the psychologist knows that the child has been in Ward B (with the restricted visiting) then any marginal comment made by the child might be scored as negative, whereas if the child had been in Ward A (with extensive visiting), marginal comments may be scored as positive.

The researcher may reduce validity by asking the child leading questions like 'were you really unhappy at being parted from your mum?' They might try to make the child say things that make it look like one way of doing things was better than the other when this wasn't really the case and was just because the person doing the interviews was biased.

Both candidates have provided appropriate answers <u>and</u> explained why this would reduce validity, so the **full 3 marks** for both of them.

(d) This study was a field experiment. Give **one** strength and **one** limitation of using this method to investigate the effects of disruption of attachment. *(3 marks + 3 marks)*

A strength is that it allows the researchers to study things that would be unethical (or impractical) to study in a lab experiment. For example, because it is generally well known that children are more likely to become distressed with restricted visiting, they could not deliberately manipulate contact as part of the study.

A limitation is that demand characteristics may affect the outcome of the study. For example, staff in Ward A may know they are part of a study and may try harder to look after the emotional well-being of the children in their charge otherwise it reflects badly on their ward.

Because the experiment is carried out in an actual hospital rather than in a laboratory this means that it has higher ecological validity.

A limitation is that the researchers can't really control all the other variables that might affect the outcome of the study. This means that any conclusions they draw may be wrong because children's contentment scores may be affected by other things rather than just how much they saw their parents in hospital.

Craig has given a strength of a natural experiment rather than a field experiment, so **0 marks**. Craig's limitation is appropriate and well explained, so the **full 3 marks**.

Charlotte has gone for ecological validity but hasn't explained why the hospital would be better nor has she explained why ecological validity is a good thing, so **1 out of 3 marks**. The limitation is appropriate and well explained for the **full 3 marks**.

Extended writing question

'Some children fail to form attachments, which may have lifelong consequences. Disruption of attachment is more commonplace but could sometimes also have severe effects.'

Outline and evaluate research into the disruption of attachment. *(12 marks)*

AO1

Not a good beginning – there is no credit for defining the terms in the question. Your understanding of the terms will be apparent in your answer.

The answer starts here with a very muddled account of the Robertson's research observing the young boy called John.

Before I start I will define the terms used in the question. Attachment refers to the bond that forms between a caregiver and an infant. This usually happens in the first year of life and is vital for healthy psychological development. Disruption means breaking this bond by physically separating the child from its primary attachment (usually the mother). This can happen in lots of different ways, such as if the child has to go to hospital or if the parents leave the child alone when they go on holiday. There has been lots of research on this, for example a man and his wife bought a camera and went into a nursery where a young boy called John was left by his parents for two weeks while they went away. John cuddled a big teddy bear a lot to try and replace them and couldn't make friends with the other children so became very upset. When his mother came to pick him up he didn't want anything to do with her and later wet the bed when he went home. His parents were so distressed they withdrew him from the study and so we don't really know what happened to him in the long term. It is possible that he would have problems forming relationships later in life. That is one of the reasons why studies like this are so unethical, because a young boy has been sacrificed just to find out something that is pretty obvious anyway. It is also unethical because he would now have relationship problems. It is also a case study so can't be generalised to other children. We don't know how other children would have reacted in the same situation.

(285 words)

AO2

The point about ethics is inappropriate – the researchers' behaviour was not unethical because they did not put the boy in this situation – they observed a naturally occuring event.

The point about case studies is appropriate and briefly elaborated.

Examiner's comments

The description of research (AO1) is muddled but there is some relevant information, so a generous **2 out of 6 marks**.

The evaluation (AO2) is a little better than 'just discernible' but there is also a lack of specialist terms, so a slightly mean **1 out of 6 marks** (which balances out the generous **AO1** mark).

Total = **3 out of 12 marks**, which would not be a pass.

Failure to form attachment and institutional care

Question 1 Explain what is meant by the term 'privation'. *(2 marks)*

Joey's answer

It is when a child loses its attachment figure, e.g. if the mother dies or there are lots of separations.

Philippa's answer

It is a failure to form an attachment during the sensitive period of development.

Examiner's comments

Many studies confuse disruption with privation, as Joey has – so he gains **no marks**. Philippa is awarded the **full 2 marks**.

Question 2 A team of American psychologists studied the effects of institutional care by following a group of children who had spent their early lives in an orphanage. The children were all adopted when they were more than two years old.

(a) Explain what is meant by 'institutional care'. *(2 marks)*
(b) Outline what previous research has shown about the effects of institutional care. *(6 marks)*
(c) Based on this previous research, write a suitable hypothesis for the current study by the American psychologists. *(3 marks)*

(a) Being raised in an institution like an orphanage.

(b) The most famous case of institutional care is Genie. She was locked in a room by her father until she reached the age of 13. When she was discovered she could barely speak and never fully recovered from her ordeal. The other famous study is of the Czech twins who spent seven years being locked up by their stepmother. When they were discovered, however, they were put in the care of two sisters who really looked after them well, and they seemed to completely recover from their ordeal and functioned normally as adults.

(c) Children who spend their early years in an orphanage will not grow into normally functioning adults.

(a) This refers to children who are looked after in an institution, e.g. an orphanage. This usually involves a stay of months or years rather than day care where children go home in the evening.

(b) Hodges and Tizard studied children who had been placed in institutional care. During childhood about two-thirds were unable to feel deeply for other people. When the children were studied at age 16, those who had now been adopted were more likely to have formed attachments with their adoptive families than those who were restored to their original families. More recently, Rutter et al. studied a group of Romanian orphans who have been adopted by families in the UK. If these children were adopted before the age of six months, the children were likely to show normal emotional development compared to UK children of the same age. However, many of the children continued to experience problems with social relationships.

(c) Children in the institutional group show less mature emotional development and more relationship problems compared to a group of children raised within an intact family setting.

(a) Joey's answer is too brief and just saying institutional care is being in an institution is circular, so just **1 out of 2 marks**, whereas Philippa gains the **full 2 marks**.

(b) Joey has not selected appropriate research. Both case studies are examples of privation but not of institutional care. Philippa has provided findings from two appropriate studies in sufficient detail, so the **full 6 marks** for her and **no marks** for Joey.

(c) Joey will get **1 out of 3 marks** because he is on the right track but his hypothesis lacks operationalisation and a control condition, unlike Philippa's, which receives the **full 3 marks**.

Question 3 Explain the difference between disruption of attachment and failure to form attachment. *(4 marks)*

Disruption of attachment is when an attachment is disrupted for some reason. Failure to form attachment means an infant hasn't managed to form an attachment bond with someone.

Disruption of attachment refers to the breaking of an existing attachment bond (e.g. through prolonged physical separation), whereas failure to form attachment refers to a situation where an infant fails to form an attachment with a primary caregiver during the sensitive period of 6–12 months.

Philippa's answers contains the key word 'whereas' but that alone does not gain marks. She should have contrasted disruption and failure on the same dimension. For example, disruption is breaking an existing bond whereas privation is not having the bond in the first place. Joey has done this but his answer lacks detail so **2 out of 4 marks**. Philippa receives just **1 out of 4 marks**.

Question 4 Outline **one** study related to the failure to form attachment (privation). *(6 marks)*

Genie was a girl of 13 who had been locked in a small room in California by her father. She wasn't spoken to at all by her parents. Genie wasn't her real name, but this was the name given to her to protect her identity. Genie was discovered at the age of 13 when her mother ran away from her father after a violent quarrel. Her mother was partially blind and applied for social security and so Genie was discovered by the social worker. Her parents were then accused of abuse and her father subsequently shot himself.

Rutter et al. (2007) studied a group of Romanian orphans who have been adopted by families in the UK. When these orphans first arrived in the UK as babies, more than half of them showed severe delays in psychological development compared with UK children of the same age. These orphans were assessed at ages four, six and eleven. If the children were adopted before the age of six months, they tended to show normal psychological development. However, those children who were adopted after six months of age developed various problems, including disinhibited attachment and problems with peer relationships. This research showed that the consequences of privation can be less severe if children have the opportunity to form attachments.

The case study on Genie is appropriate here, so Joey's answer can gain credit – but not much as his account omits key information such as the aims or findings of the study, it is therefore 'basic' and gets **2 out of 6 marks**. Another excellent, detailed answer from Philippa, for the **full 6 marks**; Rutter's study is relevant to both privation and institutional care.

Question 5 Emma and Jane were friends who discovered they had a special bond. Their mothers had both died when they were small babies. Emma feels this has permanently affected her whereas Jane does not feel there have been any long-term effects.

Use your knowledge of psychology to explain why the two girls appear to have responded differently to the same experience. *(6 marks)*

Jane doesn't feel that there are any long-term negative effects in her development as a result of losing her mother when she was young, whereas Emma does feel that this event has affected her. This could be because Jane either isn't aware of any long-term effects or is denying these. This is a common psychoanalytic defence mechanism where some people deny that they have problems when they really do have problems. Maybe they have both suffered as a result of losing their mothers but only Emma acknowledges that this could have anything to do with losing her mother.

There are several possible reasons why Emma and Jane have responded differently to the same situation. Research has shown that not all children who suffer privation show impaired psychological development. For example, in Rutter's study of Romanian orphans, one-third recovered well and developed normal emotional development. Because of these individual differences, it is likely that other factors in Jane and Emma's childhood, as well as a failure to form an attachment, determine psychological problems in adulthood (e.g. temperament differences, childhood poverty etc.). Research by Schaffer and Emerson discovered that many children form their primary attachment bond with someone other than the mother, therefore it is possible that Jane formed an attachment bond with a sensitive father or grandparent, and Emma did not.

Given that this question is worth 6 marks, it is important that Philippa has offered more than one explanation and explained both of them clearly and with reference to research, so **6 out of 6 marks**.

Joey's answer starts with the classic mistake of just writing out the question again, which is wasting time. However, he does then go on to provide a psychologically informed answer; enough for **3 out of 6 marks**.

Question 6 (a) Describe how psychologists have studied the failure to form attachment (privation). *(4 marks)*
(b) Identify **one** ethical issue that has arisen in such research and explain why it is an issue. *(3 marks)*
(c) The BPS Code of Ethics publishes a code of ethics. Explain the purpose of this code. *(3 marks)*
(d) Explain **one** limitation of the code of ethics. *(3 marks)*

(a) Psychologists have studied failure to form attachment by carrying out research. Research tests assumptions that the researchers may have about the importance of attachment in development. Therefore they can be more certain that something is true rather than just thinking it might be.

(b) An ethical issue is protection from harm. In the case of Genie, her mother complained that Genie was harmed because of all the psychological testing.

(c) The purpose of the BPS code of ethics is to stop psychologists from carrying out research that is unethical. There are different sections that offer guidance on deception (not telling lies or misleading participants), informed consent (telling participants all the risks of taking part) and protection from harm, which might be psychological harm or physical harm.

(d) A problem with the code is that not everybody conforms to it and it is very difficult to punish them. They can be struck off for carrying out unethical research, but that may be insufficiently tough.

(a) Psychologists have studied failure to form attachment by using longitudinal studies, where a child or group of children is followed over a long period of time to study the impact of early experiences on later development. For example, Hodges and Tizard (1989) followed a group of children who had spent their early years in an orphanage through to adolescence. Another way is to use a case study of children who have been isolated and therefore unable to form an attachment, as in the case of Genie, who was locked in a room.

(b) An ethical issue is confidentiality, where insufficient attention is given to protecting the identity of the person in a case study. In the case of Genie, confidential information about her upbringing, including film of her as an adolescent is widely available, and may well be a source of great embarrassment to her as she tries to rebuild her life.

(c) The BPS code of ethics exists to preserve the dignity and well-being of those who participate in research, to offer guidance as to appropriate conduct for those who carry out the research and to protect the subject of psychology from being brought into disrepute.

(d) A problem with the BPS code of ethics is that it is doesn't encourage individual responsibility. Psychologists can feel they are behaving ethically by simply following the guidelines, instead of actively considering the particular issues raised by any research study. The code closes off discussions.

(a) Perhaps Joey hasn't fully understood the question – it's not just about the research method but specifically how the method was used to study failure to form attachment. Furthermore, all he has talked about is 'research' which is not sufficiently detailed, so **0 marks**. Philippa has provided plenty of detail about two methods and linked these to actual studies for the **full 4 marks**.

(b) Both candidates have identified an ethical issue and explained why it is an issue in the research mentioned in (a). However, Joey hasn't provided enough information whereas Philippa has gone on to explain why it is an issue (see three-point rule on page 10). So **2 out of 3 marks** for Joey and the **full 3 marks** for Philippa.

(c) Both candidates have again written an appropriate answer, explaining the purpose of the code for 'guidance', so the **full 3 marks** for both.

(d) Both are fully correct answers for **3 out of 3 marks**.

Question 7 (a) Outline what research has shown about the effects of failure to form attachment (privation). *(4 marks)*
(b) Explain **one** criticism of this research. *(3 marks)*

(a) Research has shown that children who fail to form attachments (e.g. children in an orphanage) grow up with many psychological problems. These problems include not having friends and finding it difficult to fall in love and having a mental disorder such as disinhibited attachment disorder.

(b) A criticism of this sort of research is that unless these children have actually been through the Strange Situation, it is very difficult to know whether they have formed an attachment or not. It is a bit of an assumption to claim that just because someone has been brought up in an orphanage this means they haven't formed an attachment. Bruce Oldfield was brought up in a children's home and he went on to become a famous fashion designer!

(a) Studies of isolated children (e.g. the Curtiss' study of Genie) have suggested that children who are raised in situations devoid of any emotional care experience long-term problems with their emotional and social development. Research with children raised in institutions (e.g. Hodges and Tizard's study of children raised in orphanages) confirms that such children lacked social skills and were unpopular at school, and showed signs of disinhibited attachment, i.e. a failure to discriminate between people they choose as attachment figures.

(b) A criticism of this research is that frequently psychologists have no information about how these children cope later in life as adults. For example, Genie was withdrawn from the study by her mother, and Hodges and Tizard were unable to contact many of the children later in life. It is possible that children who fail to form attachments when young simply need more time to mature sufficiently and to learn how to cope with relationships.

(a) Joey's answer does contain some findings but these are fairly brief, although he does name reactive attachment disorder, so **1 out of 4 marks**. By contrast, Philippa's answer has lots of detail about findings linked to specific studies, so **4 out of 4 marks**.

(b) Both candidates have identified an appropriate criticism and Philippa has provided a full explanation (remember the three-point rule) for the **full 3 marks**. Joey has given some elaboration of his basic point but the anecdote about Bruce Oldfield is not creditworthy, so **2 out of 3 marks**.

Question 8 Georgina became severely depressed after she had her second baby, Angela. She already had a young boy, Edward, who was four years old. Her severe depression meant she was unable to give the children much love and affection but she cared for them reasonably well in terms of their physical needs.

(a) Outline the possible long-term effects of Georgina's depression on both Angela and Edward. *(3 marks + 3 marks)*
(b) Select **one** effect outlined in **(a)** and outline **one** piece of research evidence that supports this. You should include details of how the study was conducted. *(5 marks)*

(a) Research into disruption of attachment has shown that they may wet the bed, and later have relationship problems.

Another problem they may have is that they may have problems forming friendships with other children, and forever remain vulnerable to disorders such as depression and anxiety.

(b) One of these effects is bed-wetting. This was discovered in Robertson's study of John, who was left in a residential nursery while his mother was away having another baby. He stayed there for nine days and became very distressed and even rejected his mother when she came to pick him up. After he was taken home he wet the bed for a long time, so this is a long-term effect of the disruption of his attachment bond with his mother.

(a) Because Edward was already four years old when Angela was born, it means that his attachment had already been formed. What he would be experiencing is emotional disruption. The effects would be slowed development, relationship problems and a vulnerability to disorders such as depression and anxiety disorders. Angela would have failed to form an attachment, because during the sensitive period of 6–12 months, her mother was already severely depressed. Her mother was therefore incapable of showing sensitivity to Angela's emotional needs, therefore she would either fail to form any attachment or would be insecurely attached.

(b) Hart et al. (1998) studied 100 one-year-old infants and their mothers using the Strange Situation. They found that infants whose mothers were classified as depressed showed many of the typical characteristics of insecure attachment. During the different Strange Situation stages, these infants showed less separation anxiety, avoided their mothers upon reunion and were more likely to be comforted by a stranger, all typical of infants who are insecurely attached.

(a) Joey has misunderstood the question which required a separate answer for Angela and Edward, who would be affected differently because of their age, as Philippa has recognised. Joey would gain some credit for two brief answers; **1 out of 3 marks** and **1 out of 3 marks**, whereas Philippa gets the **full 3 marks** both times.

(b) Philippa has selected an excellent study but has not stated what characteristic she is linking this to. In this case Joey's answer, even though less sophisticated clearly answers the question although he didn't give details of how the study was conducted. So **3 out of 5 marks** for each of them as their answers lack key details.

RESEARCH METHODS QUESTION

A natural experiment was conducted investigating the effects of institutional care on later emotional development. The researcher identified 20 young adults who had spent their early lives in an institution and compared their emotional development with a group of other young adults who had spent their entire childhood with their natural families. The 'natural families' group were matched with participants in the institutionalised group.

(a) Outline the aims of this study. *(3 marks)*

Joey's answer	Philippa's answer	Examiner's comments
The aim was to see whether young adults who have been brought up in an institution have normal emotional development.	The aim of the study was to see whether people brought up entirely in an institution are more or less emotionally healthy than a comparable group of people brought up in 'normal' families.	Philippa has included key information about the comparison group, so the **full 3 marks**. Joey's answer gets **2 out of 3 marks**.

(b) Identify **one** factor that could have been used when matching participants and explain why this factor would be important. *(3 marks)*

One thing they should be matched on is gender because girls and boys may have different emotional development, so if all the institutionalised adults were male and all the adults from normal families were girls, this would affect the results of the study.	It would be important to match the adults in terms of temperament because research has shown that children who are friendly and happy tend to form attachments more easily, and are more likely to be securely attached, so this would have an important influence on the emotional development of members of both groups.	Oh dear – gender is a bit of an obvious choice. At least Joey has put forward a possible reason why there might be a difference, so **2 out of 3 marks**. Philippa has selected a much more intelligent factor and provided detailed evidence, so **full 3 marks**.

(c) Explain **one** strength and **one** limitation of using a matched participants design to study the effects of institutional care. *(3 marks + 3 marks)*

A strength is that by matching participants on things that are important, you can prevent those things from affecting the study (for example, age, gender, intelligence, etc.). A limitation is that it is difficult to do, and the researchers may not know things like the intelligence, etc. of the participants. A lot of the records of the children in the institutions may not be available to them, so this makes it very difficult to match effectively.	A strength is that it can control participant variables. For example, with an independent groups design there may have been important temperament differences between the two groups, and this variable could then have acted as a extraneous variable. A limitation is that it is often difficult to match effectively on all the variables that might potentially affect the outcome of the study. For example, as well as temperament, there are other important variables, illness record, gender, age, etc., all of which may affect the outcome of the study, and it becomes impossible to match all of these.	Both students have identified the same strength and the same limitation but Philippa has given much more detail each time and used the appropriate technical terms, so **2 out of 3 marks** each time for Joey and **3 out of 3 marks** for Philippa.

(d) Explain why this study was a natural experiment. *(2 marks)*

This was a natural experiment because it was carried out in the natural environment (i.e. the real world) rather than in the artificial setting of a lab.	It was a natural experiment because the independent variable (whether raised in institutions or in normal families) has not been manipulated by the researchers but has occurred naturally.	Joey has got it wrong (it's not the environment that is significant) so **no marks** whereas Philippa's answer is correct for the **full 2 marks**.

(e) Explain **one** strength and **one** limitation of using a natural experiment to study the effects of institutional care. *(3 marks + 3 marks)*

A strength is that it is more realistic to use a natural experiment to study the effects of institutional care and so this study has higher ecological validity. A limitation is that if the adults become aware that they are taking part in a study they may change their behaviour to fit with what they think the experimenter wants to find out. This is called demand characteristics.	A strength of using a natural experiment in this area is that it enables researchers to study problems of real significance rather than being restricted to problems that can be manipulated by the researchers. The long-term effects of institutional care are important in determining the upbringing of children, therefore this offers an opportunity to find out something of real social value. A limitation is that there are many extraneous variables. These include early childhood experiences that may have had an impact on emotional development, experiences with peers etc. These variables may cloud the relationship between the IV (upbringing) and the DV (emotional development in adulthood).	There is an element of truth to Joey's answer – a naturally occurring independent variable would be more realistic which could lead to enhanced ecological validity – but why is this a strength? His answer is repetitive and not really an explanation, so he receives only **1 out of 3 marks**. Philippa's answer is considerably clearer as she has explained the strength and also said why it is a strength, so **3 out of 3 marks**. Joey's limitation is just about worth the **full 3 marks** while Philippa coasts there.

(f) The researchers conducted a pilot study before the main research study. Explain why they decided to do this. *(3 marks)*

They would carry out a pilot study because this would make the main study better. A pilot study is a small-scale study that tests all the procedures prior to the main study so that they can be changed before embarking on the main study.	They decided to carry out a pilot study to check whether all aspects of the study 'worked' before conducting the main study. For example, if they were interviewing adults, did the questions get the information they were hoping to get, did they cause embarrassment etc. They can change any procedures in the light of what they learn from the pilot study.	Joey has made the mistake of saying <u>what</u> a pilot study is and only briefly trying to answer the 'why', and his answer is not sufficient to score any marks. Another excellent answer from Philippa for the **full 3 marks**.

(g) Identify **one** possible extraneous variable in this study and suggest how it might be dealt with. *(3 marks)*

It is possible that some of the people who were raised in orphanages had been abused and so this might affect their emotional development. They would have to confidentially ask all the adults whether they had been abused as children and exclude those who had.	An extraneous variable is that the person who does the testing and/or interviewing might be aware of whether the adult is in the institutional group or the normal family group, and this may bias their judgements of the person's emotional development. This can be dealt with by using a single blind procedure, so the person doing the testing is not aware of which group the person comes from.	There's enough detail in Joey's answer for the **full 3 marks** as he has identified a possible extraneous variable and clearly explained how it could be dealt with. Philippa also gets the **full 3 marks**.

Extended writing question

Discuss research related to failure to form attachment *(privation).*

(12 marks)

AO1

> The first paragraph contains a description of the Genie study which is basic in terms of detail. No marks are subtracted for the fact that researchers' names and the date have been omitted. However, this kind of information would count as 'detail'.

> In paragraph two a second study is described in a reasonable amount of detail, although again it is mainly related to procedures.

> A third study is covered but only in basic detail.

There has been lots of research related to failure to form attachment. Some of these studies have been of children who have been raised in isolation. One of these was Genie, who was kept locked in a room until she was 13. When they discovered her she couldn't speak, and even after lots of support from the psychologists she stayed retarded. This can be thought of as an unethical study because it is wrong to subject someone who has been through a hard time to research.

Another study was of children who had been raised in orphanages. This was carried out by Hodges and Tizard in 1969. They studied children who were brought up in orphanages and then when they were about two they were either given back to their mothers or adopted. When the researchers later checked on them, they found that those who had been put back with their natural parents were doing much better than those who had been adopted. This is also an unethical study because it is wrong to break confidentiality about these children's upbringing. This should be kept private.

Another study was carried out by Rutter. He studied Romanian orphans who had spent the first years of their life in an orphanage and were then were adopted. They found that these children were able to recover completely because they were in loving adopted families. These studies show that failure to form attachments can lead to negative consequences for the children, but not always, as shown by Rutter's study of Romanian orphans.

(257 words)

AO2

> One critical point is made with some brief elaboration.

> Another critical point is presented at the end of this second study, however it is not appropriate because confidentiality was not breached as consent was given.

> The final sentence offers important commentary on what we can conclude from these three studies.

Examiner's comments

This answer is rather short, which is not surprising because there really is too little evaluation (**AO2**). Despite the competent conclusion at the end, in total the evaluation is a restricted in range but better than 'just discernible' (see mark scheme on page 9), so **2 out of 6 marks**.

The descriptive (**AO1**) content is relevant and there are some detailed passages. Even though some of the material is basic, the <u>amount</u> of AO1 makes it worth **4 out of 6 marks**.

Total = **6 out of 12 marks**, a **Grade D** answer.

Extended writing question

Discuss the effects of institutional care.

(12 marks)

AO1

> A detailed description of an appropriate study by Hodges and Tizard, covering procedures and results.

> The first sentence deals directly with the demands of the question – what are the effects of institutional care?

> The phrase 'this supports' would lead you to think this might be AO2, but in this case it is a further answer to the question of the possible effects of institutional care.

> A short but clear description of the research by Rutter et al.

Hodges and Tizard (1989) studied children who had been in institutional care before they had formed attachments. When the children were studied at age 16, those who had now been adopted were more likely to have formed attachments with their adoptive families than those who were restored to their original families. The majority of the adoptive mothers felt that their child was deeply attached to them. By contrast only a half of the children restored to their original families were described in the same way. However, both sets of children experienced problems with forming relationships and were less likely to be liked by other children.

This research suggests that early privation when in the orphanage had a negative effect on the children's future development, particularly their ability to form and maintain relationships. This supports Bowlby's claim that failure to form an attachment during the sensitive period had an irreversible effect on the future emotional development of those children. Although this study suggests that institutional care has such negative effects, it should be remembered that institutions have changed a great deal since these children were there, largely as a result of research such as this, therefore modern institutions may no longer have the same negative effects on development.

Rutter et al. (2007) studied a group of Romanian orphans who have been adopted by families in the UK. If these children were adopted before the age of six months, the children were likely to show normal emotional development compared to UK children of the same age. However, many of the children continued to experience problems with social relationships. This more modern research challenges the assumption that institutional care inevitably leads to long-term negative effects on development. This suggests that privation alone cannot explain these negative outcomes, and that long-term damage only occurs when there are multiple risk factors (e.g. parental drug taking, poverty or abuse), followed by poor subsequent care.

(318 words)

AO2

> The final sentence is an excellent AO2 point, with some elaboration.

> The final sentence offers analysis.

Examiner's comments

This would be an excellent answer to the question 'Discuss research related to the effects of institutional care', but that wasn't the question. The information about how institutional care has affected children counts as the descriptive (**AO1**) content. There is certainly <u>some</u> relevant material here which is sound but less detailed in terms of breadth, so **4 out of 6 marks**.

There is relatively little evaluation (**AO2**) although the research studies could have been used as support for the points made. As it stands they gain some credit but have not been used effectively, so **3 out of 6 marks**.

Total = **7 out of 12 marks**, a **Grade C** answer
(this is a shame as the candidate clearly knows a lot but has failed to answer the question set).

Day care

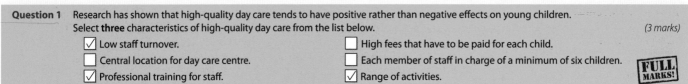

Question 1 Research has shown that high-quality day care tends to have positive rather than negative effects on young children. Select **three** characteristics of high-quality day care from the list below.   *(3 marks)*

☑ Low staff turnover.

☐ Central location for day care centre.

☑ Professional training for staff.

☐ High fees that have to be paid for each child.

☐ Each member of staff in charge of a minimum of six children.

☑ Range of activities.

FULL MARKS!

Question 2 Explain what is meant by the terms 'day care' and 'social development'.   *(2 marks + 2 marks)*

Jay's answer

Day care is any form of temporary child care which is given by people who are not family members and which usually takes place outside of the home.

Social development is about the development of sociability, which includes learning how to relate to others as well as with socialisation, where the child learns the knowledge and skills important in their culture.

Alicia's answer

Day care is looking after the child during the day when the parents may be at work.

Social development is the development of social skills like getting along with other children.

Examiner's comments

Jay has provided two detailed and informed answers for the **full marks**. Alicia has made the mistake of using the same term to define a term, i.e. day care is care during the day – never a good idea. It may be true but doesn't explain the concept, so **no marks**. Her answer for the second term, social development, is slightly better, so **1 out of 2 marks**.

Question 3 Outline possible effects of day care on children's peer relations.   *(4 marks)*

The Minnesota longitudinal study found that securely attached infants go on to be more popular with peers, but there is evidence that children in day care are less likely to be securely attached (Belsky and Rovine, 1988) and therefore less successful in peer relationships.

Day care, however, also gives children the opportunity to spend time with their peers and so develop social strategies and make friends. Field (1991) found that the amount of time spent in full-time day care was positively related to the number of friends that a child had. Clarke-Stewart found that children who had attended day care were better at settling disputes with other children.

Day care has been shown to make children more aggressive. For example, in the NICHD study, the more time children spent in day care, the more aggressive they became. Melhuish's study also showed that children who spent lots of time in day care showed more anti-social behaviour. Day care has also been shown to make children more independent and obedient. This was in a study by Clarke-Stewart. She also found that children who had experience of day care could get on better with their peers.

Jay has again provided a detailed answer to the question, focusing on the findings (rather than the procedures) and providing evidence related specifically to peer relations. His answer is nicely balanced, but there is no requirement to present negative and positive evidence. **Full marks**.

Alicia has made a common mistake – she has ignored the fact that the question is not about the effects of day care in general – it specifies peer relations, but she has presented evidence related to the effects of day care on aggression. This could have been linked to peer relations; for example, you could argue that children who are aggressive won't get on as well with peers – but this link has not been made. There is a brief mention of peer relations in the final sentence, so she just scrapes **1 out of 4 marks**.

Question 4 Outline what research has shown about the effects of day care on children's aggressive behaviour.   *(4 marks)*

Several studies have shown that children who attend day care for more than 30 hours a week are more aggressive than those who don't. In the NICHD study, children in full-time day care were more likely to show behaviour problems when they eventually went to school. These included temper tantrums and hitting other children. This was also the case in a UK study (Melhuish, 2004), who found that children who spent a lot of time in day care in the first two years were more at risk of developing anti-social behaviour later on, including aggression towards peers.

The NICHD study (National Institute of Child Health and Development) in the USA studied 1,000 children since 1991. One of the main findings was that the more time these children spent in day care centres, particularly in the first two years of life, the more aggressive they became. A problem with this finding is that it is just correlational, and not causal. Therefore this does not prove that time in day care caused the aggression. It is likely to be a number of other factors as well. It may be that aggressive people are more likely to leave their children in day care longer.

Jay's answer to question 4 is shorter than his answer to question 3 but there is still sufficient information here and it is all related to the effects of day care on aggression. Unlike many student answers, Jay has not included anything irrelevant so, it would get the **full 4 marks**.

By contrast, Alicia has wasted time and space with irrelevant material, such as a brief description of what the NICHD study entailed and the criticisms of the findings. This means that, even though her answer looks like it is as good as Jay's, most of it is not creditworthy. She would receive **1 out of 4 marks**.

Question 5 (a) Outline how **one** research study has investigated the effects of day care on children's social development. *(6 marks)*
(b) Explain **one** limitation with this research study. *(3 marks)*

(a) The NICHD study is a longitudinal study of over 1,300 children from many different types of family in 10 different locations across the US. This was started in 1991 and the intention was to study many different aspects of child development, including their social development. Children and their parents were assessed using many different techniques including observations, interviews, questionnaires and psychological testing. They were assessed at various intervals (ages 3, 6, 12 and 15) and different aspects of development (e.g. increased aggression) can then be related to children's experiences at home, in child care and later on, in school. Of the original 1,300+ children, 1,100 were followed through to adolescence.

(b) A limitation of this study is that the data it provides are not causal, therefore it does not show that high levels of day care have caused an increase in aggressive behaviour. Some critics have argued that such correlational data showing a relationship between day care and aggression is essentially meaningless if it does not indicate the processes by which aggression is increased as a result of day care.

(a) Gregg et al. studied children in Bristol as part of the 'Children of the '90s' study. They studied 14,000 children and their parents. They were interested in whether children whose mothers worked when their children were very young had any effect on the children's development. They found that for the majority of the children they studied any effects were small and were only found in certain circumstances. This was a longitudinal study which follows a group of children over a long period of time.

(b) A problem with this study is that they didn't find what they were expecting to find. The researchers wanted to show that children whose mothers worked were less well-off psychologically than children whose mothers didn't work. However, this was not what they found, therefore their findings contradicted their hypothesis and so the study was a failure.

(a) In contrast with questions 3 and 4, this question now asks for how the study was conducted, not what was found, but Alicia has continued to disregard the specific demands of the question and just written anything related to the study including some material on the procedures ('how') but also information about the aims and the findings. She gains just **1 out of 6 marks**. This is a shame because, despite apparently knowing lots, she has failed to use her knowledge appropriately and might well fail the exam because of poor exam technique. Jay, on the other hand, has done very well to provide **6 marks'** worth of information on how this particular study was conducted, although he too has included uncreditworthy information about the aims of the study.

(b) Another excellent answer from Jay exemplifying the three-point rule, for the **full 3 marks**. Alicia should really know what counts as a limitation – not getting the result you expected is not a limitation, it may be a disappointment but not a limitation of the methods used which is what was required, so **0 marks**.

Question 6 Fatima has been attending a day care centre since she was nine months old. When she started she was a very happy, outgoing child but gradually she changed to being passive and unsettled.

Use your knowledge of psychology to explain why her behaviour may have changed since she started day care. *(4 marks)*

Belsky and Rovine (1988) showed that children who received more 20 hours a week of day care before they were one year old were more likely to become insecurely attached. This might explain why Fatima has become passive and unsettled, as these are characteristics of insecure attachment. Research has also shown that there are individual differences in the impact of day care on children. For example, Pennebaker et al. (1981) found that shy children often find the experience of day care quite frightening which, if Fatima is of a shy disposition, might explain her change of behaviour.

Studies have shown that day care can increase aggression in children if they are there for more than 30 hours a week. It is possible that those children who are there full-time are becoming aggressive towards other children, and bullying them. Therefore, Fatima has become passive because she is being bullied and unsettled because she is frightened to go to day care, and may well cry when it is time to go each day.

Jay has cited two research findings that are both relevant and linked both of them to Fatima's behaviour, thus satisfying the demands of the question. His answer is far more than is required for the **full 4 marks** as just one of the studies would have been sufficient, perhaps with a little more elaboration.

Alica's answer has some merit but not much. She has cited a study and linked this to Fatima's behaviour. However, she has missed key elements of the question's stem – there is nothing that says any of the children were there for more than 30 hours so that is an assumption. It is also an assumption that the aggressive behaviour might lead to bullying. So this answer has only some relevance for **2 out of 4 marks**.

Question 7 Brian and Tina plan to place their baby son in day care when Tina goes back to work. They obviously wish to find the best possible place for their son.

What advice would you give them? Refer to psychological research in your answer. *(6 marks)*

Research has shown that children who receive high-quality day care are better able to interact with the world around them. Based on research of what constitutes high-quality day care, I would advise Brian and Tina to look for somewhere with a low staff turnover, high adult–child ratio and a positive emotional climate. For example, Melhuish found evidence of increased aggression among children whose carers were constantly changing. Research has also shown that children who spend more than 30 hours a week in day care show more problem behaviours and had more episodes of minor illness, so I would advise them to leave their son for less than 30 hours. Leach et al. found that babies fared worst when they were given day nursery care, whereas those cared for by childminders were rated second only to those cared for by their mothers. Childminders tend to provide one-to-one care, which is considered to be better for children, therefore I would advise a childminder rather than a day nursery.

I would suggest that it would be better to leave their baby with a grandparent because they would be more likely to provide a similar level of love and affection because they are related to the baby. If they can't leave the baby with a grandparent, they should look for a childminder who they trust. It is difficult to get good childminders and research suggests that children are more likely to suffer if they are looked after by a bad childminder. They can become delinquent and have more temper tantrums. However, if they are looked after by a good childminder, they develop much better. Their baby is probably too young to go to playgroup, but playgroups can be good at getting a child used to other children, which is good for a child's social development.

Alicia has tried hard to produce an answer to this question and written many useful suggestions – but there are almost no links to psychological research, as required in the question. This is, afterall, a psychology exam so your answers must demonstrate evidence of what you have learned. Her one reference to research is too vague to gain much credit. There is no requirement to give names and dates but the research must be identifiable rather than just being a vague statement that 'research shows children suffer if they are looked after by a bad childminder', so a generous **2 out of 6 marks** for a 'commonsense' answer to the question which lacks psychology.

Jay has made three suggestions and backed up each with specific research. He has given the researchers' names but not the dates – dates add more detail to your answer but as there is plenty of detail here, the lack of dates does not detract – so the **full 6 marks**. Two suggestions probably would have been sufficient for the full marks or at least 5 out of 6 marks.

A group of psychology students wish to find out more about people's experiences in day care and therefore they decide to ask their friends about their experiences in day care.

(a) The students could collect data using a questionnaire or an interview but they decide to use the interview technique. Give **one** strength of choosing to use an interview rather than a questionnaire when collecting data related to day care. *(3 marks)*

Jay's answer

A strength of using an interview in this study rather than a questionnaire is that the researchers have the opportunity to follow up on someone's answer by asking a supplementary question (e.g. if a person reports that they were unhappy during day care, they can ask them what was it about day care that made them feel like that). This would give the researchers greater depth of understanding than they would get with a fixed questionnaire.

Alicia's answer

Interviews can provide lots of detailed information about whatever it is the researchers are interested in. If the interviewer is very skilful, they can get an awful lot out of the person they are interviewing, sometimes more than the person intended to reveal. You can't really do this in a questionnaire.

Examiner's comments

Jay's answer again illustrates the three-point rule (see page 10) – he has identified the strength, given evidence from this specific case (and therefore contextualised his answer) and explained why this is a strength – for the **full 3 marks**.

Alicia's answer is also good but lacks contextualisation, i.e. reference to this particular interview involving questions about day care, so **2 out of 3 marks**. Note that contextualisation is not always required – but it is good just to get into the habit of doing it as it elaborates your answer.

(b) (i) Describe **two** possible factors that may affect the validity of their study. *(2 marks + 2 marks)*
(ii) Explain how you could deal with one of these problems. *(2 marks)*

(i) It is possible that some of the participants will respond in a way that they feel is socially desirable, e.g. not wanting to admit that they found day care terrifying and had no friends. A second problem is if the interviewer uses leading questions such as 'Were you upset being left with strangers every day while your mother went to work?' this would predispose them to answer in a certain way.

(ii) I would deal with the possibility of leading questions by trying them out in a pilot study and then reviewing (and possibly changing) any that consistently tend to produce an answer in one particular direction.

(i) A problem for validity is a lack of ecological validity. If they decided to carry out the study in a laboratory then it wouldn't have ecological validity. Another problem would be to internal validity, for example, all questions should be assessing the same thing. If they aren't then the study lacks internal validity.

(ii) I would deal with the lack of ecological validity by interviewing people in a more realistic setting such as their own homes. This would make their answers more realistic and so more valid.

(i) Alicia is wrong about ecological validity here. A laboratory is simply a space where variables can be well controlled, such as a classroom – conducting an interview in a laboratory shouldn't make any difference to the answers that a person gives, so **0 marks** for the first problem but **2 out of 2 marks** for her comments on internal validity. Both of Jay's answers are correct for the full **4 out of 4 marks**.

(ii) Jay also gains the **full 2 marks** here but Alicia receives **no marks** because ecological validity was not credited in (i).

(c) The students decide to summarise their data using a content analysis. Explain how they might do this. *(4 marks)*

They could look for particular behavioural categories such as interactions with other children, behaviour towards parents, interaction with day care providers, etc. They could then look for any responses made by their friends that fit into each of the categories because they have similar content. When they have fitted each of the responses into the different behavioural categories, they can analyse each category, looking for common themes that emerge, e.g. that day care was more likely to lead to more aggressive interactions with peers.

They could carry out a content analysis by taking all the things that are said in the interview, and then analysing the content of what is said to see if the people they interviewed had positive or negative experiences while they were in day care. This is an example of qualitative analysis – rather than just collecting numbers, the researchers are concentrating on what the people are saying instead.

Most students find questions about content analysis difficult because they have had little experience of conducting them. Our candidates have fared quite well here. Jay's answer is very clear starting with his use of behavioural categories (and giving examples) through to how the data could be analysed, so the **full 4 marks**.

Alicia's answer is less sophisticated but communicates a reasonable understanding of content analysis. However, her answer lacks detail as she just suggests that there might be two categories – positive and negative experiences. It might have helped to give some examples of the things people might say and how it would be categorised. The final sentence is not really relevant to the question 'how'. Her answer is worth **2 out of 4 marks**.

(d) (i) Name a method that is used to assess reliability. *(1 mark)*
(ii) Explain how the students might use this method to assess the reliability of their interviews. *(3 marks)*

(i) Test–retest.

(ii) They could assess the reliability of the interviews by carrying out the same interview with the same people a week later. If the interview is reliable then the answers the second time around should be more or less the same (i.e. consistent with) the answers from the first interview.

(i) One way is the split-half method.

(ii) All the questions should be assessing the same thing. The researchers would have to convert each answer into a numerical score, e.g. 5 for very upset, 4 for quite upset and so on. If answers are split in half, the mean score for each half should be the same.

(i) Both students will receive **1 mark** for this answer.

(ii) Jay has described how the test–retest method could be used in this context and gains the **full 3 marks**. Alicia has selected a different method for assessing reliability, the split-half method – a method of assessing reliability but one that is not appropriate in an interview because different questions may well be assessing different things, so **0 out of 3 marks** for the second part of this question.

Extended writing question

'Psychological research has shown that day care has positive as well as negative effects.'
Outline and evaluate research relating to the effects of day care on peer relations.

(12 marks)

AO1

The answer starts with an appropriate point linked to two different pieces of research.

A further study is briefly described.

The Swedish study counts as further description of research.

The Minnesota longitudinal study found that securely attached infants go on to be more popular with peers, and as there is evidence that children in day care are less likely to be securely attached (Belsky and Rovine, 1988), therefore they are likely to be less successful in peer relationships. However, day care also gives children the opportunity to spend time with their peers and so develop social strategies and make friends, therefore day care could also make children more successful in peer relationships. This conclusion is supported by Field (1991), who found that the amount of time spent in full-time day care was positively related to the number of friends that a child had. Clarke-Stewart found that children who had attended day care were better at settling disputes with other children.

Not all studies have shown that day care has any significant effect on children's long-term peer relations. For example, Larner et al. (1989) carried out a longitudinal study of 120 Swedish children until the age of 10. Half of these children had been through high-quality state-run day care centres, whereas the other half had been cared for at home. At age 10, there was no evidence that the day care children were any more negative in their interactions with other children compared to the children cared for at home.

The study of peer relations among infants is a relatively new area of study. Prior to the development of universal day care, infants rarely spent time in close proximity with each other. Much of the research in this area has been carried out in laboratory settings, but infants studied in laboratories do not show the same behaviours as children studied in natural environments.

(283 words)

AO2

The conclusion ('therefore they are …') counts towards AO2.

The following sentence is more AO2 than AO1, making a contrasting point/comment which is further elaborated 'This is supported by …'.

The first sentence in this paragraph is AO2 commentary.

The final paragraph is evaluation, but not very effective as children did spend time together even before day care, e.g. collectivist communities.

The final point about lab studies isn't relevant here without giving some specific examples of day care research conducted in a lab.

Examiner's comments

The quotation suggests that both positive and negative effects should be discussed, as has been done in this answer but there would be no penalty for ignoring this. The quotation simply is there to remind students that this is one way to present **AO2** material.

The description (**AO1**) of research is accurate and appropriately related to peer relations. It is better than basic though not sufficiently detailed for the top band, so **5 out of 6 marks**.

The evaluation (**AO2**) is not as good. A few creditworthy points have been made but only the second one has 'depth' – all the others are superficial – so we might be tempted towards the 5–4 mark band (see mark scheme on page 9), but the answer is best described as a restricted range and generally superficial, so **3 out of 6 marks**.

Total = **8 out of 12 marks**, a **Grade B** answer.

Extended writing question

Outline and evaluate research relating to the effects of day care on aggressive behaviour.

(12 marks)

AO1

A short outline of one piece of appropriate research.

In the second paragraph two further studies are presented, covering important and relevant details.

Several studies have shown that children who attend day care for more than 30 hours a week are more aggressive than those who don't. In the NICHD study, children in full-time day care were more likely to show behaviour problems when they eventually went to school. These included temper tantrums and hitting other children. A limitation of this study is that the data it provides are not causal, therefore it does not show that high levels of day care have caused an increase in aggressive behaviour. Some critics have argued that such correlational data showing a relationship between day care and aggression is essentially meaningless if it does not indicate the processes by which aggression is increased as a result of day care.

A UK study (Melhuish, 2004) found that children who spent a lot of time in day care in the first two years were more at risk of developing anti-social behaviour later on, including aggression towards peers. A Canadian study (Baker et al., 2008) found that following the introduction of universal day care in Quebec, aggression among two to four year olds in Quebec increased by 24% compared to 1 per cent in the rest of Canada.

There are always methodological problems associated with research into the effects of day care. Carrying out experimental research that could demonstrate a causal relationship between day care and aggression would create ethical problems where it would be considered unethical and impractical to randomly allocate children either to a day care group or to remain with their mothers. It is also possible that children who are raised in aggressive environments are more likely to be sent to day care than children who are raised in less aggressive environments. It may well then be the backgrounds of the children rather than any day care experiences that influence the development of aggressive behaviour.

(307 words)

AO2

The second half of the paragraph makes a good critical point, elaborated effectively.

The final paragraph presents an excellent analysis of the general problems with day care research. There is overarching criticism (there are methodological problems) and then an explanation of two such problems: the ethical issues of manipulating variables so causal research is not possible, and the possibility of an intervening variable (children who go to day care are more aggressive).

Examiner's comments

Three studies are presented each in some detail, therefore **6 out of 6 marks** for **AO1**.

The evaluation (**AO2**) also receives the **full 6 marks**. The range may be slightly narrow but each point is given in depth, therefore **6 out of 6 marks** for **AO2**.

Total = **12 out of 12 marks**, a clear **A grade** answer (and not that long).

Influence of research into attachment and day care

Question 1   Describe the influence of research into attachment on child care practices.   (6 marks)

Austin's answer

Research into attachment has influenced child care practices in many ways. One influence has been on day care practices. For example at the Soho Family centre they base their child care on attachment theory and make sure children all have secondary attachment figures.

Another influence has been on caring for children in hospital. Attachment research has shown that children need substitute emotional care from other adults when they are separated from their parents, even for short periods of time. This means they do not experience the negative effects of disruption of attachment.

A third influence has been on adoptions, which often used to take place when babies were quite old. Attachment research showed that attachments may not form after six months, so adoptions are done earlier than this if at all possible.

Vanessa's answer

The Robertsons conducted research on the effects of disruption of attachment. In this study they filmed young children who were separated from their parents and also recorded their observations. They found that substitute emotional care helped the children recover.

Another study was done by Hodges and Tizard. They followed a group of children who had been placed up for adoption and found that the children did later form good attachments with their adopted families but still had difficulty with friendships with their peers. This shows that early failure to form attachment can have long-term, permanent effects, or at least it looks that way.

Quinton et al. found that ex-institutional women lacked warmth when interacting with their children. It is likely that these women had failed to form attachments and this privation had affected their ability to form relationships later in life.

Examiner's comments

The key to producing a good answer to this question is being able to demonstrate the *influence* that attachment research has had on child care practices. Austin does this well, linking research theories to applications such as care of children while in hospital and adoptions. (Remember that the term 'research' refers to theories or studies – so both theories and studies are creditworthy.)

Vanessa has selected appropriate research studies and described them in reasonable detail. Unfortunately, however, she has failed to explain what kind of influence these studies might have on child care practices. Such influences are more or less implicit in what she has written but needed to be made explicit to gain better marks.

So **6 out of 6 marks** for Austin but only **3 out of 6 marks** for Vanessa.

Question 2   Describe the influence of research into day care on child care practices.   (6 marks)

There have been a number of studies that have looked at the effects of day care. In the US, a large study found that children who were in day care for more than 30 hours a week tended to become more aggressive. However, this is only correlational, and so it doesn't tell us that one thing caused the other, only that the two things (day care and aggression) are related.

Other research, e.g. Clarke-Stewart et al. found that day care can have positive effects as well. They found that children who went to day care were better developed socially than children who did not. However, this is also correlational, so we can't say that it was the day care that had a causal effect on the children's social development.

Research studies such as the NICHD study in the US have shown that children prosper with high-quality day care. Melhuish (2005) has identified some of the characteristics of high-quality day care and these have been used by Ofsted to check on standards in UK day care providers. High-quality day care includes low levels of staff turnover and low adult to child ratios in day care.

Field (1991) found that the more time children spent in day care, the more friends they had and the more extracurricular activities they engaged in. This finding that high-quality day care can have positive effects for the child, has led to a government sponsored initiative, SureStart being introduced specifically to enhance the life chances of children growing up in families identified as being 'at risk'.

This time both candidates are in difficulty with the concept of 'influence'. They have both provided lots of research evidence but kept missing the clinching statement – what does the research tell us about how children should be looked after?

Austin has provided some criticisms of the research, which are not creditworthy. He has also provided two findings but has not explained how these might further influence child care practice. Such influences may be implicit but that is insufficient as an answer to this question, so **1 out of 6 marks**. He could have simply added 'This could influence child care by...'.

Vanessa's answer is a little bit better – more findings and some mention of influences e.g. checking the quality of day care by Ofsted and setting up the SureStart initiative, so **4 out of 6 marks** for Vanessa.

Question 3 (a)   Outline **one** research study that has investigated attachment.   (4 marks)
(b)   Explain how the findings of this study could be used to improve child care practices.   (3 marks)

(a) Ainsworth studied attachment using the Strange Situation. Mothers and their babies were observed in a special room through a one-way mirror. Infants who were securely attached behaved differently compared to infants who were insecurely attached. For example, they were more willing to explore and were more distressed when their mother left the room. Securely attached children were more easily comforted when their mother returned.

(b) These findings could be used to identify whether children are securely attached or insecurely attached and so how they will react in certain situations. For example, if children are insecurely attached they will have more difficulties if they are left in day care. It would also predict how the child will be when they are picked up, so special attention can be made of the child by the mother to make up for this.

(a) Schaffer and Emerson (1964) observed 60 babies in their own homes for a period of one year. The mothers were interviewed during each visit to the home and asked about when the infants showed separation distress and with whom. This was an indication of their primary attachment figure. They found that these babies were not always attached to the person that fed them (usually the mother), but were attached to the person who was most responsive to their needs and who interacted with them the most. This was often the father or a grandparent.

(b) This study might be used to show how sensitive responding to a child's needs rather than mere physical care in child care settings is important to emotional care, and therefore child care staff should provide such responsiveness. It also raises the possibility that if the mother has to work, high-quality emotional care can be provided by other family members such as the father.

(a) Our candidates are back on safer ground here, because they just have to describe a study. Both have described appropriate studies in more than enough detail for the **full 4 marks**. The question does not specify whether only procedures or only findings are required so both are creditworthy – in fact any details of the studies would be creditworthy.

(b) Vanessa has done a slightly better job of saying how the findings could be used to improve child care practices, and deserves **3 out of 3 marks**. Austin hasn't clearly made suggestions about what might be done, he has really just said what we might expect, so only **1 out of 3 marks**.

Question 4 (a) Outline how **one** research study has investigated the effects of day care on children's social development. *(4 marks)*

(b) Explain how the findings of this study could be used to improve child care practices. *(3 marks)*

(a) The EPPE project studied 3,000 children in a variety of different day care settings. The children were assessed at about age three to four and again when they started school to assess the contribution that receiving day care had made to their development. The researchers found that day care can have positive effects on children's social development, particularly their sociability and cooperation. They also found that disadvantaged children did particularly well if they received high-quality day care.

(b) This study is important because it is 'evidence-based', using actual evidence to inform child care practices. This has led to a government sponsored project called SureStart which is designed to provide high-quality day care for children who are in disadvantaged areas. This is based on the finding that disadvantaged children make the most of high-quality day care.

(a) The NICHD study is a longitudinal study of over 1,300 children across the US. The intention is to study many different aspects of child development, including social development. Children and their parents are assessed at various intervals up to when the children are 15, using observations, interviews and psychological testing. In this way, different aspects of development (e.g. increased aggression and relationships with peers) can then be related to children's experiences at home, in child care, and later on, in school. Of the original 1,300+ children, 1,100 were followed through to adolescence.

(b) The NICHD study found that day care providers could only provide sensitive care for children in their charge if the child–adult ratio was three to one or less. This shows the importance of not overcrowding any day care provision without having sufficient dedicated staff to maintain this ratio. The study found that 20% of staff failed to provide sensitive care and were emotionally detached from infants in their care. This could be something that Ofsted check and may require more stringent licensing and training for child care providers.

(a) Again, both candidates have provided detailed descriptions of appropriate studies. The question specified that the studies should relate to children's social development (rather than being specifically on aggression or peer relations) so both studies are appropriate. The **full 4 marks** for both our candidates.

(b) Austin has answered the question by showing how the findings have been used as opposed to how they might be used, but that is quibbling with words. However, his answer lacks detail, so he gains **2 out of 3 marks**. Vanessa's answer is more detailed and also a more explicit answer to the question, so the **full 3 marks**.

Question 5 Sunnyday nursery school is very well regarded by parents. The children who are looked after at Sunnyday all appear happy and rarely show signs of distress. They arrive at the nursery beaming with smiles and leave their parents without a backward glance. At the end of the day they enthusiastically greet their parents.

Use your knowledge of psychology to explain how this day care facility has ensured that the children are so contented. *(6 marks)*

Sunnyday is obviously a very happy place to be. The children are probably in purpose-built buildings, with lots of new toys to play with, rather than being in a draughty village hall playing with broken and boring toys. Children are also unhappy if they are bullied, therefore the staff must stop any bullying from taking place. Maybe the staff take them out to interesting places and so the children look forward to going there. Psychology has told us a great deal about what makes children happy (e.g. doing interesting things and having attractive toys) and what makes them unhappy (e.g. being bullied). It also suggests that the children who go to Sunnyday are all securely attached, which is why they are happy and enthusiastic towards their parents. This could be because Sunnyday is an expensive place to send your children and only middle class parents can afford it.

Based on research by Melhuish, who identified the characteristics of high-quality day care, Sunnyday will have provided a low adult–child ratio. This was also a finding of the NICHD study, which found that sensitive care could only be provided when the ratio was three to one or less. Children are most happy in situations where there are low levels of staff turnover. Schaffer found that when staff change frequently, children suffer the anxiety associated with disruption of the attachment bonds they have formed with staff. Sunnyday is therefore likely to have low staff turnover because the children are so contented and show no signs of anxiety. Sylva et al. found that the quality of provision was associated with the qualifications of the staff. Therefore Sunnyday would have well-qualified staff capable of delivering developmentally appropriate activities and sensitive care to infants in their charge.

Austin has certainly tried to construct a good answer to this question, but the main issue is 'where is the psychology?' There is a rather general statement that 'Psychology has told us a great deal about what makes children happy…'; even with the examples this is too general to be worth much credit. Austin also refers to secure attachment, correctly judging this from the question stem. However his explanation of why they are securely attached is not based on psychology either, so only **1 out of 6 marks**.

Vanessa's answer is spot on; linking research studies directly to features that are likely to have made Sunnyday so successful, so the **full 6 marks**.

Question 6 One of the aims of psychological research is to produce findings that can be applied to improve people's lives.

(a) Outline **two** ways that research into attachment could be used to improve child care practices. *(6 marks)*

(b) Outline **two** ways that research into day care could be used to improve child care practices. *(6 marks)*

(a) Robertson's research on maternal separation has changed hospital practices involving young children. Robertson's research focused on the importance of providing high-quality emotional care during separation, and hospitals now make it easier for a close relative to stay with the child at all times. Bowlby's work on the formation of attachments during a sensitive period of development, and Hodges and Tizard's research on adopted children have both emphasised the importance of adoption, wherever possible, taking place before rather than after the first six months of a child's life.

(b) Research such as the NICHD study has shown that children prosper with high-quality day care. Melhuish (2005) has identified some of the characteristics of high-quality day care and these have been used by Ofsted to check on standards in UK day care providers. Field (1991) found that the more time children spent in day care, the better their social development. This has led to the SureStart programme being introduced to enhance the life chances of children growing up in families identified as being 'at risk'.

(a) Research into attachment can be used to improve child care if children are looked after more sensitively so their emotional well-being is looked after as well as their physical well-being. Research has also shown that children suffer when they are separated from their mother, therefore the mother should try not to separate herself from her child until they reach school age.

(b) There have been lots of ways that research into day care has been used to improve child care practices. The NICHD study found that children who go to day care for more than 30 hours a week become aggressive, therefore they should be stopped from going for more than 30 hours. Research has also shown that some day care workers are not very caring; they could be trained to be more caring.

(a) An excellent answer from Austin linking three examples of attachment research to improving child care practices, for the **full 6 marks**. Vanessa has looked at two ways research can be applied, as required in the question. In both cases there isn't a clear link to research but it is implicit particularly in the second 'way', so **3 out of 6 marks**.

(b) Austin again provides an excellent, detailed answer with research linked to improving child care practice, so the **full 6 marks**. This time Vanessa has managed to describe a piece of research (the NICHD study) but her suggestion for improvement is rather weak. Her final suggestion has very little mention of the research and again a rather weak improvement – she could have given more detailed information about what such training would involve related to research findings. So a mark of **3 out of 6**.

RESEARCH METHODS QUESTION

A study was conducted to see how children aged between two and four years reacted to their mother's voice, compared with the voice of a stranger. The children listened to the voices through a headset. Some children heard their mother's voice, first reading a short passage, and then the stranger's voice, reading the same passage. Other children heard the voices in reverse order.

The children's responses were assessed through observation and a 'happiness' score was calculated. The results are shown in the table on the right.

Results showing happiness scores for each child.

Child	Happiness score listening to mother's voice	Happiness score listening to stranger's voice
1	6	4
2	5	4
3	8	3
4	8	6
5	7	3
6	9	7
7	5	5
8	5	6
9	6	4
10	4	4

(a) (i) Explain why this is a repeated measures design. *(2 marks)*
(ii) Give **one** strength of using a repeated measures design rather than independent groups to study children's behaviour. *(3 marks)*

Austin's answer

(i) This is repeated measures because children take part in both parts of the study.

(ii) A strength of the repeated measures design is that it used fewer participants so is economical.

Vanessa's answer

(i) This is a repeated measure design because there are two conditions (mother's voice and stranger's voice) and the same participants (the children) experience both conditions.

(ii) A strength of this design is that it controls for participant variables that might affect the outcome of the study, such as whether the children are securely or insecurely attached to their mother, or whether they are used to listening to voices on tape.

Examiner's comments

(i) Vanessa has provided a clear and detailed answer, whereas Austin's answer is less detailed – it is not entirely clear what he means, so **1 out of 2 marks**. Participants can take part in both parts of a study even if it isn't repeated measures. The key is that they have experienced both conditions of the IV. However, there is enough understanding in Vanessa's answer for the **full 2 marks**.

(ii) Austin's answer is correct and he has added a further explanation (it 'is economical') but there is no context, so a generous **2 out of 3 marks**. Vanessa's answer has everything for the **full 3 marks**.

(b) Explain why it was a good idea to play the voices in a different order to some of the children. *(3 marks)*

So the order is counterbalanced to stop order effects.

This would be to minimise order effects. The children might find hearing a voice as novel the first time but less so the second time and so react differently because of that (rather than whose voice it was). Playing the voices in a different order would overcome this problem by randomising this effect.

Again, a much too brief answer from Austin. His answer is correct which suggests he knows and understands the material but he hasn't made the effort to explain it fully, as Vanessa has done. On the other hand, Austin has used the technical terms 'counterbalancing' and 'order effects' effectively so **2 out of 3 marks** for Austin and the **full 3 marks** for Vanessa.

(c) Explain which measure of central tendency would be the best to use with the data in the table. *(3 marks)*

It would be best to use the mode as a measure of central tendency because this would show which is the most frequently occurring score, which for the mother's voice is 5 and for the stranger's voice 4.

The median would be the best measure to use, because this is the middle score when the scores are ordinal. This data is ordinal rather than interval therefore would require the median. The median isn't affected by extreme scores, for example if one child was frightened by the voices and produced very low happiness scores.

The mode would not be appropriate here because there are several modes for each data set so we wouldn't see a clear picture of the results, so **0 marks** for Austin.

Vanessa is correct in saying this is not interval data and therefore the median is appropriate. However, there are arguments that say such data can be treated as interval so the mean would also be acceptable. It doesn't make her answer wrong (so she receives **3 out of 3 marks**) but a candidate who gave the mean as an answer could also score full marks.

(d) Explain how you would calculate the range for both sets of happiness scores. *(3 marks)*

The range is the difference between the highest score and the lowest score in a set of data.

The range would be calculated by finding the difference between the highest happiness score for one condition and the lowest score for that condition. For example, for the mother's voice condition, the highest score is 9 and the lowest score 4, so the range is 5.

Austin has not answered the question 'how'. Instead he has answered the question 'what', however the 'how' is implicit and he has identified which scores would be used to calculate it, so **2 out of 3 marks**. Vanessa's answer is spot on, including the fact that she has explained how it would be done for each set of scores, so **full marks**.

(e) Explain why it would be desirable to conduct this study in a laboratory. *(2 marks)*

By conducting the study in a laboratory it means the researchers can demonstrate a causal relationship between the IV and DV.

It is desirable because the laboratory gives the researchers the opportunity to control any extraneous factors (such as the presence of distractions or the loudness of the voice) that might influence the child's behaviour.

Austin again has got it wrong – this time he is showing a lack of understanding. Causal relationships are shown in experiments whereas any kind of method may be conducted in a lab, not just experiments, so **0 marks**. Control is the key issue which has been well explained by Vanessa for the **full 2 marks**.

(f) (i) Explain what is meant by validity. *(2 marks)*
(ii) Explain **one** possible factor that might lower the validity of this study. *(2 marks)*

(i) This is whether a test is really measuring what it is supposed to be measuring.

(ii) This could be the risk of demand characteristics, the children might react in the way they think the experimenter wants them to react.

(i) Validity refers to how legitimate a measurement is, for example, whether measuring 'happiness' is a valid way of assessing reaction to the two voices.

(ii) A problem with validity might be the fact that the laboratory is a contrived set-up and the child might react to the presence of strangers (the researchers) rather than the voices.

(i) Vanessa's answer is better because it applies to all kinds of validity, however Austin's answer is sufficient for the **full 2 marks**.

(ii) Both candidates have described a possible problem with validity in sufficient detail for the **full 2 marks**.

Extended writing question

Outline and evaluate the influence of research into attachment on child care practices.

(12 marks)

AO1

The first paragraph offers a reasonably detailed description of one influence of attachment research.

A second relevant influence is described in this paragraph, again in reasonable detail.

A third influence is covered in the penultimate paragraph.

AO2

Research into attachment has influenced child care practices in many ways. One influence has been on day care practices. For example at the Soho Family centre they base their child care on attachment theory and make sure children all have secondary attachment figures.

This is supported by Bowlby's theory. He claimed that primary attachment figures are important in a child's emotional development. However, according to Bowlby, if the child's primary attachment figure is absent, secondary attachment figures create an emotional safety net.

Another influence has been on caring for children in hospital. Attachment research has shown that children need substitute emotional care from other adults when they are separated from their parents, even for short periods of time. This means they do not experience the negative effects of disruption of attachment.

This is supported by research such as the Robertsons' study. They showed that the children who were given a good level of substitute emotional care while their mothers were absent, appeared to experience no ill effects from separation.

A third influence has been on adoptions, which often used to take place when babies were quite old. Attachment research showed that attachments may not form after 6 months so attachments are done earlier than this if at all possible.

This is supported by the research by Rutter et al. studying Romanian orphans adopted by UK families. Those orphans adopted before the age of 6 months appear to have recovered well, whereas the same is not true of later adoptions. This supports the importance of early adoptions.

(256 words)

The second paragraph presents support for the description in paragraph one. Separating AO1 and AO2 in this way makes it clear to the examiner what is AO1 and what is AO2. The lead in sentence 'This is supported…' also flags up AO2.

The fourth paragraph contains more AO2, research support. However, the point is not fully explained or supported by specific evidence.

One final evaluative point, well elaborated and following the three point rule (i.e. identify, justify and explain – see page 10)

Examiner's comments

Much of the description (**AO1**) in this essay is reasonably detailed. Material has been selected appropriately and presented clearly. So the answer would receive **6 out of 6 marks.**

In this essay evaluation (**AO2**) marks are awarded for research support. The three pieces of research support in this essay are reasonably elaborated except for the second one. Coverage of just three points lies somewhere between 'broad' and 'narrow', so overall this is worth **5 out of 6 marks.**

Total = **11 out of 12 marks**, a **Grade A** answer.

Extended writing question

Outline and evaluate the influence of research into day care on child care practices.

(12 marks)

AO1

In this paragraph Field's research is used as a means of explaining the point rather than evaluating it. The content is detailed and relevant.

Further description is covered in the second and third paragraphs by looking at what research has told us about how to improve quality of care care. Thus it is answering the question as required – considering how day care research can influence chid care practice.

AO2

Research into day care suggests that quality is the most important factor in ensuring that children experience benefits rather than drawbacks from attending day care. For example, Field (1991) found that the greatest benefits of day care on peer relations were for those children in high-quality care. Therefore if we wish to maximise these positive effects we need to maximise the quality of care. Offering sensitive care is an important aspect of this.

Research has further found that the ratio of staff-to-children is one way to improve quality. For example the NICHD study (1999) found that day care staff could only provide sensitive high-quality care if the ratios were as low as 1:3.

Research has also found that the experience of the staff is a key factor in ensuring high quality. For example Sylva et al. (2003) found that the quality of care provided was positively correlated with the qualification levels of the day care staff.

Each of these points is further supported by research theories. The importance of high-quality care is explained by Bowlby's theory. He argued that healthy, secure attachments are formed with adults who respond with the greatest sensitivity. Such sensitivity is a characteristic of high-quality care and is likely to be enhanced by having good staff-to-child ratios.

The importance of high-quality care may explain why many children experience negative rather than positive effects. It seems that many day care centres are not providing adequate care. The NICHD study (1999) found that only 23% of infant care providers give 'highly' sensitive infant care. If this is also the case in the UK it would explain why so many children appear to experience negative rather than positive effects. This underlines the influence of research and the importance of high-quality care.

295 words

In this answer all of the evaluation has been placed in the second half of the answer. This is a good strategy because it helps you to see whether you have written equal amounts of AO1 and AO2.

The second evaluation point is a tricky point and the student has tried reasonably well to explain it.

Examiner's comments

In this essay three areas of research have been considered in reasonable detail (in paragraphs 1–3). Three points is reasonable for an extended writing question but possibly a little more detail is needed, so **5 out of 6 marks.**

The evaluation is not as thorough as the essay above. There's simply less of it, so clearly a 'narrow range' but in depth. A generous **4 out of 6 marks.**

Total = **9 out of 12 marks**, a **Grade A** standard.

Extra questions for you

Some further examples of questions requiring you to apply your knowledge to novel situations.

Question 1 Aleisha's older sister had her first child six months ago. Now that Aleisha is studying developmental psychology she sees this as an ideal opportunity to consider attachment behaviour first-hand. She decides to see whether her sister's baby is securely or insecurely attached.

    (a) Identify **two** behaviours that would convince Aleisha that her sister's baby is securely attached and **two** behaviours that might convince her that her sister's baby is insecurely attached. *(2 marks + 2 marks)*

    (b) Identify **one** ethical issue that Aleisha should consider when carrying out this study and outline how she might deal with this. *(3 marks)*

Question 2 A psychologist is going to conduct research into attachment in older children (aged between 8 and 12 years). In order to do this the psychologist needs a method to assess attachment in these children. He could do this either by observing the children's behaviour with their mother or by using a questionnaire.

Using your knowledge of psychology, describe how you might use either of these methods to assess attachment in these children. *(4 marks)*

Question 3 Maria and Misaka are studying A level psychology. At the moment, in their Psychology class, they have been discussing research on cultural variations in attachment and are interested in how this relates to their own experiences. Maria comes from a fairly traditional Spanish family whereas Misaka's family are Japanese.

Use your own knowledge of psychology to suggest how Maria and Misaka might have had different attachment experiences. *(4 marks)*

Question 4 Naseem is one of five children, the youngest of whom, Parveen, has had considerable health problems, necessitating frequent hospital stays of over a week at a time. The first time this happened, when she was 18 months old, Parveen's parents were unable to visit and Parveen showed a number of emotional and behavioural problems when she returned home. Naseem, who has studied psychology, tries to explain to his parents why this has happened.

    (a) Using your knowledge of psychological research, suggest why Naseem feels his sister was so badly affected by her hospitalisation. *(4 marks)*

    (b) Suggest **two** things that Naseem might suggest to his parents to make Parveen's next stay in hospital less distressing. *(2 marks + 2 marks)*

Question 5 Angelina spent the summer working as a volunteer in an orphanage in Eastern Europe. She was deeply distressed by the plight of the children in the orphanage, so decided to set up an adoption programme in the UK to allow these children to be adopted by British families.

Explain **two** factors that might be important in determining whether these children might recover from their early privation after being adopted. *(4 marks)*

Question 6 A young couple, Sue and Greg Morgan, decide to set up their own day nursery for young children aged between one and five years. They have read reports that day care can harm young children's development and want to ensure that the children in their care will be happy and emotionally well-adjusted.

With your knowledge of psychology, describe **two** things they might do to ensure that the children in their care will be happy and well-adjusted. *(4 marks)*

Question 7 Angelina goes on to become a government advisor on child care. She is asked to give a short presentation on the influence of research into attachment for child care provision.

    (a) Outline **two** research studies that she might include in her presentation. *(2 marks + 2 marks)*

    (b) Explain how each of these research studies might be transformed into practical changes in child care provision that could be implemented by the government. *(2 marks + 2 marks)*

Question 1 Research into failure to form attachment (privation) has often relied on case studies as a way to gain insights into the effects of privation.

(a) Explain what is involved in conducting a case study.	(4 marks)
(b) Explain why case studies are often used to study privation.	(2 marks)
(c) Outline **one** aspect of a case study that is likely to affect the validity of the data collected.	(3 marks)
(d) Identify and explain **one** ethical issue that is likely to arise in a case study of privation.	(3 marks)
(e) Outline an alternative method that could be used to study privation.	(3 marks)

Question 2 Research on day care has found that high-quality day care is clearly better for young children than low-quality care. One feature of high-quality day care may be the child–staff ratio. In order to investigate this, a researcher compared two day care centres. In one centre each adult worker had special responsibility for two children whereas in the second day care centre each adult worker had special responsibility for four children. In others words, Centre 1 had a low ratio (2:1) whereas Centre 2 had a high ratio (4:1).

(a) Describe the operationalised independent variable in this study.	(2 marks)
(b) Describe how they might assess the young children at the end of the study to compare the effects of low and high staff ratios.	(3 marks)
(c) This study could be described as a natural experiment. Explain how a natural experiment differs from a field experiment.	(4 marks)
(d) (i) Explain what is meant by 'demand characteristics'.	(2 marks)
(ii) Explain how demand characteristics might affect the validity of this study.	(3 marks)

RESEARCH METHODS QUESTION

Question 3 A psychologist decided to investigate whether children who were adopted were more emotionally well adjusted if they were adopted earlier rather than later. To do this he placed an advertisement in several newspapers asking adopted children to contact him. He gave each participant a psychological test that measured emotional adjustment (the higher the score, the better the individual's adjustment). He also recorded the age at which they were adopted in months. He found a negative correlation between emotional adjustment score and age.

(a) Outline the aims of this study.	(2 marks)
(b) Draw a sketch of what a negative correlation would look like on a scattergram.	(2 marks)
(c) Explain what he could conclude from this scattergram in terms of his original aims.	(3 marks)
(d) (i) Identify the method used to select participants.	(1 mark)
(ii) Outline **one** limitation of using this method of selection.	(2 marks)
(iii) Suggest an alternative method and explain how you would use this to select participants for this study.	(4 marks)

SPECIFICATION BREAKDOWN

Specification content

Comment

Stress as a bodily response

- The body's response to stress, including the pituitary-adrenal system and the sympathomedullary pathway in outline.

- Stress-related illness and the immune system.

This section of the specification starts with a rather frightening set of technical terms – 'pituitary-adrenal' (HPA) and 'sympathomedullary'. There's no need to be alarmed; once you get used to using these long terms, you'll realise they are just describing what's going on in your body when you're aroused!

Research has shown that stress is associated with various illnesses. Some stress-related illnesses are caused by the effects of stress on the immune system, for example getting a cold. Stress causes the immune system to underfunction, making people (and animals) more susceptible to infectious illnesses.

There are other stress-related illnesses, such as heart disease or depression, which cannot be explained in terms of immune system functioning.

Stress in everyday life

- Life changes.

- Daily hassles.

- Workplace stress, including the effects of workload and control.

- Personality factors, including Type A and Type B behaviour and hardiness.

- Psychological and biological methods of stress management, including stress inoculation therapy and drugs.

There are many sources of stress in our lives. One source is life changes – events such as marriage, moving house and even Christmas – which have a psychological 'cost'. It isn't just the big events that are stressful – everyday hassles also wear you down and act as stressors.

A further common source of stress comes from the workplace – job demands and responsibilities are linked to illness.

Some people are more affected than others by stress. One such personality type is called 'Type A' – people who are competitive and assertive, and also in a rush to do things. The opposite of this is the Type B personality, characterised by a relaxed and more easygoing approach to life. The concept of hardiness has also been used to explain why some people cope better with stress.

Methods of stress management aim to provide more comprehensive techniques for dealing with stress. These may be psychological and deal with the subjective experience of stress, or biological and deal with what is happening in your body when you experience stress. We will look at different examples of each of these, as well as the strengths and limitations of each method.

Chapter 3

BIOLOGICAL PSYCHOLOGY seeks to explain behaviour in terms of the systems that operate in our bodies – such as the action of blood, hormones, nerves and the brain, and also in terms of genes. The way we think and feel has important influences on these biological systems, illustrated by the study of stress.

CHAPTER CONTENTS

Biological psychology: stress

The body's response to stress

Question 1 The following statements all relate to the way that the body responds to stressors.

A Long-term, chronic response.

B Short-term, acute response.

C Involves the adrenal medulla.

D Involves the adrenal cortex.

In the table below write write which statement applies to which type of bodily response to stress. *(4 marks)*

Pituitary-adrenal system	A, D
Sympathomedullary pathway	B, C

Question 2 Explain what is meant by stress. *(2 marks)*

Asif's answer

Stress is experienced when there is a difference between the perceived demands of a situation and an individual's perceived ability to cope with that situation.

Wendy's answer

Stress is an unpleasant feeling when a person feels unable to deal with the demands of a situation.

Examiner's comments

Wendy's answer lacks the psychological edge of Asif's, so just **1 out of 2 marks** for her and the **full 2 marks** for Asif.

Question 3 Outline the main features of the pituitary-adrenal system. *(3 marks)*

It involves the hypothalamus, which leads to the production of CRF. This causes the pituitary gland to release ACTH into the bloodstream, which travels to the adrenal cortex which releases cortisol into the bloodstream.

The main features are the pituitary gland, known as the master gland, and the adrenal gland, which releases stress hormones, which allow the body to deal with the source of stress.

Asif's answer contains plenty of detail, more than enough for the **full 3 marks**. Wendy has mentioned two key components and might have scored full marks if they had been linked together, so just **2 out of 3 marks**.

Question 4 Outline the main features of the sympathomedullary pathway. *(3 marks)*

Short-lived stressors arouse the sympathetic branch of the autonomic nervous system, which arouses the person for fight or flight. At the same time, the adrenal medulla releases adrenaline into the bloodstream, boosting the supply of oxygen and glucose to the brain.

If we come across something scary, like a snarling bear, the ANS prepares us to either fight the bear or to run away from it. This is also known as the fight or flight response. The medulla supports this response and makes it easier to fight or run away.

Wendy's answer is largely irrelevant – she is not describing the sympathomedullary pathway but instead discussing what might trigger it. Just about worth **1 out of 3 marks**; compared with a detailed account from Asif worth the **full 3 marks**. Note that it is fine to use common abbreviations, such as CRF and ACTH.

Question 5 Ailsa is at school studying for her GCSEs. She has spent the last four weeks revising and has been feeling quite stressed. Describe the likely response of her body to this stressful period in her life. *(3 marks)*

Because her stress is ongoing, the likely response involves the pituitary-adrenal system. The hypothalamus stimulates the production of CRF, which in turn causes the pituitary gland to release ACTH into the bloodstream. ACTH travels to the adrenal cortex, which releases the stress hormone cortisol.

She is going to feel stressed, and maybe get stress-related problems such as headaches. It is also possible that her immune system functions less well, and she could end up having a nervous breakdown as her body struggles to cope with the stress.

Asif has correctly recognised that this is ongoing, chronic stress and described the pituitary-adrenal system for **3 out of 3 marks**. Wendy has included a lot of irrelevant information but she is correct in mentioning possible stress-related illness and immune system problems, but her answer lacks detail and focus, so just **1 out of 3 marks**.

Question 6 I dislike watching scary films. My heart pounds, my hands feel clammy and I am just generally uncomfortable.

(a) Explain how bodily processes are producing these symptoms. *(2 marks)*

(b) Once the film is finished I feel much better. Explain what is likely to be going on in my body after the film is over. *(2 marks)*

(a) Because watching a scary film is an acute stressor, that means that the sympathetic branch of the autonomic nervous system is activated and causing the body to sweat and heartbeat to increase.

(b) Once the acute stressor has passed, the parasympathetic branch of the autonomic nervous system takes over, restoring the resting equilibrium resulting in an overall feeling of calm.

(a) Scary films make you feel aroused, and it is the arousal (e.g. increasing heartbeat and sweating) that leads to these feelings. Some people do not find these films scary, therefore would not react in the same way.

(b) When the film has finished, the arousal levels drop, as does heartbeat and sweating. You now feel less stressed and calmer.

Asif's answers are spot on and detailed for the **full 2 marks** for (a) and (b). Wendy's answers are not wrong but she hasn't explained the bodily processes – she hasn't explained what is causing the arousal, sweatiness or feelings of being calm, so **0 marks** for both parts.

Question 7 Outline what research has shown about the body's response to stress. *(6 marks)*

Taylor et al. (2000) suggest that the fight or flight response is mainly a male response to stress and that females are more likely to display a 'tend and befriend' response, where females respond to stressful situations by protecting their young, and seeking social contact and support from other females when threatened. Taylor et al. found that higher levels of the hormone oxytocin in females are responsible for making women more sociable and less anxious under conditions of stress. Oxytocin is associated with reduced cortisol responses to stress and faster recovery following acute stress. Male hormones appear to reduce the effect of oxytocin.

Research has shown that the body responds to stress in two main ways. It responds to acute stress by activating the sympathetic nervous system and it responds to chronic stress by the pituitary-adrenal system. The activation of the sympathetic nervous system is what is known as the fight or flight response. This involves the pituitary system, which releases ACTH and the adrenal gland, which releases cortisol. Cortisol is a stress hormone, which is part of the body's response to stress.

Our candidates have given two quite different responses. Asif describes research related to gender differences and focuses, appropriately, on what the research has shown for the **full 6 marks**.

Wendy has not identified a particular researcher but the contents of her answer are derived from research and therefore creditworthy. She has covered both acute and chronic stress but only provided details for the latter, so **5 out of 6 marks** because of the breadth of points covered.

A researcher investigated the differing levels of certain hormones at times of stress. To do this he measured the levels of certain hormones in the blood – the day before an exam and just before the start of the exam. The results for one person are shown in the table.

	Measurement on the day before an exam	Measurement just before the start of an exam
Adrenaline	2	9
Cortisol	4	1

(a) What difference would the researcher expect to find between stress the day before the exam and stress immediately before the exam? *(3 marks)*

Asif's answer

Because the exam is an acute stressor, the researcher would expect to find that levels of adrenaline would rise in response to the onset of the exam and reduce after the exam.

Wendy's answer

The researcher would expect to find that stress levels are higher just before an exam therefore the stress response would be more as well.

Examiner's comments

Wendy's answer lacks the detail given by Asif but neither candidate has mentioned cortisol levels. Just **1 out of 3 marks** for Wendy and **2 out of 3 marks** for Asif.

(b) What might the researcher conclude from the results in the table? *(4 marks)*

They might conclude that these results show that revision is a chronic stressor, because cortisol levels are higher in the lead up to the exam and cortisol is related to the chronic stress response. The rise in adrenaline levels show that the exam is acting as an acute stressor. Adrenaline is part of the sympathomedullary response to stress.

They would conclude that adrenaline levels rise when someone takes an exam. They would also conclude that cortisol levels drop just before an exam, compared to the day before an exam.

Wendy has made the common mistake of simply describing the results rather than offering an interpretation of them, as Asif has done. Conclusions are an interpretation – you should be trying to describe what the results show us. **Full marks** for Asif and **1 out of 4 marks** for Wendy for her rudimentary answer.

(c) Explain **one or more** ethical issue that might arise in this study. *(4 marks)*

An ethical issue is protection from harm. It is possible that the stress of being tested, and possibly knowing that such an extreme reaction is taking place inside the body, might create added stress of the individual(s) being tested, which, in turn, might impact on their performance in the exam, an outcome which is potentially harmful for the individual.

An ethical issue is informed consent. Participants would have to be told what the study was about and how they might be affected by it, before agreeing to take part. There might be risks associated with taking part, so they should be told about these.

Both candidates have just focused on one issue and provided sufficient detail for the **full 4 marks**. Some candidates might just say 'Informed consent because they should be told what the study is about'. An answer like this would only receive 2 marks – you must always be prepared to supply further details if there are more marks available.

(d) Aside from ethical issues, identify **one** limitation to this study and explain how you would correct it. *(4 marks)*

A limitation is that there is an assumption that any change in adrenaline and cortisol levels is due to the examination. This is not necessarily the case, as there may be other factors in the person's life that are causing the stress and influencing these hormone levels. This can be corrected by having all participants complete a questionnaire the day before and just before the exam indicating other stressors in their life, whether they have slept well, etc.

A limitation is that the study only uses students. Students are not typical of the overall population, and this should be overcome by using a wider range of participants from lots of different ages and occupations.

Again, both candidates have identified an appropriate issue. Asif's answer is detailed but he hasn't offered an appropriate way to deal with the issue because even if we know about other stressors we cannot claim a causal relationship. To do this we would need to deliberately vary stress, so **3 out of 4 marks** for Asif. Wendy's answer lacks detail so also **2 out of 4 marks**.

Extended writing question

'The big question about the body's response to stress is whether it is the same in all people.' Describe and evaluate the body's response to stress. *(12 marks)*

AO1

In the first paragraph the body's response to chronic stress is outlined in reasonable detail.

In the third paragraph the acute response to stress is outlined in slightly less detail – but it is a less complex system.

The pituitary-adrenal system operates under conditions of chronic stress. It involves the hypothalamus, which leads to the production of CRF. CRF causes the pituitary gland to release ACTH into the bloodstream, which travels to the adrenal cortex which then releases cortisol into the bloodstream. Cortisol is secreted in higher levels during the body's fight or flight response to stress, and is responsible for a number of stress-related changes in the body.

Research has found some gender differences in cortisol responses to stress. For example, Kunz-Ebrecht et al. (2004) found that women are particularly sensitive to the anticipation of chronic stress, and this influences their cortisol output.

The sympathomedullary system operates in response to acute stress. Short-lived stressors arouse the sympathetic branch of the autonomic nervous system, which arouses the person for fight or flight. At the same time, the adrenal medulla releases adrenaline into the bloodstream, boosting the supply of oxygen and glucose to the brain.

Recent research by Taylor et al. (2000) has challenged the view that the fight or flight response is a universal response to stress, and claims that females are more likely to display a 'tend and befriend' response, where they respond to stressful situations by protecting and nurturing their young, and seeking social contact and support from other females when threatened. Taylor et al. found that higher levels of the hormone oxytocin in females are responsible for making women more sociable and less anxious under conditions of stress. Oxytocin is associated with reduced cortisol responses to stress and faster recovery following acute stress. Male hormones appear to reduce the effect of oxytocin.

(267 words)

AO2

In this essay gender differences have been used as a way to consider whether all people respond the same.

The first piece of research evidence is effective but limited in depth.

The second piece of research evidence is again effective – it is clearly used to show how men and women are different. There is also considerable elaboration of this point.

Examiner's comments

The outline (**AO1**) contains appropriate material. It is reasonably detailed but limited in terms of breadth, so would receive **5 out of 6 marks**.

The evaluation (**AO2**) is effective but a narrow range of points are covered which are (on average) presented in reasonable depth, so **5 out of 6 marks** – not enough depth for the top band (see mark scheme on page 9).

Total = **10 out of 12 marks**, a **Grade A** answer.

Stress-related illness and the immune system

EXAM ADVICE
Take care with this topic because some studies are not creditworthy if the question specifies the immune system (see, for example, question 2 below).

Question 1 Explain what is meant by 'the immune system'. *(2 marks)*

Ricky's answer

This is the part of the body that fights infection and keeps us healthy.

Rebecca's answer

This is a system within the body, which protects it from infectious agents such as viruses and other toxins.

Examiner's comments

Ricky's brief answer is worth **1 out of 2 marks** but Rebecca's is sufficient for **full marks**.

Question 2 (a) Explain how psychologists have investigated the relationship between the immune system and stress-related illness. *(6 marks)*

(b) Identify **one** threat to validity that might occur in research on the relationship between the immune system and stress-related illness, and explain how it could be dealt with. *(4 marks)*

(a) Russek (1962) asked different types of doctor whether they had experienced heart disease. He compared those who had relatively low-stress medical occupations (e.g. dermatologists) with those in relatively high-stress medical occupations (e.g. GPs), in order to see whether those in high-stress occupations were more likely to develop coronary heart disease than those in low-stress occupations.

(b) A threat to validity in this study is the fact that some of the different branches of medicine could attract different types of person or could pay more, therefore there are other factors that might determine illness rather than just the level of stress. This could be overcome by making sure (e.g. from a personality test) that doctors were matched in important personality characteristics (e.g. Type A personality).

(a) Keicolt-Glaser et al. (1984) carried out a natural experiment with medical students facing an important examination. Researchers assessed immune system functioning by measuring natural killer cell activity one month before the examinations (the low-stress phase of the study) and during the exam period itself (the high-stress phase of the study). They also asked the students to fill in questionnaires about other life stressors they were experiencing during both phases of the study. This was to assess whether any change in natural killer cell activity could be attributed to the stress of the examination, or other life stressors.

(b) A threat to validity concerns the problem of population validity. This study used students, who might be considered a restricted sample. For example, students tend to be mainly in the 18–22 age bracket. This can be dealt with by repeating the study with other occupational groups and age groups facing a stressful event that is equivalent to the examination in this study.

(a) Ricky has made the mistake of writing about a stress-related illness that is <u>not</u> associated with immune system dysfunction. Heart disease is linked to stress for other reasons (e.g. stress causes high blood pressure which increases the risk of heart disease). So Ricky receives **0 marks**. Rebecca has selected an appropriate study and focused just on the procedures, as required in the question, so **full marks**.

(b) As Ricky's answer to (a) is not creditworthy, his answer to (b) is also going to receive **no marks**. Rebecca has identified an appropriate threat to validity and a means of dealing with it, and both have been explained/elaborated, so the **full 4 marks**.

Question 3 Describe what research has shown about the relationship between the immune system and stress-related illness. *(6 marks)*

Kiecolt-Glaser carried out research using people looking after patients with Alzheimers disease. She found that if they had a small wound on their arm, it took longer to heal than people who weren't Alzheimers carers. Other research has shown that students suffer more from illness when they are in the middle of examinations than when they are revising for their examinations. This is because their immune system wasn't working as well when they were stressed, which is why they became ill.

Kiecolt-Glaser et al. found that students experienced more suppression of their immune systems during important examinations than in the period one month before, demonstrating that it was the acute stressor that caused a drop in immune system functioning. Marucha et al. also showed that wounds took longer to heal during exam periods than during the summer holidays. Research on the link between chronic stressors and illness (Kiecolt-Glaser et al., 1987) showed that women who had been separated from their partners had much poorer immune system functioning than married couples.

Rebecca has identified three appropriate studies and provided details for each of these, so the **full 6 marks**. Ricky has identified just two pieces of research. The first study is described in reasonable detail but the second study is only just identifiable which means it is only just creditworthy (it is the study described by Rebecca). He has, however, focused appropriately on findings/conclusions, so **3 out of 6 marks**.

Question 4 Ivana has had three bad colds this year. She has noticed that each time she gets ill she has also been feeling quite stressed at work. Use your knowledge of psychology to explain why Ivana has been having frequent colds. *(4 marks)*

Ivana has more colds because she is stressed and so her immune system isn't working that effectively, which is why she gets ill. There have been lots of studies that have shown that people get ill when their immune systems are not working properly and stress is thought to be one of the reasons why this happens. Ivana finds her job stressful (e.g. she may have had an argument with her boss) and so this affects her immune system, which makes her ill.

Ivana most probably has frequent colds during times of ongoing stress (e.g. workload or job demands) because her immune system is suppressed. Research has shown that during times of chronic stress, immune system functioning is lowered. For example, Kiecolt-Glaser et al. (1987) found that recently separated women had lower immune system functioning than matched married couples.

An excellent answer from Rebecca providing the two key elements – an explanation of why Ivana is ill and a link to specific psychological research. Ricky's answer is reasonable but lacks the specific research link, so **3 out of 4 marks** for Ricky and **full marks** for Rebecca.

Question 5 (a) Explain the link between stress, immune system activity and illness. *(3 marks)*

(b) On the basis of psychological research into the relationship between the immune system and stress-related illness, what recommendation would you make to someone who has recently been in hospital for major surgery? *(3 marks)*

(a) The link means that when people become stressed, their immune system is suppressed (e.g. Kiecolt-Glaser). When a person's immune system is suppressed, the body can't fight off infection and so the person becomes ill.

(b) I would tell them to avoid situations where they might become stressed, because then their immune system would work more effectively and they might recover more quickly.

(a) Immune system activity can cause illness in one of two ways. It can be under vigilant, letting infections enter the body, or over vigilant, so that it is the immune system itself (for example, as in Crohn's disease), rather than a virus or infection that causes an illness.

(b) Based on studies by Kiecolt-Glaser et al. (2005) and Marucha et al. (1998), we know that wounds heal more slowly when individuals are stressed. Therefore I would recommend that anyone who has undergone major surgery should take steps to manage their stress (e.g. through relaxation or meditation) and avoid situations that they find stressful until they are completely recovered.

(a) An extremely well informed answer from Rebecca but Ricky's answer also contains sufficient detail so they would both receive the **full 3 marks**.

(b) In this case Ricky's answer is just a little too brief (lacking detail), so just **2 out of 3 marks**. It could be improved by mentioning research as Rebecca has done – her answer is certainly worth **3 out of 3 marks**.

EXAM ADVICE

In this essay any research on stress-related illness will be creditworthy, whereas in the essay below only research related to the immune system and stress will be creditworthy.

Extended writing question

Outline and evaluate research into stress-related illness.

(12 marks)

AO1

The essay starts with a detailed description of one study.

Kiecolt-Glaser et al. (1984) carried out a natural experiment to see if a short-term acute stressor suppressed immune system functioning, decreasing resistance to infection. Medical students gave two blood samples to measure natural killer cell activity: one a month before an important exam and one during the exam period itself. The students also completed questionnaires at each phase of the study to see if they were experiencing any other significant life stressors. The results showed that natural killer cell activity, and therefore immune system functioning, was significantly reduced during the exam period compared with the period one month before. Immune system functioning was also significantly reduced in those individuals who were suffering other (i.e. chronic) life stressors.

A limitation of this study might be that it used medical students, who might be considered a non-representative section of society, so that generalisations cannot be made to other sections of society. However, Kiecolt-Glaser has carried out similar research on other groups, such as people caring for a partner suffering from Alzheimers disease and women going through a divorce.

Two further studies are outlined, both are appropriate.

Research has also shown a correlation between stress and other forms of illness. For example, Brown and Harris (1978) found that chronic stress may lead to depression. Women exposed to chronic stressors such as long-term unemployment and three or more children at home, were more likely to develop depression. Melchior et al. (2007) carried out a survey of people in high- and low-stress jobs, and found that a much higher proportion of those in high-stress jobs had developed the symptoms of depression compared to those in low-stress jobs.

However, it is difficult to determine whether the link between stress and depression is a causal one, as most studies have used retrospective methods, relying on people's recall of events in the past, something that is notoriously unreliable. Prospective studies where people in different types of jobs are followed over a period of time are rare. It is also difficult to determine a causal relationship between stress and illness generally because health tends to be fairly stable in people, and slow to change. As a result, it is difficult to demonstrate that exposure to a particular stressor has caused a change in health for that individual.

(370 words)

AO2

One limitation is identified and elaborated using other research, but it would have been better if a conclusion from this research had been stated (e.g. 'This shows that other groups of people also respond to stress like students do').

The final paragraph contains two separate evaluative points – they are separate because they deal with two different aspects of the causation issue. Each point has been well elaborated.

Examiner's comments

The description (**AO1**) includes three studies, each in reasonable detail or better, so **6 out of 6 marks**.
The evaluation (**AO2**) covers a relatively narrow range of points but in considerable depth so also **6 out of 6 marks**.

Total = **12 out of 12 marks** – which might appear to be a 'model' answer but there isn't such a thing. This is just an answer that is sufficient for full marks.

Extended writing question

Discuss research into the relationship between the immune system and stress-related illness.

(12 marks)

AO1

The Kiecolt-Glaser study is appropriate as it did deal with the effects of stress on the immune system, however the description of this study is basic.

There have been lots of studies that have shown a relationship between the immune system and stress-related illness. Kiecolt-Glaser studied medical students who were taking an examination. She gave each of them a blood test a month before the exam, and then during the exam itself to test their immune system. What she found was that when she took the first blood sample, their immune system was working fine, but when she took the second blood sample she found that their immune systems were not working properly.

This is a good study because it was an experiment. That means the researcher can make a causal connection between the stress of the examination and their immune system functioning. It also had good ecological validity because it was carried out with real students. A limitation of this study is that there may be other things going on in the students' lives (e.g. illness or money problems) that might be causing their immune system to not work, so the researcher should have checked for that.

VERY IMPORTANT POINT

The second study is not creditworthy because the cause of heart attacks is not related to the immune system – the statements made regarding immune system involvement are wrong.

Another study that looked at the relationship between the immune system and stress-related illness was by a psychologist who studied doctors who were either in stressful jobs or not. The stressful jobs were like a GP and the non-stressful jobs were like a pathologist. The psychologist who did the research found that the doctors who were in the high stress jobs like a GP had immune systems that didn't work properly and so they were more likely to have had heart attacks.

A problem with this study is they were doctors, and so this might not be generalised to the rest of the population. It also isn't an experiment so the psychologist couldn't tell whether it was the stress that had caused their immune systems to pack up. Also it could be considered unethical to study doctors without telling them why they were doing the study (i.e. it might cause them more stress so they become more ill).

(330 words)

AO2

The study was an experiment – but it was a natural experiment and therefore causal conclusions are not acceptable. Therefore no credit can be given.

The second point about ecological validity is superficial although there are a few extra words of elaboration.

The final point is more effectively made.

The criticisms are not creditworthy because the study is not creditworthy.

Examiner's comments

The description (**AO1**) is just 'basic'. There is only one creditworthy piece of research which has been described in some detail but that is not sufficient to be drawn upward to the 5–4 mark band (see mark scheme on page 9) so this answer is awarded **2 out of 6 marks** rather than 3 out of 6 (which would signal being tempted towards the band above).

The evaluation (**AO2**) is also basic. Essentially, two points are made and only one of them is in any reasonable depth, so **2 out of 6 marks**, again because there is no temptation to be drawn towards the band above.

Total = **4 out of 12 marks**, which is not even equivalent to a **Grade E**.

Life changes

EXAM ADVICE

Sometimes questions have two parts (as in question 2 here). Candidates often do one part and seem to forget about the other.

Question 1 Give **one** example of a 'life change' and explain why this might cause stress. *(3 marks)*

Patrick's answer

An example of a life change is divorce. This might cause stress because it requires a major transition in the person's life, and it is this transition that causes stress. Divorce is often stressful because it is accompanied by other life events (e.g. arguments, financial stress) that are stressful in their own right.

Judy's answer

A life change that causes stress is the death of a spouse. The SRRS scale has this as the most stressful life change because it affects a person the most, whereas other life changes such as changing school are not as stressful for the individual.

Examiner's comments

Both candidates have identified a life change but Judy has failed to explain why it might cause stress, so **1 out of 3 marks**. Patrick's answer is worth the **full 3 marks**.

Question 2 (a) Outline **one** study that has investigated the relationship between life changes and stress. *(6 marks)*
(b) Give **one** criticism of the study you outlined in **(a)**. *(3 marks)*

(a) Rahe et al. (1970) used a version of the SRRS scale on US sailors. This scale contains items ranked in terms of how much readjustment would be needed by an individual. The SRRS then gives a total number of life change units for that individual, for example death of a spouse is 100 LCU and divorce is 73 LCU. Rahe et al. found a small but significant correlation between the number of life change units experienced by the men and their illness over the same period. The correlation was +.118. As the SRRS measures both positive and negative life changes, this study indicated that it was not whether a life change was positive or negative that caused stress but the amount of energy that was needed to deal with the event in question.

(b) A criticism of this study is that it only provides correlational data, therefore cannot show a causal relationship between life changes and stress-related illness. It is possible that a third factor affects both, for example, that individuals who are more anxious are both more likely to report negative life events and also more prone to illness.

(a) A study that investigated the relationship between life changes and stress was carried out by Holmes and Rahe. They used the social readjustment rating scale (SRRS). This is a list of 47 different life events. They found that the ones that caused the most stress were death of a spouse and divorce, and the ones that caused least stress were Christmas and minor violations of the law. People indicated which of these life events they had experienced over the previous year. Death of a spouse scored 100 and marriage 50. Those people who scored more in terms of these life events were more likely to have been ill over the same period.

(b) A criticism is that the SRRS does not take into account individual differences in the impact of different life events. For example, for some people divorce might be extremely stressful but for others it is a liberating experience.

(a) Patrick's answer receives the **full 6 marks** as it is detailed and all appropriate – the question does not ask for just procedures or just findings/conclusions, so any aspect of the study is creditworthy. Judy has made the mistake of writing about the SRRS rather than writing about a study that used this to investigate the relationship between life changes and stress. However, as Holmes and Rahe's original work in constructing the scale could count as a 'study' she will receive some credit. For full marks she should have given details of how the scale was constructed not how the scale is used, so **2 out of 6 marks**.

(b) An excellent answer from Patrick, illustrating the three-point rule (see page 10), so **full marks**. Judy's answer is a criticism of the scale not the study, so **0 marks**.

Question 3 Outline what research has shown about the relationship between life changes and stress. *(4 marks)*

Rahe et al. used a version of the SRRS scale on US sailors. Rahe et al. found a small but significant correlation between the number of life change units experienced by the men and their stress-related illness over the same period. Hurst et al. found that life change scores based on an individual's personal ratings of an event (rather than normative ratings) more accurately reflect the potential stressful impact of different life changes.

Holmes and Rahe studied people using the SRRS and found that the more life changes (like divorce) they had experienced, the more illness they had. Rahe used the SRRS to study people in the US Navy, and also found that those sailors that had the most life changes over the previous year also had the most illness.

Both Patrick and Judy have identified two studies each and outlined the findings from these studies – it would be equally acceptable to provide lots of findings from just one study. Patrick's answer is more detailed for **full marks**, but Judy's answer contains almost enough for full marks (the first study is rather weak in detail) so **3 out of 4 marks**.

Question 4 This year has been a very happy year for Sanjay. He got married at the beginning of the year and now his wife has just given birth to twin boys. However, it has also been a sad year because his father died soon after the wedding.
(a) What is the term used by psychologists to describe these stress-related events? *(1 mark)*
(b) Explain why Sanjay has found he has been ill more frequently this year. Make reference to psychological research in your answer. *(4 marks)*

(a) Life changes.

(b) Sanjay has experienced three critical life changes in a relatively short time. Research (e.g. Holmes and Rahe) has shown that a combination of critical life changes, such as death of a close relative and marriage create stress in the individual because they involve a major transition in the person's life. These life changes are associated with an increase in stress-related illness, which would explain why Sanjay has been ill more frequently.

(a) They are called stressors.

(b) Sanjay has been ill because he has been so stressed having to deal with these different events in his life. Having to experience three major stressors in a year has made him ill, although having a baby and getting married would ward off some of the stress caused by the death of his father.

(a) Only Patrick's answer is right.

(b) Another excellent answer from Patrick for **full marks**. Judy has produced a basic answer to the question but not referred clearly to research in her answer – in fact she's wrong in saying that positive events would not be stressful, so just **1 out of 4 marks**.

Question 5 Sarah has a twin sister Jane who has been ill quite a lot over the past two years. Sarah wonders whether this is related to all the upheavals in their lives – her parents were divorced, they both changed schools and their grandmother died. However, Sarah hasn't been ill. Sarah wonders why Jane has been ill but she hasn't.
Use your knowledge of psychology to explain why Sarah and Jane might have responded differently. *(4 marks)*

There are several reasons why Jane has been ill and Sarah hasn't. One reason is that there are individual differences in the impact of life stressors, so Sarah has coped better with these life changes than Jane. It is possible that Sarah shows more evidence of hardiness in her personality, which makes her more resistant to the negative impact of life stressors, and so more resistant to stress-related illness.

Sarah copes better with stress than Jane does. There are individual differences in how people deal with stress, but it is also possible that Sarah is less close to her parents and grandparents and didn't like school, so was less affected by these life changes.

The key to Patrick's answer is that he has mentioned hardiness, so he not only identifies individual differences as the explanation (as Judy has) but also provides some specific psychological information. **Full marks** for Patrick and **2 out of 4 marks** for Judy.

RESEARCH METHODS QUESTION

A recent study demonstrated a strong negative correlation between the incidence of life changes and illness.

(a) Explain what is meant by a 'strong negative correlation'. *(3 marks)*

Patrick's answer

It means that high life-change scores were related to low levels of illness and low life-change scores were related to high levels of illness. On a scattergram the dots would be closer together than in a weak correlation.

Judy's answer

This means that illness is less likely to be caused by life changes.

Examiner's comments

Patrick has explained each of the three words as required (strong + negative + correlation), for **full marks**. Judy's answer is completely wrong as she has described a causal relationship, **0 marks**.

(b) Explain whether this finding would be expected or unexpected, making reference to other psychological research. *(4 marks)*

This finding would be unexpected because most research has found that more life changes have been associated to higher levels of illness. For example, the SRRS scale (Holmes and Rahe) was based on the research finding that individuals who had experienced high numbers of life changes over a given period were more likely to suffer illness over the same period. Rahe's research with US sailors also found a significant positive correlation between life changes and illness.

If it was a directional hypothesis (saying that there would be a positive correlation between life changes and illness), then this would be unexpected. Previous psychological research would suggest that there would be a positive correlation, so this would be unexpected.

Judy's answer is muddled – it is a directional hypothesis so her statement is wrong. However, she is right in saying that previous research does suggest a positive correlation so a negative correlation is unexpected – but doesn't give the details of the previous research – as Patrick has. **Full marks** for Patrick and **1 out of 4 marks** for Judy.

(c) Outline **one** strength and **one** limitation of using correlations in stress research. *(4 marks)*

A strength is that a correlation can be used when it would be unethical or impractical to manipulate the variables. For example, it would be impractical to subject individuals to life changes and unethical to subject them to illness.

A limitation is that there may be other variables that influence both the life changes and the illness. For example, people who are anxious by nature may be more likely to experience negative life events such as divorce, and also more likely to become ill.

Correlations can give a visual representation of two variables (a scattergram) so that it is easy to see if there is a relationship between them.

Correlations can't show a causal relationship between two things, so just because they are correlated doesn't mean that one has caused the other.

Patrick's answers are detailed and contextualised, as required by the question, for the **full 4 marks**. Judy's answers lack detail which could have been provided by contextualisation – which is required – so **4 out of 6 marks**.

(d) Outline how psychologists have measured life changes. *(3 marks)*

Psychologists use the Social Readjustment Rating Scale (SRRS) devised by Holmes and Rahe. There is a list of critical life events and each event has a score for life change units (LCUs). In order to assess stress a person indicates which events they have experienced. Their LCU score can then be calculated.

Holmes and Rahe produced a questionnaire called the SRRS. It was used by Rahe to find out if stress was correlated with illness. He did this by giving the questionnaire to men in the US Navy and also asking them about any illness.

Patrick's answer is clear and accurate for the **full 3 marks**. Judy hasn't read the question carefully and has only implicitly given us some information about how life changes are measured, so **1 out of 3 marks**.

Extended writing question

Outline and evaluate research related to life changes and stress. *(12 marks)*

AO1

The only descriptive material in this essay is in this first paragraph, a detailed account of the study by Rahe *et al.*

Notice how this answer is constructed from smaller building blocks on the rest of this spread.

Rahe et al. (1970) used a version of the SRRS scale on US sailors. This scale contains items ranked in terms of how much readjustment would be needed by an individual. The SRRS then gives a total number of life change units for that individual, for example death of a spouse is 100 LCU and divorce is 73 LCU. Rahe et al. found a small but significant correlation between the number of life change units experienced by the men and their illness over the same period. The correlation was +.118. As the SRRS measures both positive and negative life changes, this study indicated that it was not whether a life change was positive or negative that caused stress but the amount of energy that was needed to deal with the event in question.

A limitation of the SRRS scale is that there are individual differences in the impact of a life event, therefore it is difficult to predict illness from SRRS scores alone. Hurst et al. (1978) found that life change scores based on an individual's personal ratings of an event (rather than the normative ratings used in the SRRS) more accurately reflect the potential stressful impact of different life changes.

A criticism of studies such as these is that they only yield correlational data, therefore they cannot show a causal relationship between life changes and stress-related illness. It is possible that a third factor affects both, for example that individuals who are more anxious are both more likely to report negative life events and are more prone to illness.

Some critics argue that major life changes as measured by the SRRS are relatively rare in people's lives, therefore it is more likely that daily hassles are the more significant source of everyday stress.

(294 words)

AO2

In this second paragraph one critical point is identified and well elaborated.

A second critical point is identified and again explained in depth.

The third and final critical point lacks depth – although is better than 'superficial' (see mark scheme on page 9).

Examiner's comments

This answer provides a detailed description (**AO1**) of one study which is sufficient for full marks in an essay asking for 'research'. Full marks are only awarded for one study if it is sufficiently detailed; on the previous spread only one study received 2 out of 6 marks because of the lack of detail. 'Detail' can be provided in terms of lots of studies or the specific details given for each study. In this case the detailed description of Rahe *et al.* received 6 marks on the facing page and gets **6 out of 6 marks** here.

The evaluation (**AO2**) is relatively narrow in range but in places there is considerable depth. On balance it is worth **5 out of 6 marks**.

Total = **11 out of 12 marks**, a **Grade A**.

Daily hassles

Question 1 In the table below, list two examples of life changes and two examples of daily hassles. *(4 marks)*

Life changes	Example 1– Divorce	Example 2 – Getting married
Daily hassles	Example 1 – Bad weather	Example 2 – Heavy traffic

Question 2 (a) Explain what is meant by a 'daily hassle'. *(2 marks)*
(b) Explain the possible link between daily hassles and illness. *(3 marks)*

Elliott's answer

(a) A hassle is something like dropping your iPhone or missing a bus.

(b) Daily hassles can make people ill because they are stressful. A study of university students found that the more hassles they had, the more depressed they became.

Nadja's answer

(a) Frustrating everyday experiences (e.g. a malfunctioning computer) that occur regularly in a person's work, home or personal life.

(b) Daily hassles may lead to an accumulation of minor stressors, which overload the individual and lead to anxiety or depression. Chronic stress caused by life events may also deplete an individual's resources, making them more vulnerable to daily hassles and subsequent illness.

Examiner's comments

(a) Nadja's answer is clearly more detailed including an explanation plus an example (**full marks**), whereas Elliott's answer just has an example and no explanation (**1 out of 2 marks**).

(b) There is some creditworthy material in Elliott's answer (the mention of stress and of depression), so **1 out of 3 marks** and the **full 3 marks** for Nadja.

Question 3 (a) Outline **one** study that has investigated the relationship between daily hassles and stress. *(6 marks)*
(b) Give **one** criticism of the study you outlined in (a). *(3 marks)*

(a) Gervais carried out a study where nurses kept a diary of all the things that happened to them during the week. They recorded all the daily hassles, such as breaking things or rude patients, and all the daily uplifts, such as compliments from members of the public or their ward manager. Gervais found that, provided they received an equal number of uplifts, they could deal with the hassles without them becoming too stressful.

(b) A criticism of this study is that it used nurses who may not be typical of the rest of the population. For example, they may experience more daily hassles than most people, but simply get used to it so they are not as stressed.

(a) Bouteyre et al. studied the relationship between daily hassles and mental health in French students. These students completed a hassles questionnaire and a depression inventory. The researchers found that about 40% of the students tested showed some symptoms of depression and that there was a positive correlation between scores on the hassles scale and scores on the depression inventory. This study demonstrated that the transition to university involves many hassles for new students (e.g. sorting out classes, looking after themselves for the first time), and that these may well be a contributing factor in the development of depression.

(b) Research such as this relies on participants assessing the impact of hassles they have experienced over a particular period (e.g. the previous month). For many people who are suffering from depression there is a 'search for meaning' as they look for reasons why they feel the way they do. Consequently, they are more likely to recall more experience of hassles and a greater negative impact of these hassles.

(a) Again, Nadja's answer is clearly more detailed, containing information about procedures and results, so the **full 6 marks**. Elliott's answer is good – he has selected an appropriate study and also described process and findings. His answer is less detailed but better than basic, so **4 out of 6 marks**.

(b) Elliott's answer just falls short of full marks. He has identified his criticism and explained why it is a criticism but he needed to go a bit further for the full marks. For example, he might have said 'This means you can't really generalise the findings to other people'. So a rather mean **2 out of 3 marks**. Nadja's answer provides all three key elements of a criticism (see the three-point rule on page 10), so **3 out of 3 marks**.

Question 4 Outline what research has shown about the relationship between daily hassles and stress. *(6 marks)*

Research has shown that daily hassles, such as arguments with family and cars breaking down, can be as stressful, if not more stressful, than life events such as divorce or the death of a spouse, and so can be a contributory factor in the development of stress-related illnesses such as depression.

Bouteyre et al. (2007) found a positive correlation between scores on a hassles scale and depressive symptoms among first-year university students, suggesting that the transition to university is stressful for new students. A study by Gulian et al. (1990) found that the effect of daily hassles accumulates over the course of a day and adds to the impact of subsequent stressors. Participants who had experienced a number of daily hassles at work during the day reported a more stressful journey home.

Nadja has tried to provide enough detail by using the findings from two studies and for each of them reported two findings/conclusions – but not quite enough for full marks, so **4 out of 6 marks**. Elliott's answer is rather general (i.e. no specific study is mentioned) but his answer is better than 'very brief' or 'flawed', so **2 out of 6 marks**.

Question 5 Sue Ellen has had nothing but problems all day – her car wouldn't start this morning, she had a difficult meeting at work and then she found she'd left her purse at home and had no money for lunch. When she got home she snapped at her husband.

(a) Use your knowledge of psychology to explain why Sue Ellen was so short-tempered with her husband. *(3 marks)*
(b) Give **one** limitation to the explanation you have provided in (a). *(3 marks)*

(a) Sue Ellen was short-tempered with her husband because they are possibly going through a divorce. Divorce is a significant life event, therefore a major source of stress. Holmes and Rahe suggested that divorce was a major cause of stress for most people.

(b) A limitation of this explanation is that it may not be divorce but just that her husband is irritating her at the time, therefore is one of her daily hassles. Research has shown that daily hassles can be every bit as stressful as life changes like divorce, particularly if (as here) several are experienced at once.

(a) Research has shown that the effect of daily hassles tends to accumulate over the course of a day, and adds to the impact of subsequent stressors. In the case of Sue Ellen, although each of the hassles she experienced during the day was relatively minor, the cumulative effect of them meant she was under a considerable amount of stress, resulting in her snapping at her husband, probably because he had irritated her in some relatively innocent way.

(b) A limitation of this explanation is the assumption that her behaviour towards her husband was caused by the frustration of the daily hassles experienced during the day. It is possible that her behaviour towards him was caused by some long-running argument between the two of them, and even that some of the hassles she had experienced at work (e.g. the difficult meeting) were a product of her continuing negative mood.

(a) Elliott has lost the plot a bit – first of all he ignores the information in the stem and instead focuses on Sue Ellen's husband as the source of her stress, and second he ends up describing research on life events whereas the stem is clearly about daily hassles, so **0 marks**. Nadja clearly uses information in the stem to answer the question for **full marks**.

(b) Since Elliott's answer to (a) is not creditworthy he can receive **0 marks** for (b). Nadja's answer again demonstrates the three-point rule (see page 10) and is worth the **full 3 marks**.

A researcher investigated the relationship between daily hassles and levels of stress. He used a questionnaire to find out which hassles people were experiencing on the day they were questioned and also to asked them to rate how stressed they were feeling. His results are shown in the scattergram.

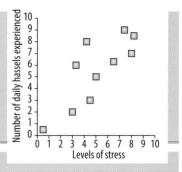

(a) What conclusion could you draw from the scattergram? *(2 marks)*

Elliott's answer

The more daily hassles people experience, the more stressed they become.

Nadja's answer

That there is a moderate positive correlation between the number of daily hassles experienced and the perceived level of stress.

Examiner's comments

Both answers are correct but neither candidate has given enough detail for 2 marks. Nadia has described the graph but not provided a conclusion. **1 out of 2 marks** for both.

(b) Give **one** strength and **one** limitation of using a questionnaire to find out about daily hassles. *(3 marks + 3 marks)*

A strength is that questionnaires are more likely to be answered honestly, especially if they are anonymous. People would be happier to answer questions about the things that stress them in a questionnaire than they would be in an interview.

A limitation is that people are less likely to be honest in questionnaires because they would answer in a way that makes them look good. For example, they might not like to admit that some things cause them stress.

A strength of using a questionnaire is that it allows the researcher to repeat the questionnaire easily and economically. This means that they can gather data concerning the effect of daily hassles from large numbers of respondents in order to establish trends about the relationship between hassles and stress for different groups of people.

A limitation is that there may be a sampling bias in any use of questionnaires to find out about daily hassles. Many people find filling out questionnaires a hassle, therefore those who are most stressed may be least likely to complete the questionnaire, meaning that any conclusions may not be valid.

Both candidates have provided contextualised answers, i.e. they have referred to the specific context of daily hassles. Nadja has given plenty of other information so the **full 3 + 3 marks**. Elliott's answers, even though they are clearly shorter, also contain enough detail for **full marks** – for example he identifies the strength (honest answers), points out that this is related to anonymity and makes a comparison with interviews. Contextualisation is not always required on Unit 2 but it does increase elaboration so is always worthwhile.

(c) Outline how psychologists have measured daily hassles. *(3 marks)*

Psychologists have measured daily hassles by giving people questionnaires which have questions about daily hassles, and people then indicate which hassles they have experienced.

The most common way is to use a questionnaire called the Daily Hassles and Uplifts Scale. This scale has 53 items which are either hassles or uplifts and a person has to indicate if the item is experienced as a hassle or an uplift and how frequently on a scale of 0–3 where 3 is a great deal.

There is sufficient detail in Nadja's answer for the **full 3 marks** but Elliott only gets **1 out of 3 marks** because really the only relevant thing he has said is that a questionnaire is used.

Extended writing question

Outline and evaluate research relating to the relationship between daily hassles and stress. *(12 marks)*

AO1

A reasonably detailed description of an appropriate study is presented. The greatest danger is that students will write about studies on life changes rather than daily hassles. If they do, they get no credit.

A second appropriate study is again described in reasonable detail.

Bouteyre et al. (2007) studied the relationship between daily hassles and mental health in French students who were making the transition between school and university. The researchers found a positive correlation between scores on a hassles scale and scores on a depression inventory. This study demonstrated that the transition to university contains many hassles for new students (e.g. sorting out classes, looking after themselves for the first time), and that these may well be a contributing factor in the development of depression.

Research such as this relies on participants assessing the impact of hassles they have experienced over a particular period (e.g. the previous month). For many people who are suffering from depression there is a 'search for meaning' as they look for reasons why they feel the way they do. Consequently, they are more likely to recall more experience of hassles and a greater negative impact of these hassles.

A study by Gulian et al. (1990) found that the effect of daily hassles accumulates over the course of a day and adds to the impact of subsequent stressors. They found that participants who had experienced a number of daily hassles at work during the course of their working day reported a more stressful journey home.

Daily hassles may well be a more significant source of stress than life changes, such as divorce and redundancy. This view is supported by evidence from Ruffin (1993), who found that daily hassles were linked to greater physical and psychological dysfunction than even major negative life events. However, it is possible that the greater stress associated with daily hassles could be due to the reduced social support provided by others compared to the level of support provided for major life changes.

(287 words)

AO2

The second paragraph counts as evaluation (general commentary) on the research – however it could be made more effective by explaining in which way this challenges the results of research (it reduces the validity of the research).

The final paragraph contains one more point of evaluation which is very well elaborated using supporting research and by looking at an alternative explanation of this research.

Note that the research study is not described in great detail – which is a good thing because description would otherwise count as AO1.

Examiner's comments

The descriptive (**AO1**) content consists of two studies in reasonable detail – but the issue is whether this counts as 'sound' knowledge and understanding (which would gain 6 out of 6 marks – see mark scheme on page 9). It is probably not 'sound' but closer to that than only 'some relevant' (which would gain 3 out of 6 marks), therefore **5 out of 6 marks**.

The evaluation (**AO2**) is limited in terms of the range of points covered, although these are provided in considerable depth. **4 out of 6 marks.**

Total = **9 out of 12 marks**, enough for a **Grade A** – even though it is a short answer, the <u>quality</u> of the description and evaluation gains the necessary marks.

Workplace stress

Question 1 Explain what is meant by 'workplace stress'. *(3 marks)*

Adam's answer

Aspects of the working environment that the individual perceives as placing demands or pressures on them that they find difficult to cope with, for example having too much work to do or not having enough control over working practices.

Eve's answer

Workplace stress is experienced when somebody is stressed at work, for example when the job is too difficult for them.

Examiner's comments

Eve's answer doesn't really explain anything – obviously workplace stress is stress at work, although her example provides a little insight so the answer is just about worth **1 out of 3 marks**. Adam's answer is worth the **full 3 marks**.

Question 2 Workers' absence is a major problem for employers because it reduces productivity and therefore costs money. One of the reasons for absenteeism is that workers experience stress in the workplace. Psychologists have been called on to identify possible sources of workplace stress.

(a) Outline **two** psychological sources of stress in the workplace. *(3 marks)*

(b) Choose **one** of these sources of stress and explain how an employer might reduce the problems caused by it. *(3 marks)*

(a) Workload, having too much work to do in the time available; because the demands of the workplace then become greater than the resources the individual has available. Control, having too little responsibility for working practices although some employees are less stressed in situations where they have little control over working practices.

(b) An employer may reduce some of the stress associated with the issue of control by introducing a psychological profiling exercise to discover whether employees are happy in positions where there is a great deal of control or where there is very little. By matching each employee with the right position, this should reduce stress and absenteeism through stress-related illness.

(a) Too much work, not enough pay.

(b) If the workers feel stressed because they are not paid enough, this creates stress because they cannot make ends meet. The employer could reduce the problems associated with this by giving them a pay rise. This would enable them to live more comfortably and so they would not be as stressed.

(a) As this is a psychology exam we are looking for psychologically informed answers. Adam's are and Eve's aren't, so full marks for Adam and only **1 out of 3 marks** for Eve (because, even though her answer is lacking psychology, it is appropriate).

(b) Eve has chosen 'poor pay' which is a source of stress and obviously increasing pay would deal with this, but again the answer doesn't demonstrate psychological knowledge so only **1 out of 3 marks**. At this rate there is no way she is going to pass the exam. Adam's answer is detailed and clear; **full marks**.

Question 3 Outline what psychological research has shown about workplace stress. *(6 marks)*

Marmot et al. (1997) found that civil servants in the highest grades reported the highest levels of control over their work and were the least likely to develop heart disease.

Schaubroeck et al. (2001) found that workers respond differently to lack of control, with some workers actually showing higher immune responses in low-control situations.

A meta-analysis by Kivimaki et al. (2006) found that employees with high levels of work stress were 50% more likely to develop heart disease than employees with low levels of work stress.

Marmot carried out a study of civil servants. He asked 7,000 of them to complete a questionnaire about their workload and the amount of control they had over their work. He also checked to see if any of them had any cardiovascular disease. He found that workload wasn't related to heart disease but control was. A problem with this study is that some people find lack of control stressful, whereas other people find having lots of control very stressful. Therefore we can't draw too many conclusions from this study.

Adam's answer focuses entirely on results/conclusions. He has selected three appropriate studies and provided detailed information for each. It is not necessary to include names and dates to gain full marks but it is a means of providing detail; **full marks**. Eve has selected just one study, which is fine if she knows enough detail about the findings/conclusions – however, she has padded out her answer with irrelevant information about the procedures and criticisms, so just **1 out of 6 marks**.

Question 4 A psychologist looked at a range of studies on workplace stress. Some of these studies found that high levels of responsibility led to increased stress, whereas other studies found the opposite was true – that people who had high levels of responsibility had lower levels of stress.

Explain why research has produced such contradictory results. *(3 marks)*

The main reason for these contradictory results is because of individual differences in preferences for responsibility. Some people who are high in hardiness may see high levels of responsibility as 'challenging', whereas people low in hardiness see such responsibility as stressful. Schaubroeck et al. (2001) found some people feel less stressed by having no responsibility and show better immune responses in such situations.

If a study discovers something (e.g. that high levels of responsibility lead to increased stress) and another study finds the opposite, this could be due to sampling error (e.g. that one study has used only students who hate responsibility) or the fact that other extraneous variables haven't been controlled (e.g. the nature of the work, or the consequences of their decisions).

Both candidates have provided insightful and plausible answers, demonstrating psychological knowledge. Adam has again cited specific research making his answer more detailed but Eve has referred to psychological concepts and in this way provided detail. The question doesn't require just one explanation so both of Eve's explanations are creditworthy. **Full marks** for both answers.

Question 5 Katie runs a small business producing greeting cards. Her employees all work in a bright, cheerful, quiet office. Recently she has had some problems with illness – a number of her employees have taken time off work because they have had colds and 'flu. Katie thinks they may have become ill because they are stressed at work.

Use your knowledge of psychology to suggest what Katie might do to reduce illness in her office. *(4 marks)*

Schaubroeck et al. (2001) found some people feel less stressed by having no responsibility and show better immune responses in such situations. Therefore Katie might interview each employee to establish their preferred work situation (i.e. high or low responsibility). Johansson et al. (1978) found that workers who had repetitive jobs with an unrelenting pace were those who experienced the most stress. As the production of greeting cards would follow a similar pattern, she could introduce a scheme whereby each worker produced complete cards rather than being part of a production line.

Some studies have found that people are more stressed when they have little or no control over their working environment. For example, a study of civil servants found that low levels of control led to stress-related illness. Also, a study of a Swedish sawmill found that workers who had to perform repetitive tasks that required high levels of attention were more stressed and more likely to have stress-related illness. So, Katie could introduce more control and less repetitive tasks in her office.

Both candidates have given far more information than required for a 4-mark question – and likely to have wasted important examination time for thinking, planning and writing. One study, described in some detail is enough as long as it is linked to suggestions about what Katie could do. Eve's answer doesn't provide the researcher's names but the research is described in sufficient detail to be identifiable. Therefore the **full 4 marks** for each candidate.

RESEARCH METHODS QUESTION

(a) Outline **one** research study that has investigated workplace stress. *(3 marks)*

Adam's answer

Marmot et al. conducted a study looking at coronary disease in civil servants, comparing those in high-grade jobs with those in low-grade jobs. They answered a questionnaire on workload, job control and amount of social support, and were checked for cardiovascular disease. This was repeated five years later.

Eve's answer

Marmot et al. studied civil servants and found that those who had lots of responsibility in their job were less likely to feel stressed compared to those who had very little responsibility.

Examiner's comments

Full marks to Adam for a sufficiently detailed description. Eve this time has identified the researcher but really only given limited information about the study, so **2 out of 3 marks**.

(b) Explain **one** possible problem with the validity of this study and say how it might be dealt with. *(4 marks)*

A problem is that questionnaires that are used in studies such as this might only include the stressors that researchers feel are important, and might exclude those that are more personally stressful to the participants in this study (e.g. violence from patients). This can be dealt with by using interviews and allowing civil servants to mention those aspects of their role that they find most stressful, and allowing researchers to follow up on their answers.

A problem with validity was that this sample (civil servants) is biased and it may not generalise out to a wider population. For example, a lot of their work is boring, which makes the role conflict they experience more intense. This can be dealt with by using other occupations as well, particularly those whose work is less boring.

Both are excellent answers worth the **full 4 marks**. Notice particularly how Eve has said that a sample of civil servants is biased – but then explained why this group of people differ from the general population, i.e. she has explained her claim that it is a biased sample.

(c) Identify **one** ethical issue that might arise in this study and explain how it would be dealt with. *(3 marks)*

An ethical issue is confidentiality, particularly as much of the material given in the questionnaires would be of a sensitive nature. This can be overcome by making all responses completely anonymous, and ensuring no personal information is collected that could identify an individual from their responses.

An ethical issue is lack of informed consent. The civil servants may not have been given the choice about whether they took part in the study. This can be dealt with by asking them to sign an informed consent form before the study.

Again, both answers are different but both worth the **full 3 marks**. What is important is that the ethical issue has been identified and two further, distinct points made about how this could be dealt with, for the **full 3 marks**.

(d) Identify **one** way in which psychologists have investigated workplace stress and give **one** limitation of this method. *(4 marks)*

Most studies of workplace stress use questionnaires such as the Health and Safety Executive (HSE) stress at work questionnaire. These questionnaires measure the relationship between aspects of the working environment and the experience of stress. However, traditional questionnaires may only include those aspects of working life that researchers feel are important, and may exclude those that are more personally stressful to the participants in a particular environment.

Psychologists have investigated workplace stress using naturalistic observations, for example researchers observed workers in a sawmill. A limitation of this method is that the researchers can't control variables that might affect the results, and so can't draw any causal relationships between aspects of the workplace and stress.

This question is different from (a) because you are only required to focus on methods. It would be fine to describe the procedures of a particular study or, as our candidates have done, to focus on research methodology more generally.

Both answers are worth the **full 4 marks** although Eve's answer only just makes it – she has elaborated both points and so deserves full marks.

Extended writing question

'A number of psychological factors have contributed to stress in the workplace.'
Discuss the contribution of **two or more** factors to workplace stress. *(12 marks)*

EXAM ADVICE

Some extended writing questions begin with a quotation, which is there to guide you. You can ignore it but it might give you some useful ideas about how to answer the question.

AO1

Two studies are described that relate to workplace stress – which makes us think that the student is answering a different question, i.e. 'Discuss research into…'

So, we have to look carefully to see if factors have been identified – control, social support and role conflict are mentioned and for each their contribution is noted – but the presentation of this information is not clear and coherent.

Marmot et al. (1997) carried out a questionnaire study of civil servants to investigate the relationship between work stress and cardiovascular disorders. In a follow-up study five years later they found that those in the highest grades and who reported the highest levels of control over their work and the most social support were the least likely to develop heart disease. Those in the lower grades had reported less control over their work and the poorest social support, and were the most likely to develop heart disease and hypertension. Johansson et al. (1978) studied workers in a sawmill. They found that a group of men who were responsible for finishing timber had the most stressful job because they were responsible for the output of the whole sawmill. They also had the highest levels of illness.

A problem with studies that focus on stressors such as control and role conflict is that they might not tell us anything about stressors that are associated with more modern working practices, such as 'virtual offices' and working from home. As a result, research might always lag behind actual working practices. There are also individual differences in the impact of these work stressors, for example high levels of control and workload may be seen as challenging by an individual high in hardiness, but as stressful by someone low in hardiness, making them more vulnerable to stress-related illness. The importance of the workplace as a source of stress is supported by a meta-analysis of 14 studies by Kivimaki et al. (2006), who found that employees with high levels of work stress were 50% more likely to develop heart disease than employees with low levels of work stress.

(281 words)

AO2

For this question the evaluation could consist of looking at research support, or looking at the soundness of the research.

In this essay the commentary actually manages to focus on the factors themselves, and provides three critical considerations in depth.

Examiner's comments

The description (AO1) of workplace stress factors is relevant but the answer is not coherently presented, so **4 out of 6 marks**.

The evaluation (AO2) is excellent. The range is possibly 'narrow' instead of 'broad' (see mark scheme on page 9) but the depth is better than 'reasonable' and the actual points raised are insightful and effective, so **6 out of 6 marks**.

Total = **10 out of 12 marks**, a **Grade A** answer.

Personality factors and stress

Question 1 Three of the following statements apply to individuals with a Type A personality. Indicate the correct statements. *(3 marks)*

- ☑ Time pressured.
- ☑ Competitive.
- ☐ Relaxed.
- ☐ Wish to please others.
- ☑ Hostile.
- ☐ Gloomy.

FULL MARKS!

Question 2 (a) Explain what is meant by 'Type A behaviour'. *(2 marks)*
(b) Outline **one** method that psychologists have used to measure Type A behaviour. *(2 marks)*

Adrian's answer

(a) This is the behaviour shown by people with a Type A personality, people who are always trying to hit deadlines.

(b) One method is to observe people while they are working to see if they display the characteristic Type A behaviours.

Caroline's answer

(a) Behaviour that is characterised by competitiveness, achievement striving, impatience and hostility.

(b) Type A behaviour is measured by means of semi-structured interviews, such as the Rosenman semi-structured interview. The interviewer has set themes to explore but can add new questions during the interview as a result of what the interviewee says.

Examiner's comments

(a) Adrian has given us a circular definition (Type A is shown by Type A people) but he has provided an example, which would give him **1 out of 2 marks**. Caroline's answer is detailed and accurate for **full marks**.

(b) Adrian's answer is correct but lacking detail so **1 out of 2 marks**, whereas Caroline again gets **full marks**.

Question 3 Outline two personality factors that may explain why some people experience higher levels of stress than others. *(4 marks)*

Type A and internal locus of control. Type A people are always chasing deadlines so are more likely to experience stress. Internals worry that they are responsible for everything that happens to them, so are more likely to experience anxiety and stress.

Type A personality, characterised by competitiveness, achievement striving, impatience and hostility, is believed to lead to an increase in stress hormones and coronary heart disease.

Some people are more resistant to stress because they have a hardy personality. People who are low in hardiness (low in control, challenge and commitment) are, however, less resistant to stress.

Caroline gains **full marks** here. Even though Adrian's answer is clearly less detailed, he has identified two personality factors and linked each of them to stress. However, the general lack of detail means that he receives **3 out of 4 marks**.

Question 4 Outline what psychologists have found out about the relationship between personality factors and stress. *(6 marks)*

Psychologists have found that people who have a Type A personality are very achievement oriented and are always chasing deadlines. This means they are more likely to have high blood pressure and are more vulnerable to heart attacks. Psychologists have also found out that some people are more resistant to stress if they have a hardy personality. Kobasa found that these people don't get as stressed because they see work as a challenge and are more committed to their work. Consequently they don't get as stressed as people who are low in hardiness.

In a study of 3,000 Californian men, Freidman and Rosenman (1960) found that over a period of eight years, twice as many men with Type A personalities had died with cardiovascular problems than those without Type A characteristics.

A meta-analysis of 35 studies (Myrtek, 2001) found an association between coronary heart disease and just one aspect of Type A personality, hostility.

Kobasa (1979) assessed hardiness and stress scores among 800 executives using Holmes and Rahe's SRRS. She found that 150 of the executives were classified as being highly stressed, yet differed in terms of their illness record. Those with the lowest illness record tended to score the highest on the three components of the hardy personality.

Caroline's answer certainly looks better because she has included names and dates and it is longer but, in fact, the results/conclusions cited by Adrian are all clearly identifiable without giving researchers' names. Caroline has presented four findings and it's a shame she hasn't expanded any of these, for example by drawing conclusions, therefore **5 out of 6 marks**. She might have said, for example, 'Myrtek (2001) found an association between coronary heart disease and just one aspect of Type A personality, hostility. <u>This suggests that the harmful effects of Type A behaviour aren't related to competiteness or impatience</u>'. (The conclusions have been underlined.)

Adrian has actually provided five findings/conclusions, each of which is reasonably detailed and accurate, so he also gains **5 out of 6 marks**.

Note how Caroline has used paragraphs to make her answer more readable – examiners find this makes it much easier to read and mark a student answer.

Question 5 Outline how psychologists have investigated the relationship between personality factors and stress. *(6 marks)*

Friedman and Rosenman carried out a study to see if men who had the Type A personality were more likely to become ill from heart disease. They interviewed the men and decided whether they were Type A or Type B personality. Type A were very achievement motivated and aggressive, Type B were more relaxed. They followed them over eight years and found that those with Type A were more likely to develop heart disease.

Friedman and Rosenman (1960) carried out a natural experiment in which a group of men with Type A personality (assessed by interview) were compared to a group of men who did not have Type A personality to see if one group was more likely to develop heart disease. In order to determine which aspects of the Type A personality were more associated with coronary heart disease, Myrtek (2001) carried out a meta-analysis of 35 studies.

Kobasa (1979) used the SRRS to determine the stress scores of 800 executives and a hardiness test to determine hardiness. The most stressed of the executives then had their illness records checked to see whether those high in hardiness had better or worse illness records than those low in hardiness.

Caroline has again extended her answer by looking at a range of studies and wisely focused only on the methods used, as required in the question. This answer is sufficiently detailed for the **full 6 marks**.

Adrian's answer relies on just one study, which would be fine if he knew the procedures in detail. As it is, only two of the sentences concern procedures – he has included information about the aims and results as well. This is a basic answer, closer to 'very brief' than 'detailed' so **2 out of 6 marks**.

Question 6 Explain why people who display Type A behaviour are more likely to suffer negative effects from stress. *(3 marks)*

They are more likely to suffer negative effects of stress because they are more likely to develop heart disease as a result of their behaviour, e.g. always chasing deadlines and being impatient with other people.

The characteristics of the Type A personality, such as achievement striving, impatience and hostility, lead to an increase in blood pressure and levels of stress hormones, both of which have been shown to lead to coronary heart disease.

Caroline has included the key element here – which is the rise in blood pressure. Adrian has failed to explain why stress is linked to heart disease beyond saying that it leads to chasing deadlines, etc. So just **1 out of 3 marks** for Adrian and **full marks** for Caroline.

Question 7 Psychologists have found that people who display Type A behaviour experience higher levels of stress than other personality types. Give **one** criticism of this explanation. *(3 marks)*

One criticism is that there are other reasons why people experience stress. It may not be the Type A personality that makes them stressed but that they tend to find themselves more in situations that make them stressed because they get impatient with others.

A follow-up study of Friedman and Rosenman's study 22 years later found no significant difference in the rate of death from heart disease between men with Type A personality and those with non-Type A personality. This challenges the claim that Type A personality is a significant risk factor for death from stress-related illness.

Both candidates score their marks in the second sentence. In Adrian's case just saying 'there are other reasons' is not really a criticism without explaining the point – he identifies Type A as a potential intervening variable. His answer could perhaps be clearer so **2 out of 3 marks**.

Caroline starts with a statement about the study but in her second sentence she actually answers the question, providing a clear explanation of why this is a criticism, so **full 3 marks** for clarity and elaboration.

Question 8 Ted and Martin work in a busy office. They are under a lot of pressure to complete tasks on time and make money for the company. Ted often gets quite stressed whereas Martin always seems very relaxed.

    (a) Identify the personality type of each of these men. *(2 marks)*

    (b) What are likely to be the consequences of this personality type for Ted? *(3 marks)*

(a) Ted has a Type A personality because he feels stressed when under pressure. This is characteristic of the Type A personality, always chasing deadlines and being impatient with other people.

Martin is more likely to have a Type B personality because he is more relaxed when at work. He shows none of the signs of a Type A personality.

(b) Ted is more likely to feel stressed all the time and more likely to die of a heart attack before Martin does.

(a) Ted has a Type A personality, whereas Martin has a Type B personality.

(b) Because of the hostility aspect of his Type A behaviour, Ted is likely to experience an increase in blood pressure and levels of stress hormones. Both of these are linked to ill health, including coronary heart disease.

(a) Both candidates receive the **full 2 marks**. It seems that Adrian has not noticed that this question is only worth 2 marks and that only a brief answer was required – there are no extra marks available, he has just wasted valuable time.

(b) Conversely, Adrian has written a lot less for this part despite the fact that it is worth more marks. The first statement 'Ted is more likely to feel stressed all the time' is just repeating material in the stem, so just **1 out of 3 marks**. Caroline's answer provides plenty of detail for the **full 3 marks**.

Question 9 It is examination time and, when you look around you, you will see many students who are feeling very stressed. But not everyone is stressed. Of course this might be because they simply don't care, but psychologists suggest the reason why some people get stressed is down to their personality. Use your knowledge of psychology to explain why people differ in terms of how stressed they are. *(4 marks)*

Some people have Type A personalities so are more likely to be stressed. They are always in a hurry and get impatient with other people and so are more likely to be stressed. Type B people just let it all wash over them, so wouldn't be as stressed in the same situation.

Some people are not particularly hardy so are more likely to be stressed, whereas people who are hardy are resistant to stress.

Some people are internals so are more likely to be stressed because they feel they are responsible for things that happen around them.

Some people have used stress management techniques which reduce the stress that they feel.

People differ in how stressed they are because of two different personality factors. People with a Type A personality are characterised by competitiveness and impatience, therefore will find examinations and other similar situations more stressful than those people with a Type B personality, who tend to be more relaxed.

Some students will be more resistant to stress during examinations because they have a hardy personality. These students see themselves as being more in control and see potentially stressful situations such as examinations as a challenge to be faced rather than a stressor to be feared. Because the hardy personality is also characterised by increased commitment to a task, such students are more likely to have stuck to their revision and consequently would experience less stress in the exam.

Caroline displays detailed knowledge about individual differences in stress but, in fact, Adrian has shown a better range of explanations (depth versus breadth). Caroline's answer has given us plenty of psychology whereas Adrian has focused more on the second part of the question – how people differ. So which answer is better?

Adrian's answer has breadth and it also has some psychology – he refers to Type A behaviour and to hardiness, so he has provided a good answer to the question of individual differences plus he has covered psychology. This answer gets the **full 4 marks**.

Caroline has focused more on psychological knowledge but she hasn't ignored the other requirement entirely (explaining why people differ) and there is enough here for the **full 4 marks**.

The key point is that you must provide psychology and also answer the question in order to get full marks.

RESEARCH METHODS QUESTION

A psychology class decide to test their own personalities to see which class members have a Type A personality and which haven't. They design a questionnaire to test for Type A personality and use it with students in their class and also some teachers. The bar chart shows the mean scores for males and females.

(a) Write **one** question that they could use on their questionnaire, which would help assess whether someone has a Type A personality. *(2 marks)*

Adrian's answer

Do you get impatient with other people if they slow you down?

Caroline's answer

It doesn't bother me if I can't finish what I had planned for the day. Yes/No

Examiner's comments

The key point is that the question must be related in some way to Type A behaviour, thus demonstrating knowledge about Type A – both questions have demonstrated this – so **full marks**.

(b) Explain whether the question you wrote in part **(a)** would produce qualitative or quantitative data. *(2 marks)*

The question would produce quantitative data because you could count whether people answered yes or no.

The answers would be quantitative.

This is a tricky one because Adrian's question might produce qualitative or quantitative answers – but he has dealt with this by explaining his answer. It could be argued that people might give more than a yes/no answer, in which case it would be qualitative but he has said the answers would be just yes/no and that these could then be counted, so **full marks**. Caroline gets **1 out of 2 marks** for a correct answer which lacks an explanation (the question does say 'explain').

(c) They used mean scores rather than just giving the total scores for boys and girls. Why is the mean score better to use than a total? *(2 marks)*

The mean is the total divided by the number of scores, so gives an average score.

The mean gives an average score for the two groups. If there were more boys than girls they would probably get a higher score even though, on average, their scores might be lower.

Oops, Adrian hasn't answered the question so **0 marks**. This is an excellent answer from Caroline for the **full 2 marks**.

(d) What does the bar chart suggest about Type A behaviour? *(4 marks)*

Male students score higher on Type A behaviour than female students, and students generally score a little bit higher than teachers.

The bar chart suggests that Type A behaviour is more common in males then females. This applies to both student and teacher groups. It also suggests that there is no real difference between the incidence of Type A behaviour among teachers and students.

Caroline's answer is better in several ways. First she is dealing with conclusions (what the results 'show') rather than describing what the results are ('males score higher'). More importantly she has grasped that there isn't much difference between students and staff whereas Adrian has mistakenly reported that the students scored higher (the females didn't). So **1 out of 4 marks** for Adrian and the **full 4 marks** for Caroline.

(e) A good questionnaire should be reliable. Explain why reliability is important. *(3 marks)*

Reliability is important because if a questionnaire wasn't reliable then it couldn't be relied upon. If a questionnaire is reliable, then it will be answered in the same way by people if they take it on more than one occasion.

For a questionnaire to be reliable, it should produce the same results every time it is used. If it does (as in the case of a reliable questionnaire) then it can be trusted to produce data that is consistent and an accurate reflection of the behaviour being measured by the questionnaire.

This is not an easy question – but quite likely one, so be prepared! Adrian's first sentence is meaningless but he makes a better effort the second time – although he still hasn't said why reliability is important, just so **1 out of 3 marks** for a muddled attempt.

Caroline's answer gets to the main issue – it means we can trust the data (notice that she has not said we can 'rely' on the data – because that would be a circular explanation). **Full marks** for Caroline.

(f) Identify **one** ethical issue and explain why this might be an issue in the case of this study. *(3 marks)*

An ethical issue is confidentiality. This is an issue because people wouldn't want other students reading about them.

An ethical issue is the right to withdraw. This might be an issue in this study if participants are not told both at the start of the questionnaire that they can withdraw at any time, and at the end of the questionnaire that they can withdraw their data without penalty.

Adrian's answer is appropriate but there is insufficient detail for the full 3 marks – he might have added that the information could be 'sensitive' which is why people wouldn't want others to read about it. So just **2 out of 3 marks**.

Caroline has given the extra detail for the **full 3 marks**.

Extended writing question

Outline and evaluate research studies relating to personality factors and stress.

(12 marks)

AO1

The first paragraph contains a description of an appropriate piece of research, reasonably detailed.

Another study is briefly outlined.

A final study is outlined in reasonable detail.

Friedman and Rosenman (1960) carried out a natural experiment in which a group of 3,000 Californian men with Type A personalities were compared to a group of men who did not have Type A personalities to see if one group was more likely to develop heart disease. They found that over a period of eight years, twice as many men with Type A personalities had died with cardiovascular problems than those without Type A characteristics.

However, a follow-up study of Friedman and Rosenman's study 22 years later found no significant difference in the rate of death from heart disease between men with Type A personalities and those with non-Type A personalities. This challenges the claim that Type A personality is a significant risk factor for death from stress-related illness.

A meta-analysis of 35 studies (Myrtek, 2001) found an association between coronary heart disease and just one aspect of Type A personality, hostility. This study showed no evidence to support the claim that Type A personality as a whole was associated with coronary heart disease.

Kobasa (1979) assessed hardiness and stress scores among 800 executives using Holmes and Rahe's SRRS. She found that 150 of the executives were classified as being highly stressed, yet these men differed in terms of their illness record. Those with the lowest illness record tended to score the highest on the three components of the hardy personality, control, challenge and commitment. Kobasa's conclusion that hardiness acts as a buffer against stress has been supported in a study by Maddi et al. (1987). In a company where individuals faced the constant threat of redundancy, those who showed most evidence of stress-related illness were those low in hardiness, whereas those who thrived were high in the three components of the hardy personality. A problem for studies like this, that rely on self-reports as a source of data, is that people could exaggerate their symptoms to make the situation seem worse, or under-report them, to make it appear they are coping well with stress (and are therefore more employable).

(340 words)

AO2

A further study is referred to but mainly used as evaluation. Depth is provided with a further comment on what the study demonstrates.

The second sentence of this paragraph is an AO2 comment.

The conclusion and supporting study are credited as evaluation.

A criticism of the studies is identified and elaborated.

Examiner's comments

The outline of research (**AO1**) shows appropriate selection of material and a variety of studies. Some of these are presented in reasonable detail and some are less detailed, so **5 out of 6 marks**.

The evaluation (**AO2**) provides a broad range of issues again with a range of quality from limited to reasonable, so **5 out of 6 marks**.

Total = **10 out of 12 marks**, a **Grade A** answer.

Extended writing question

Outline and evaluate the relationship between personality factors and stress.

(12 marks)

AO1

The answer starts by clearly addressing the question rather than just describing a research study. The findings of the study are part of the answer. The fact that the study has not been specifically identified is not of key importance because other details are provided and these make it identifiable.

In this third paragraph the relationship between stress and the hardy personality is outlined in reasonable detail.

A Type A personality describes people who are always trying to hit deadlines and who get impatient and hostile with others who get in their way. The main study in this area was a study of men in California who were interviewed and then classified as either Type A or Type B (relaxed and non-competitive). The researchers then followed these men over a period of eight and a half years. They found that twice as many of the men who had been classified a having a Type A personality had died of cardiovascular problems compared with those who had been classified as Type B. The Type A men also had higher blood pressure and higher levels of cholesterol.

A problem is that, in another study, only hostility was found to be important. A follow-up study found that in the long-term the death rate from heart disease among Type A men was not significantly higher than among Type B men. Some critics claim that a preoccupation with Type A personality was more an issue in the 1960s and it isn't as relevant today. Finally, the Type A personality is criticised as being gender biased because it describes typically male behaviours.

People with hardy personalities are meant to be more resistant to stress. The hardy personality has three major characteristics. The first is control, in that they see themselves as having control over their lives rather than being at the mercy of external forces. The second is commitment in that hardy people are committed to what they are doing and have a strong sense of purpose. The third is challenge, hardy people see life challenges as something that can be overcome rather than stressors that they can't cope with. Kobasa (1979) found that businessmen who were high in hardiness were better able to cope with work stress and had lower levels of absenteeism due to stress-related illness.

A problem is that negative affectivity, where people dwell more on their failures, may be a simpler explanation of these findings. Another problem is that much of the data is acquired through questionnaires, which suffer from the social desirability bias, therefore participants may not be completely honest in their responses. A final problem is that much of this research has been done with businessmen, so the results cannot be generalised to women and to other occupational groups within society. However, there is evidence to support this explanation (e.g. Maddi's study of people facing unemployment), so it is a good one.

(415 words)

AO2

Three separate points are made in this paragraph, identifying limitations with the Type A concept. These points are slightly better than 'superficial'.

The final paragraph contains a broad range of critical points related to the concept of a hardy personality, provided in some depth. For example, the answer says 'There is evidence to support the explanation' and mentions a study and also says why this is a strength (i.e. the three-point rule, see page 10 – although rather brief).

Examiner's comments

The description (**AO1**) is reasonably detailed and the evaluation (**AO2**) covers a broad range of points with some depth, so **6 out of 6 marks** for both **AO1** and **AO2**.

Total = **12 out of 12 marks**, which doesn't mean to say it is a perfect answer but certainly good enough.

Psychological and biological methods of stress management

EXAM ADVICE

The specification names drugs and Cognitive Behavioural Therapy as two methods of stress management – but the same methods are mentioned as ways to treat abnormality in the section on individual differences (see Chapter 5).

When answering an exam question, check which section the question is in. If you are asked about drugs and the question is in the biological psychology section of the exam, then only anti-anxiety drugs are creditworthy. If you are asked about drugs and the question is in the individual differences section, then think carefully about which drug would be appropriate to the question asked. The same principles apply to Cognitive Behavioural Therapy.

Question 1 (a) Explain the difference between psychological and biological methods of stress management. *(4 marks)*
(b) Give **one** example of a psychological method of stress management and **one** example of a biological method of stress management. *(2 marks)*

Rhys' answer

(a) Psychological methods try to get people to think differently about a stressful situation so it won't be as stressful for them, whereas biological methods just involve taking drugs to calm a person down when they are stressed.

(b) Stress inoculation therapy and drugs.

Amalia's answer

(a) Psychological methods attempt to change the way that people think about or react to stressful situations, therefore are an example of the problem-focused coping approach. By contrast, biological methods focus only on reducing the negative emotions associated with stress and so they are an example of the emotion-focused coping approach.

(b) An example of a psychological method is hardiness training, and an example of a biological method is the use of beta-blockers as a form of drug treatment.

Examiner's comments

(a) Amalia's answer is more clearly concerned with the difference between the two methods and also has more elaboration, so **full marks** for Amalia and **3 out of 4 marks** for Rhys.

(b) Both answers gain the **full 2 marks**. There is no need to write out the question again as Amalia has done.

Question 2 Tanya is an actress who suffers from stage fright. She consults her doctor about what she could do to manage her stress levels better. Two possible methods are stress inoculation therapy or drugs.
(a) Outline what would be involved in undergoing stress inoculation therapy to treat her stress. *(4 marks)*
(b) Explain **one** limitation of using stress inoculation therapy to treat her stress. *(3 marks)*
(c) Her doctor actually thinks that using drugs might be a better solution for Tanya. Identify a suitable drug and explain how it works. *(4 marks)*
(d) Explain **one** limitation of using drugs to treat her stress. *(3 marks)*

(a) The therapist would try to change the way that Tanya thinks about her stress by trying to inoculate her against stress. Stress inoculation therapy was invented by Meichenbaum as a way of protecting people from the adverse effects of stressors in much the same way that people can be inoculated against other diseases. This would involve changing the way she thinks about stress so that in future when she was in a similar situation (e.g. her next performance) she wouldn't be as stressed.

(b) A limitation is that stress inoculation therapy is not as effective at getting rid of stress as using drugs. Drugs like BZs and beta-blockers have been shown to be very effective for stage fright.

(c) A suitable drug would be a benzodiazepine (BZ). This works by enhancing the action of GABA. BZs slow down the action of the central nervous system, which then calms the person down so that they feel less stressed. This would make Tanya less anxious whenever she went on stage.

(d) The trouble with BZs is that people can become addicted to them if they take them for a long time. They also have a number of side effects including memory impairment. This would not be very good for an actress because she might forget her lines!

(a) Tanya might be treated using stress inoculation. This involves developing the necessary skills and confidence to deal with stressors so they are no longer stressful for the individual. In the conceptualisation phase Tanya would be taught to think differently about her performances, e.g. to think of them as a bit of fun. In the skills acquisition phase she could be taught coping skills (e.g. positive thinking and relaxation) that she can practise during and between performances. In the application phase, these learned skills can be applied in increasingly stressful situations, from rehearsals to live performances.

(b) A limitation is that it is time-consuming. Given the fact that she is already stressed about having to learn her lines, she may decide she cannot afford to spend the time and effort required to embark on this form of therapy. She may instead prefer the relatively 'quick fix' of a drug treatment such as a beta-blocker.

(c) A suitable drug would be a beta-blocker. This works by reducing the action of adrenaline and noradrenaline, which are part of the sympathomedullary response to chronic stress. Beta-blockers bind to and block receptors on the surface of the heart and in other parts of the body that are stimulated when the person is in a state of arousal. When these receptors are blocked, it is harder to stimulate cells of the heart, with the result that the heart beats slower and with less force, and the person feels calmer and less anxious.

(d) A problem with using beta-blockers to treat Tanya's stage fright is that they are only effective as long as she continues to take them. As soon as she stops taking the drug, she will be anxious again, because she has done nothing to address the cause of her stress, only applied a temporary 'bandage' to her problem.

(a) Stress inoculation therapy is creditworthy here as a form of CBT (but that may not always be the case – see exam advice at top of page). Amalia has focused on the techniques and thus gets the **full 4 marks**, whereas Rhys has given very little relevant information and would receive **1 out of 4 marks**.

(b) Rhys would receive **1 out of 3 marks** for identifying a limitation but the elaboration is really just a repetition of the point already made. Amalia's elaboration provides context and then gives a further comment (the three-point rule, so **full marks**.

(c) Amalia's answer is very detailed, more detailed than required for the **full 4 marks**. Rhys' answer is clearly less detailed but he has identified a suitable drug and given sufficient detail for the **full 4 marks**.

(d) Again, **full marks** for Amalia because she has provided appropriate elaboration of the limitation identified. Rhys has made the mistake of identifying two limitations whereas only one was required. Therefore the examiner will decide which of the two limitations will gain most credit – the second one is better, so he would get **2 out of 3 marks**.

Question 3 Outline **one** study that has demonstrated the effectiveness of stress inoculation therapy. *(6 marks)*

Meichenbaum compared the use of stress inoculation therapy to systematic desensitisation for people suffering from snake phobia. He found that, although both types of therapy were effective at relieving the phobia, stress inoculation therapy was more effective than systematic desensitisation and people were less afraid of snakes after receiving this therapy. This shows that stress inoculation is an effective form of therapy, particularly when dealing with the anxiety that people experience when faced with things they fear.

Sheehy and Horan (2004) studied the effects of stress inoculation therapy (SIT) on the stress and academic performance of first-year law students. Of the 29 students who originally volunteered to take part in the SIT treatment programme, seven withdrew at the beginning of the academic year, claiming that the time commitment was too much for an already heavy workload. The remaining students met with their counsellors for a series of 90-minute weekly sessions of SIT over a four-week period. Compared with students who received no SIT, those who received SIT showed lower levels of anxiety due to stress. More than half of the students who received SIT significantly improved their academic performance, measured in terms of predicted class rank.

Both candidates have done well to know details of an appropriate study. There is no requirement in the question for just procedures or findings/conclusions so all the material is creditworthy. Amalia's answer is clearly worth the **full 6 marks**, and Rhys' answer is not far off. He has included lots of detail but not quite enough for the full marks, so **5 out of 6 marks**.

Extended writing question

Outline and evaluate **one or more** psychological methods of stress management.

(12 marks)

EXAM ADVICE
Students often get confused in an exam between the words 'psychological' and 'biological'. When you are answering a question that says 'Discuss biological methods' read it three times to treble check you are writing the right essay – otherwise you could lose a lot of marks.

AO1

> Hardiness training is a psychological method of stress management – but here the focus is more on the hardy personality rather than on how hardiness can be trained – so this paragraph receives little credit.

> The method is described in the second paragraph.

Kobasa and Maddi (1977) identified the hardy personality as being particularly resistant to stress and believed that they could train people to increase their hardiness and so make them more resistant to the effects of stress. People who are high in hardiness see themselves as being in control of their lives, have a strong sense of commitment to whatever they are doing, and see problems as challenges to be overcome rather than insurmountable threats or stressors.

Hardiness training has three phases. In the focusing phase the client is taught to identify the sources of stress in their life, and to recognise the biological signs of stress such as increased heart rate or muscle tension. The client is then encouraged to relive previous stressful situations and to analyse how they responded to them, and whether these responses were effective. In the final phase, self-improvement, they are taught new techniques, for example how to see stressors as challenges they can take control of rather than as a problem they must give in to.

Hardiness training has been shown to be effective in many different situations and with many different populations. For example, Maddi (2002), in a study of managers, compared a hardiness training condition with a meditation condition and a placebo control condition. Hardiness training was more effective than the other conditions in increasing self-reported hardiness and job satisfaction while decreasing self-reported stress and the severity of any stress-related illness. Hardiness training has also helped Olympic swimmers to control stressful events in their life that might otherwise interfere with their training schedule (Lancer, 2000).

A limitation of hardiness training is the problem of having to overcome aspects of personality (e.g. stubbornness or reluctance to change) and maladaptive habits of coping that are difficult to modify. It cannot, therefore, be seen as a rapid method of stress management. Hull et al. (1987) argue that, whereas commitment tends to be positively related to control and both related to resistance to stress, challenge is not related, and therefore is not seen as a necessary aspect of hardiness training.

(345 words)

AO2

> Two pieces of research evidence are used to demonstrate the effectiveness of hardiness training, providing effective evaluation in depth.

> There is no requirement for both strengths and limitations but it does help to increase the breadth of the answer.

> Two limitations are discussed in reasonable depth – both points could be explained more fully.

Examiner's comments It is possible to achieve full marks with just one method of stress – as here. However, precious time has been wasted on a description (AO1) of the hardy personality rather than just focusing on the therapy. Nevertheless, the therapy is described in fair detail so **5 out of 6 marks**.

The evaluation (AO2) is quite sophisticated, covering a broad range of points in reasonable detail, so **6 out of 6 marks**.

Total = **11 out of 12 marks**, a **Grade A** answer.

Extended writing question

Outline and evaluate biological methods of stress management.

(12 marks)

AO1

> Two physiological methods are outlined. They are both examples of drug therapies but count as two methods because the different effects of each drug are presented.

Biological methods focus only on reducing the negative emotions associated with stress, e.g. by making a person more relaxed and less anxious. Drug treatments are an example of a biological method of stress management. For example, benzodiazepines (BZs) work by increasing the action of GABA, which is a natural tranquiliser in the brain. BZs slow down the action of the central nervous system, which then calms the person down so that they feel less stressed. Another type of drug used in stress management is beta-blockers. These work by blocking the action of adrenaline and noradrenaline. These hormones are part of the body's fight or flight response, and cause the heart to beat faster and blood pressure to rise. Beta-blockers reduce their action, and so make the heart beat slower and help the person to feel less anxious whenever they are in a stressful situation.

The trouble with drug treatments is that people can become addicted to them if they take them for a long time (particularly BZs). They can also have a number of unpleasant side effects, which would stop people from taking them. A problem with all drug treatments is that they do not address the problem itself, but just deal with the emotions that arise from it. If treatment ends (i.e. the person stops taking the drug), then the stressor is still there and the symptoms return. An alternative to drug treatments is stress inoculation therapy. This works by inoculating people against stressful situations and making them better prepared to deal with stress in the future. SIT has been shown to be effective with a variety of stressful situations, such as fear of snakes. Another alternative to drug treatments is hardiness training, where people are trained to take control of their lives and see stressors as challenges to be overcome rather than as threats to be feared. Both of these are effective as methods of stress management and can be used as an alternative or in conjunction with drug treatments.

(332 words)

AO2

> Two criticisms of drug therapies are given, each with some elaboration.

> A further critical point is made about an alternative treatment but there is no credit for *describing* this alternative method. There would be credit for comparing the relative effectiveness of each method.

> The final sentence has some creditworthiness.

Examiner's comments In this essay you are required to outline and evaluate a minimum of **two** biological methods, which has been done here. The description (AO1) includes enough detail for the full **6 out of 6 marks**.

The problem in terms of evaluation (AO2) is that **two** biological methods of stress management need to be evaluated – which would be achieved if both BZs and beta-blockers were evaluated, but that is not the case. This means the maximum mark is 4 out of 6 for partial performance. This would be awarded if there was a broad range of points in reasonable depth – which there isn't, so **2 out of 6 marks**.

Total = **8 out of 12 marks**, a **Grade B**.

Extra questions for you

Some further examples of questions requiring you to apply your knowledge to novel situations.

Question 1 Caspian had just started his first year at the University of Candleford. He is worried about leaving Lark Rise, about making new friends, the heavy workload, coping without his mum and even what his girlfriend would be up to while he is away. After two weeks of worry, he rings home in tears and tells his mum he can't cope with university life. His tutor tells him he is stressed and mutters something about the pituitary-adrenal system. His dad tells him he needs to grow up and stop complaining.

From your study of the effects of stress, what does Caspian's tutor mean by his claim that Caspian's state is 'something to do with the pituitary-adrenal system'? *(4 marks)*

Question 2 Caspian sticks it out for a bit longer but two weeks later he comes down with a heavy dose of 'man 'flu'. He feels listless and lethargic so phones his mum and tells her he has had enough and wants to come home. His tutor tells him his stress has affected his immune system. His mum tells him he isn't eating properly.

From your knowledge of research in this area, explain why Caspian's tutor feels that Caspian's stress has affected his immune system. *(4 marks)*

Question 3 Meanwhile, back in sleepy Lark Rise, Caspian's mother has found herself suffering from a stress-related illness since his departure. It has been an eventful year for her, her son left home, she had lost her job at the local mill, and now, at the age of 45, she has found herself pregnant! She rings Caspian's tutor who tells her she is stressed because of the life changes she has experienced over the past 12 months.

With reference to research, explain the relationship between Caspian's mother's illness and the life changes she has experienced. *(6 marks)*

Question 4 Caspian's tutor has had enough. Instead of spending a relaxing day browsing through his favourite psychology book *AS Psychology: The Complete Companion*, he has spent the morning with a sobbing Caspian, missed his lunch and then spent the afternoon counselling Caspian's distraught mother over the phone. At going home time he manages to drop his car keys down a drain, where they promptly disappear from view. He stands and screams with frustration. A passing colleague, Dr Smartass, informs him that he is probably stressed because of all his daily hassles. Caspian's tutor punches Dr Smartass.

Is Dr Smartass right? When he comes around, what evidence could Dr Smartass use to support his judgement of the reasons for Caspian's tutor's stress? *(6 marks)*

Question 5 Caspian's tutor calls Caspian to arrange to see him and tells him to sort his stress out with drugs, but is unable to explain what this means as he is busy clearing his desk, having been dismissed for assaulting a colleague.

(a) Identify **two** types of drug that might be appropriate as a form of stress management for Caspian. *(2 marks)*

(b) Outline how each of the drugs identified in (a) work in reducing stress. *(4 marks)*

Question 6 Caspian wonders which would be the best method of stress management to use and manages to catch up with his tutor, who says 'Work it out for yourself'. Which of the four methods you have outlined in question 5 is best?

(a) Outline what is meant by 'hardiness training'. *(3 marks)*

(b) Outline **two** reasons why Caspian should consider engaging in some hardiness training. *(4 marks)*

Question 7 Caspian's tutor realises that he needs help himself to cope with his increasing levels of anxiety since losing his job, and wonders if Cognitive Behavioural Therapy might help him deal with his stress.

(a) Describe what would be involved in stress inoculation therapy for treating stress. *(3 marks)*

(b) Explain **one** limitation with choosing this method. *(3 marks)*

Question 1   A psychologist who is studying stress decides to ask people about their stress experiences.

(a) Explain why it might be better to use an interview technique rather than a questionnaire. *(4 marks)*

(b) Explain why it might be better to use a questionnaire instead of interviewing the participants. *(4 marks)*

(c) (i) The psychologist also needs to think about the kind of questions she asks.
Give an example of a question that she could use that would produce quantitative data. *(2 marks)*

 (ii) Explain why it is preferable to use questions that produce quantitative data rather than qualitative data. *(3 marks)*

 (iii) Give an example of a question that she could use that would produce qualitative data. *(2 marks)*

 (iv) Explain why it is preferable to use questions that produce qualitative data rather than quantitative data. *(3 marks)*

Question 2   A study looked at the difference between men and women and their preference for psychological or biological methods of stress management. The bar chart shows the results from the study.

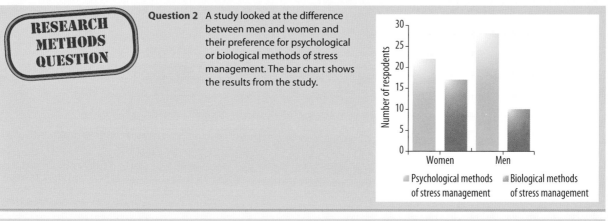

(a) (i) Outline **one** example of a psychological method of stress management. *(2 marks)*

 (ii) Outline **one** example of a biological method of stress management. *(2 marks)*

(b) What does the bar chart show about gender preferences for the different methods of stress management? *(4 marks)*

(c) The researcher decided the data might be clearer if it was placed in a table.
Draw a suitable table for the data, and place the values from the graph in your table. *(4 marks)*

(d) (i) The data for this study was collected using a questionnaire. One of the problems with questionnaires is they sometimes lack reliability. Explain what is meant by a questionnaire lacking reliability. *(3 marks)*

 (ii) Explain how you could assess the reliability of the questionnaire. *(8 marks)*

Question 3

(a) Outline **one** study that has investigated Type A behaviour. *(6 marks)*

(b) Explain **one** limitation of the method(s) used in this study. *(3 marks)*

(c) Explain **one** possible problem with the validity of this study and say how it might be dealt with. *(4 marks)*

(d) Identify **one** ethical issue that might arise in this study and explain how it would be dealt with. *(3 marks)*

SPECIFICATION BREAKDOWN

Specification content	Comment

Social influence

- Conformity (majority influence), types of conformity, including internalisation and compliance.

- Explanations of why people conform, including informational social influence and normative social influence.

- Obedience, including Milgram's work.

- Explanations of why people obey.

Your study of social influence starts with the topic of conformity – your behaviour is in part influenced by what *most* people do (i.e. majority influence). Behaviour is also sometimes influenced by the views and behaviour of single individuals (the minority). In the case of conformity individuals are usually merely *complying*, i.e. following the behaviour of others but not changing what they believe. In the case of minority influence, personal views may be changed so that the behaviour of others has become *internalised*.

You also study explanations for why people conform. The two most common explanations are informational social influence (we conform in order to do the right thing) and normative social influence (we conform to gain acceptance and to not be rejected by the 'crowd').

Your behaviour is not only indirectly influenced by others but could be changed by *direct* orders from others. The classic study of obedience was conducted by Stanley Milgram because he wanted to investigate the validity of the 'only obeying orders' defence of the Nazi war criminals. Milgram conducted a range of obedience studies in different settings which demonstrated that obedience can be explained in terms of situational factors (i.e. obedience occurs because of factors in the situation which trigger it).

Social influence in everyday life

- Explanations of independent behaviour, including locus of control how people resist pressures to conform and resist pressures to obey authority.

- How social influence research helps us to understand social change; the role of minority influence in social change

There are many explanations of independent behaviour. Some of these are based on personality differences, such as locus of control, the degree to which an individual feels they are responsible for their own behaviour or controlled by external factors. The ability to behave independently may also be governed by personal characteristics of the individual (e.g. morality) or may be a consequence of situational factors such as the presence of allies or the status of the authority figure.

We end this section by looking at how social influence research can be used to understand the process of social change – how the views and behaviour of any social group change over time. Many of these implications can be gleaned by studying the processes of minority influence and how these have been demonstrated in real-life social change.

Chapter 4

SOCIAL PSYCHOLOGY is the study of the nature and causes of human social behaviour. Social psychologists are particularly interested in the influence that other people have on our behaviour as we interact with them in our social world.

CHAPTER CONTENTS

Social psychology:
social influence

Conformity

Question 1   The statements below describe types of social influence. Tick the three statements that apply to conformity.   *(3 marks)*

- [ ] Behaving in response to direct orders from a person in authority.
- [x] Tendency to adopt the behaviour of a majority group.
- [x] Changing your views as a result of persuasive arguments.
- [x] Behaving in a way to gain social approval.
- [ ] Accepting influence because it fits in with your own thinking.

FULL MARKS!

Question 2   Explain what is meant by 'internalisation' and 'compliance' in the context of conformity.   *(2 marks + 2 marks)*

Lachlan's answer

Internalisation means going along with other people because of an acceptance of their point of view, leading to an acceptance of the group's views both in public and in private. Compliance means going along with others to gain their approval or avoid their disapproval, leading to an acceptance of the group's view in public but not in private.

Rosie's answer

Internalisation is like when someone does something because they have seen others doing it and believe it is the right thing to do. Compliance is going along with others because they have power over you.

Examiner's comments

Lachlan's answer is detailed and comprehensive worth more than the **full marks**. Rosie's answers communicate little knowledge. Her first explanation is wrong, so **0 out of 2 marks**, but her second (on compliance) shows a glimmer of understanding for **1 out of 2 marks**.

Question 3   Explain what is meant by 'conformity'.   *(3 marks)*

Conformity is when we choose to think or act in a certain way because that way of thinking or acting seems to be favoured by the majority of group members rather than being the result of our own independent judgement.

Conformity is going along with other people. Another name for it is majority influence. It means doing what everyone else is doing or thinking.

Lachlan again has provided a complete and detailed answer for **full marks**. Rosie's answer contains some elaboration and thus gains **2 out of 3 marks**. The answer is not precise enough for full marks.

Question 4   Outline how psychologists have investigated conformity.   *(6 marks)*

Asch (1956) recruited volunteers to take part in a test of vision, although really this was a study of how participants would react to a majority that gave the same wrong answer in a perceptual task. The task was to judge which of three lines was the same length as a comparison line. On 12 of the 18 trials, the confederates gave the same wrong answer out loud. Conformity was measured in terms of the number of these trials in which the participant, answering second to last, gave the same wrong answer. Other researchers have carried out meta-analyses to investigate whether there are gender differences in conformity (Eagly and Carli, 1981) and whether collectivist cultures show higher levels of conformity than individualist cultures.

Psychologists have investigated conformity using mostly experiments. One experiment was Asch's study. He used an independent groups design, testing people under different conditions, e.g. with a fellow dissenter, with different size majorities, with easy or difficult tasks and so on (independent variable). He could then compare the different levels of conformity that he got as a result (dependent variable). He controlled all other extraneous variables, such as the confederates, the task, the situation and so on.

Lachlan has correctly focused on the methods used to study conformity, as required by the question. He has used more than one study to provide sufficient detail for the **full 6 marks**. Rosie has also managed to focus on methods and not be waylaid by reporting results or conclusions, which would not be creditworthy. She has also provided a range of details although the focus is too much on general methodology and a bit too little on specifically how conformity has been investigated, so **5 out of 6 marks**.

Question 5   Outline what research has shown about conformity.   *(6 marks)*

On the 12 critical trials in Asch's study, 36% of the responses given by participants were the same wrong answer as given by the majority, i.e. conforming responses. When answering in private, participants gave the right answer 99% of the time. Asch found that when the task was made more difficult, conformity rates increased, and when a confederate gave a different answer to the majority, conformity rates dropped dramatically. In two meta-analyses, Eagly and Carli (1981) found women were more compliant than men, and Smith and Bond found that collectivist cultures showed higher levels of conformity than individualist cultures, although they also found that rates of conformity have progressively declined since Asch's original study.

Asch's work on conformity found that the level of conformity was about one-third, in that on one-third of the trials the participant went along with the majority. He also found that when there was a fellow dissenter, conformity levels dropped, even when they gave a different wrong answer to the majority. The larger the majority, the higher the conformity levels, although above four, levels didn't go up much more. When tasks were more difficult levels of conformity rose, and when they were easy levels dropped.

Again both candidates have avoided one of the biggest pitfalls – failing to answer the question by, for example, writing about procedures instead of focusing solely (as required in this question) on findings/conclusions. Lachlan's answer is extremely detailed, providing information from various studies. He deserves **full marks**. Rosie has managed to pack a lot into a short answer, often providing extra detail (e.g. 'although above four, levels didn't go up much more') which makes her answer worth **5 out of 6 marks**.

Question 6   Sumita recently moved with her family to a new town and started school there. As you probably know, it is difficult when you go to a new school because everyone has friends and you just want people to like you.
The girls in Sumita's class all wear very short skirts and Sumita thinks she should dress like this in order to fit in, but she doesn't like short skirts because her family prefer less revealing clothes (for religious and cultural reasons).
Use the concepts of conformity, compliance and internalisation to explain Sumita's behaviour.   *(6 marks)*

Because Sumita has just started her new school, she will experience considerable pressure to fit in, i.e. to conform. Asch found that people are likely to conform out of a desire to fit in and be accepted by the majority (compliance) even though it may go against their true beliefs. By wearing a short skirt she will fit in and be accepted, but this doesn't mean she agrees with the practice of wearing short skirts. It is possible that the majority of women in her family wear much less revealing clothes for religious and cultural reasons, and this is a practice that she accepts as being the right thing to do when with her family (internalisation).

Conformity is going along with the majority. Sumita is doing this by wearing a short skirt. Compliance is doing things to be accepted. She believes she will be accepted if she wears a short skirt. Internalisation is when you do something because you believe what the majority tell you, e.g. the majority may convince her that short skirts are far more fashionable than what she usually wears.

Lachlan's answer is excellent, making reference to psychological research and using his psychological knowledge to explain all three concepts, **full 6 marks**. Rosie has explained the meaning of each term and tried to link this meaning to Sumita's behaviour. Rosie's answer is reasonable for conformity and compliance (although neither is very detailed) but becomes muddled with the final term, internalisation. The question stem makes it clear that Sumita has not internalised the behaviour. Rosie's answer gains **4 out of 6 marks**.

A psychologist investigated conformity by putting smarties in a jar and then asking people to guess how many there were. The participants were asked to write their estimates on a special form, which also showed what previous people had estimated. For one group of participants the previous estimates were high (more than 80), whereas for the other group of participants the previous estimates were low (less than 50). The results are shown in the table.

Table showing the mean estimates for each group

	Group with high estimates (more than 80)	Group with low estimates (less than 50)
Boys	95	42
Girls	81	56

(a) What can you conclude about conformity from the results of this study? *(4 marks)*

Lachlan's answer

I can conclude that people are likely to conform to the majority when the task is ambiguous. This is demonstrated by the fact that both boys and girls agreed with the majority decision of over 80. The second conclusion is that girls were less influenced by the majority than the boys, indicated by the lower mean estimates when the >80 group and higher when in the <50 group.

Rosie's answer

I would conclude that girls don't conform as much as boys, because their estimates are less affected by the estimates of the majority as shown them by the researchers before they make their own estimates of how many smarties there are in the jar.

Examiner's comments

Rosie has only provided one conclusion whereas Lachlan has teased out two conclusions but both candidates have given conclusions and linked these to findings, rather than just describing the figures in the table. So **2 out of 4 marks** for Rosie and **full marks** for Lachlan.

(b) The values given in the table are 'mean' values. Explain what the 'mean' refers to. *(2 marks)*

The mean is the arithmetic average, e.g. in this case the sum total of all male estimates in the >80 condition, divided by the number of males taking part in that particular condition.

Mean means average. In this study the means are calculated for males and females in the more than 80 and less than 50 smarties conditions.

Rosie hasn't <u>explained</u> what the word 'mean' refers to beyond saying it is an average, so **0 marks** and the **full marks** for Lachlan.

(c) Identify **one** limitation of this study and suggest how you could deal with it. *(3 marks)*

A limitation of this study is that there is a possibility that the task is gender biased (i.e. a maths based estimating problem), and this might influence the levels of conformity found for males and females. This can be dealt with by using a more neutral task that favours neither males nor females, as this would give a more accurate reflection of conformity levels without the influence of a task variable.

A limitation is that they are using smarties. Some people may be more used to smarties because they like them, so would be more accurate at guessing how many there are because they are more used to handling them and know, for example, how many there are in a packet and what that many looks like when put in a jar.

A well informed answer from Lachlan for the **full 3 marks**. Rosie's answer might appear creditworthy but it really makes little sense – being familiar with smarties wouldn't necessarily make you better at guessing and it certainly doesn't explain why girls might be better than boys, so **0 marks** for Rosie.

Extended writing question

Outline and evaluate research relating to conformity. *(12 marks)*

AO1

An accurate and detailed description of the classic piece of research on conformity by Asch.

A second study by Perrin and Spencer is described – which could have been used as a form of evaluation because of the contrasting findings. But as it is this study counts as description.

A third study is described, this time a meta-analysis by Eagly and Carli.

A fourth study by Smith and Bond is described.

Asch (1956) recruited volunteers to take part in a test of vision, although really this was a study of how participants would react to a majority that gave the same wrong answer in a perceptual task. The task was to judge which of three lines was the same length as a comparison line. On 12 of the 18 trials, the confederates gave the same wrong answer out loud. Conformity was measured in terms of the number of these trials in which the participant, answering second to last, gave the same wrong answer. On the 12 critical trials in Asch's study, 36% of the responses given by student participants were the same wrong answer as given by the majority, i.e. conforming responses. When answering in private, participants gave the right answer 99% of the time. Asch found that when the task was made more difficult, conformity rates increased, and when a confederate gave a different answer to the majority, conformity rates dropped dramatically.

Perrin and Spencer (1980) attempted to replicate Asch's study with UK students. They found extremely low levels of conformity, but when they made the costs of perceived non-conforming to be high (e.g. when using youths on probation as participants and probation officers as the majority), the levels of conformity rose to nearly those obtained by Asch. They concluded that the 'costs' of not conforming in the original Asch study were largely due to the fact that when this study was carried out, US students were far more conformist because the USA was in a period known as McCarthyism, which repressed liberal thinking and non-conformity.

Eagly and Carli (1981) carried out a meta-analysis of 145 studies and found that women showed higher levels of conformity than men. However, they suggested that this may have more to do with the experimental tasks used in these studies, which favoured men. Other studies that have used more neutral experimental tasks have not tended to find gender differences in conformity levels. In another meta-analysis, Smith and Bond found that collectivist cultures show higher levels of conformity than individualist cultures, although they also found that rates of conformity have progressively declined since Asch's original study. They found a negative correlation between the date of publication and the levels of conformity found, with more recent studies showing the lowest levels of conformity.

(387 words)

AO2

The conclusion from this study counts as evaluation as it provides an interpretation of the results of the previous studies.

Two brief points of evaluation referring to methodological issues (the type of experimental task) and to other studies that have not found a gender difference.

Examiner's comments

The descriptive (AO1) material is both accurate and detailed and also plentiful – more than necessary for **6 out of 6 marks**. In fact some of the descriptive material would have been more effectively developed into evaluation.

The evaluation (AO2) consists of one well elaborated conclusion, which could have been phrased more effectively, and two brief points (superficial consideration), so **3 out of 6 marks**.

Total = **9 out of 12 marks** – which just about makes a **Grade A** answer – but the same material could have been woven into an even better answer if structured differently.

Explanations of why people conform

Question 1 The following are all explanations of why people conform.

    A The result of wanting to be right.   **C** Conformity to fit in.

    B The result of wanting to be liked.   **D** Conforming because of uncertainty.

In the table below, write which statement applies to explanations.

(4 marks)

Informational social influence	A, D
Normative social influence	B, C

FULL MARKS!

Question 2 Explain the terms 'informational social influence' and 'normative social influence'. *(3 marks + 3 marks)*

Lukas' answer

Informational social influence is when the group provides a person with information, which they then use to make their decision. It is conformity based on that information.

Normative social influence is when a person does what everybody else in the group does, because they feel that if they don't they will be ostracised by the group. It is conformity based on the need to be liked.

Marion's answer

Informational social influence occurs when an individual goes along with the majority because they believe them to be right, or that they have more information about a particular issue than the individual has. This is more likely to result in an individual changing their behaviour (in public) and their attitude (in private).

Normative social influence occurs when an individual acts in the same way as the majority or agrees with them without actually accepting their viewpoint. This is because they want to be accepted by the majority. This results in the individual changing their behaviour in public but not changing their attitude in private.

Examiner's comments

Lukas' explanation of informational social influence reads a little bit like guesswork – using the word 'information' to explain informational is both circular and uninformative, **0 marks**. Lukas' second answer is much better and worth **2 out of 3 marks** for the two points made about fear of being ostracised and need to be liked.

Marion's answer is accurate and detailed for **full marks** both times. She has also used the word 'information' in her first explanation – but there is plenty of other detail to compensate for this.

Question 3 Explain the difference between informational social influence and normative social influence. *(4 marks)*

Informational social influence is when the group provides a person with information, which they then use to make their decision, whereas normative social influence is when a person does what everybody else in the group does, because they feel that if they don't they will be ostracised by the group.

The difference between the two is that informational social influence is motivated by a desire to act in the right way based on the information that the group provides, and so produces changes in both public behaviour and private attitudes. Normative social influence on the other hand is motivated by a desire to be accepted by the group and so produces change in public behaviour only and no change in private attitudes.

The key point here is that the answer to question 3 should be different to question 2 because this time **one or more** differences are required. Marion has focused on one difference – what motivates the behaviour (and gets **full marks**). Lukas hasn't done much more than juxtapose two explanations using 'whereas', which isn't enough for more than **1 out of 4 marks**.

Question 4 Outline one research study that demonstrated normative social influence. *(4 marks)*

Asch studied whether people would give the same wrong answer as a majority when shown three lines and asked to judge which was the same length as a comparison line. About 30% of the time the individual went along with the majority and gave the same wrong answer. This level of conformity dropped dramatically when Asch introduced another person who agreed with the individual.

A study by Garandeau and Cillessen (2006) found that children with few friends (and therefore more in need of social acceptance from others) were more likely to comply to pressure exerted by a bully and other group members to victimise another child. By conforming to the actions of the bullying group they could maintain the friendship of the other group members regardless of how they felt towards the victimised child or to the practice of bullying.

Marion has dug deep with this study and provided ample detail of the study for **full marks**. Lukas' choice is the obvious one by Asch which is related to normative social influence and therefore creditworthy. The details are limited and therefore **3 out of 4 marks**. There is no requirement to explain why the study is related to normative social influence – although it's always a good idea to do this in such questions (as Marion has).

Question 5 Outline one research study that demonstrated informational social influence. *(4 marks)*

Asch studied whether people would give the same wrong answer as a majority when shown three lines and asked to judge which of them was the same length as a comparison line. He found that 36% gave the same answer as the majority, even though it was wrong. When he interviewed them afterwards, some of them said that they thought the majority must be right, so agreed with them. This is an example of informational social influence.

Fein et al. (2007) showed participants a film of a US presidential debate. They also saw what was supposedly the reaction of the other group members towards the different points that the candidates were making. When individual participants were then asked about their opinion of each of the candidates' performances in the debate, they shifted in the direction of what they thought was the opinion of the majority of other group members.

Lukas has used the same study this time but has explained why it is also an example of informational social influence. This time he has given a more precise figure for the results (it was in fact 36.8% conformity on the 12 critical trials) but this only makes a small contribution to the overall detail which again is worth **3 out of 4 marks**. Marion deserves the **full 4 marks**.

Question 6 Women today are far thinner, on average, than they used to be. One explanation that is offered for this is the fact that models in magazines are exceptionally thin.

Use your knowledge of conformity to explain how the models in magazines may be influencing the attitudes of women today. *(4 marks)*

Because many magazines feature women models in their pages who are supposed to represent what 'normal' people look like, a reader may think they have to conform to that look to be accepted. So if the model is very thin, the reader feels they are under pressure to become thin themselves otherwise they won't be accepted. Also they begin to dress like the models they see in magazines and wear their hair like them (e.g. Victoria Beckham).

Women may feel that because the models are happy and popular, that being thin must be the key to being accepted and liked by others, an example of normative social influence. As a result, they attempt to bring their weight down to that of the models they see in magazines. Women may also believe that these models are better informed about the beneficial effects of being thin (e.g. for health and well-being), and so accept that by conforming to their behaviour, they will also be healthy and will feel better about their body.

Both candidates have presented reasonable explanations and have talked about people being influenced by magazine models because they want to be liked or accepted which acknowledges psychological research. Marion has made specific mention of psychological research when referring to normative social influence – so the **full 4 marks** for her and just **3 out of 4 marks** for Lukas.

RESEARCH METHODS QUESTION

(a) Outline **one** method psychologists have used to investigate conformity. *(2 marks)*

Lukas' answer

Asch sat people round a table and all were confederates except one who was the naïve participant. They had to judge the length of lines, but the confederates all gave the same wrong answer and Asch wanted to see if the real participant followed them.

Marion's answer

Eagly and Carli's study was a meta-analysis, which looked at the results of many studies of conformity to see if there were any trends in the data (in this case gender differences).

Examiner's comments

Both answers are sufficiently detailed and focus solely on methods, as required, so **full marks** for both candidates.

(b) Describe **two** problems with validity that occur in conformity research. *(2 marks + 2 marks)*

Asch only used students in his study and students are not representative of the general population.

His research doesn't tell us how people would react in real life (e.g. in juries), as it is a lab study.

Asch's study involved a relatively trivial task, therefore the fact that there was a relatively high degree of conformity cannot be used to indicate that people would conform quite so readily in more important tasks, so the study lacks external validity.

This study took place during a very specific period of history, McCarthyism, and more modern research has found much lower levels of conformity, so the study lacks historical validity.

Marion has provided a high level of detail in her criticisms, following the three-point rule (see page 10), **full marks**.

Lukas' answers lack sufficient elaboration. For full marks we need to know why students are not representative and we need to know why a lab study wouldn't relate to real life. So **1 out of 2 marks** for each answer.

Extended writing question

Outline and evaluate one or more explanations of why people conform. *(12 marks)*

Answer 1

AO1

A basic explanation of normative social influence.

A basic explanation of informational social influence.

A third explanation is given – socialisation, which is reasonably detailed.

One explanation is normative social influence. This is when people want the group to like them so they go along with the group even though they don't want to. This is also known as compliance. This was supported by Asch's study because people went along with the majority even though they knew the majority had got it wrong. A problem with this explanation is that it might only apply to some types of conformity (e.g. comparing line lengths) and not to more important things like religion. Another explanation is informational social influence. This is when people do what the majority does because they think the majority know something that they don't or when it might be dangerous to act in the wrong way. A problem with this explanation is that there hasn't been much research on this so we don't know if this is really true. Some people conform because they are socialised into conforming. For example, they grow up in a society where they are supposed to do as they are told and not question rules. This produces a very conforming society. An example of a conforming society would be China, whereas in the USA people would be much less likely to conform. Research has supported this, with the finding that people who live in societies such as China are much more likely to conform than people who live in societies such as the USA or the UK.

(239 words)

AO2

Asch's study is used to support but no elaboration is given.

A good critical point is made, although somewhat superficial.

A very weak critical point and incorrect – there is plenty of research.

A further reference to research support, with some depth.

Examiner's comments The description (**AO1**) is generally basic but the quantity lifts this to **4 out of 6 marks**. The evaluation (**AO2**) is generally superficial and restricted in terms of range, so **3 out of 6 marks**.
Total = **7 out of 12 marks**, a **Grade C**.

Answer 2

AO1

A detailed description of informational social influence.

A detailed description of normative social influence.

Informational social influence occurs when an individual goes along with the majority because they believe them to be right, or that they have more information about a particular issue than the individual has. This is more likely to result in an individual changing their behaviour (in public) and their attitude (in private). Informational social influence is more likely when the situation is ambiguous, so that the individual is not sure what is the best course of action, and also likely when it is a crisis and so rapid action is required, and also when they believe others to be experts in that particular situation.

This explanation of conformity is supported by research. For example, Fein et al. (2007) showed participants a film of a US presidential debate and also what they were led to believe was the reaction of other group members towards the points that the candidates were making. When participants were then asked about their opinion of each of the candidates' performances, they shifted in the direction of what they thought was the opinion of the majority of other group members. This also offers an insight into how social stereotypes form, with research by Wittenbrink and Henly (1996) demonstrating that participants given negative information about African Americans that they thought was the view of the majority were then more likely to report more negative beliefs about a black individual.

Normative social influence occurs when an individual acts in the same way as the majority or agrees with them without actually accepting their viewpoint. This is because they want to be accepted by the majority or don't want to be rejected. This results in the individual changing their behaviour in public but not changing their attitude in private. Because human beings are a social species, they have a strong need for social acceptance and a fear of rejection, which explains the motivation for normative social influence.

This explanation has been used to give an insight into why some children are drawn into bullying others, even though they are clearly uncomfortable with it. Garandeau and Cillessen (2006) found that children who were more in need of social acceptance were more likely to comply to pressure exerted by a bullying group to victimise another child. By conforming to the actions of the bullying group they could maintain the friendship of the other group members regardless of how they felt towards the practice of bullying.

(403 words)

AO2

Effective research support from two studies. It is preferable to provide names and dates but not required for full marks. What is most important is that the study is identifiable in some way, i.e. there is some elaboration – but not too much description because that then becomes AO1.

Further, effective and elaborated research support.

Examiner's comments Worth **12 out of 12 marks, Grade A**.

Obedience

Question 1 Explain what is meant by 'obedience'. *(3 marks)*

Stanley's answer

Obedience is when someone carries out an order that has been given to them by a figure in authority (e.g. an army officer), something that they would not have done without having been ordered to do so.

Alexandra's answer

Obedience is when you obey someone like a policeman or a teacher.

Examiner's comments

Stanley's answer is clearly worth the **full 3 marks** whereas Alexandra's contains so little, so **0 out of 3 marks**.

Question 2 Conformity and obedience are two kinds of social influence. Explain the difference between conformity and obedience. *(4 marks)*

Conformity involves social pressure that is felt by an individual merely because they are aware of the opinions of a majority. There is no direct pressure to behave in the same way. Obedience, on the other hand, involves social pressure that is more direct, with an individual being pressured by an individual in authority to behave in a certain way.

Conformity is when someone does something because they see the majority of other group members doing it or they have the same attitudes as the majority so they can be accepted. Obedience is when someone obeys an order from someone in authority such as a policeman.

Alexandra has made the mistake of merely defining both terms and not made any attempt to identify a dimension on which they differ, so only **1 out of 4 marks**. Notice how Stanley has clearly identified a difference – social pressure – and has elaborated the difference. He receives **full marks**.

Question 3 Outline what research has shown about obedience. *(6 marks)*

Milgram (1963) found that 65% of participants followed the experimenter's orders and gave the maximum shock level to a learner in a simulated learning task. He found that this level of obedience decreased when the learner was visible to the participant and could also be heard, and decreased when the authority figure was not in the same room as the participant and gave their orders over the phone. Obedience levels (the percentage of participants who continued to the maximum 450 volts) increased to their highest level when two obedient confederates appeared happy to give shocks and decreased dramatically when two confederates refused to continue giving shocks.

Milgram used 40 male participants who had to give electric shocks to an actor who was supposed to be learning word pairs. Milgram found that 26 of the 40 participants went all the way and gave the full 400 volts. He also had a condition where the 'teacher' had to force the learner's hand to receive an electric shock. Not as many participants went to the maximum shock level under this condition. When the learner claimed he had a heart condition this made no difference to the number of participants who went to the maximum shock level.

Stanley has again provided a detailed and extensive answer for the **full 6 out of 6 marks**.

Alexandra has written a lot about the procedures ('how') and only given two findings, so perhaps a rather mean **2 out of 6 marks**.

 **RESEARCH METHODS QUESTION** Milgram conducted one of the best known studies of obedience. People have argued that his study is famous possibly because of the surprising findings or possibly because of the unethical methods he used.

(a) Outline how Milgram investigated obedience. *(4 marks)*

Stanley's answer

Milgram used male volunteers in a series of lab experiments to study the impact of orders from an authority figure. The volunteers acted as a 'teacher' in a word association task, with a confederate acting as the 'learner'. Learner errors were to be punished by increasing levels of electric shock delivered by the teacher. These were designed to investigate the effect on obedience of various situational manipulations, including bringing the learner closer to the teacher, moving the authority figure away from the teacher, and introducing compliant or resistant confederates. Obedience was measured by the percentage who went all the way to 450V.

Alexandra's answer

Milgram advertised for volunteers to take part in his study. When they got to the lab, they were introduced to Mr Wallace, who was really an actor. They drew lots to see who would be teacher and learner. It was rigged so Mr Wallace was always the learner. The teacher had to give shocks to the learner if he got questions wrong. The shocks got bigger and bigger and if they wanted to stop, they were ordered to continue by the authority figure.

Examiner's comments

An excellent and detailed answer from Stanley (it is debatable whether Milgram's study is an experiment but that certainly would not be penalised).

Alexandra's answer is well focused on procedures, as required, but is limited in it's scope (but better than basic) so **3 out of 4 marks** and **full marks** for Stanley.

(b) Explain why people described the results of Milgram's research as surprising. *(3 marks)*

Milgram's results were surprising for two reasons. First, before he started the study he had asked other psychologists to estimate the percentage of participants who would go to 450 volts. Their estimate was less than 1%, whereas 65% actually went to 450 volts. Second, it was believed at the time that only pathological people could inflict harm on others so easily, yet Milgram showed that the majority of ordinary people could be made to do this simply by manipulating aspects of the situation.

Milgram's results were surprising because they were so shocking. People found it hard to believe that ordinary people could kill an innocent person just because he got some questions wrong. This made people think that maybe the Nazis were not evil after all because Milgram's participants had just been ordinary people who, like the Nazis, had been obeying orders.

Another excellent and detailed answer from Stanley for the **full 3 marks**. In fact, he has written more than is necessary.

Alexandra has given an appropriate answer and sufficient detail to also be awarded **full marks**.

(c) Explain why some psychologists have criticised Milgram for conducting unethical research. *(3 marks)*

He was criticised for deception, in that he deceived his participants by telling them the true purpose was to test the effects of punishment on learning (rather than obedience). Participants were not told the pressure they would be put under, therefore were denied informed consent. He also put his participants under considerable stress, therefore did not protect them from psychological harm.

He deceived people by telling them the study was about something else. It was also unethical not to let people leave when they wanted to (right to withdraw). He was also accused of causing his participants harm. A lady psychologist said this wasn't justified.

Both candidates have given a number of ethical criticisms but Stanley's answer is better because he has <u>explained</u> the issues whereas Alexandra has made the mistake of listing lots of points but offering no explanation about why they are issues, so **full marks** for Stanley and just **2 out of 3 marks** for Alexandra.

(d) Milgram defended his research and claimed it was not unethical. Give **one** way he may have justified his research. *(3 marks)*

Milgram claimed that his participants were not harmed, and employed a psychiatrist to interview them looking for any signs of lasting harm. He found none. Milgram claimed the participants suffered only from 'momentary excitement'.

Milgram said he didn't stop people leaving because they were free to leave whenever they wanted and some did.

Alexandra's answer is too brief for more than **1 out of 3 marks**. Stanley's is worth the **full 3 marks**. Note how he has followed the three-point rule (see page 10).

Outline and evaluate research studies relating to obedience.

(12 marks)

Answer 1

AO1

The first paragraph is uncreditworthy as it is concerned with background information to the research. 'Research' refers to explanations as well as studies so the explanations might have been creditworthy if the essay was <u>just</u> asking for research – but here it is specifically 'research studies'.

The second paragraph gives information about Milgram's study, describing the procedures in reasonable detail.

The final paragraph describes the findings of the study, again in reasonable detail.

Obedience is when someone obeys a direct order from somebody in authority such as a teacher or policeman. Milgram claimed that obedience could explain why people did terrible things, because they have been socialised into obeying orders from authority figures. He used the example of the Nazis. Many of these were brought to court for war crimes against Jews, but claimed they had only been obeying orders. Milgram wanted to see if this claim was right and so carried out an experiment, which has become one of the most controversial experiments ever carried out in psychology.

Milgram put an advert in a newspaper and offered $4.50 to people to take part in his study. When they arrived at Yale University many of them would have been in awe of such a prestigious university so would not have acted naturally. This means the results might not have been valid. They met another man, Mr Wallace, who was actually an actor. They then drew lots to see who would be the teacher and who would be the learner, but this was rigged so the real participant was always the teacher. His job was to deliver electric shocks to the learner each time he did something wrong.

The results found that 65% went all the way to 450 volts, even when the learner said he had a heart condition. If the teachers tried to stop, the experimenter said 'you must continue' and 'you have no choice'. Milgram said that the reason so many participants did as they were told was because of agentic shift. However, some people have said that Milgram's study was unethical because he deceived the participants and caused them psychological harm. It can also be criticised because it only used students, and students are not a representative cross-section of society.

(300 words)

AO2

At the end of this paragraph two criticisms are given but these are fairly superficial.

Examiner's comments | The description (**AO1**) presented in the second and third paragraphs is appropriate, clear and coherent, and it is reasonably detailed, so **6 out of 6 marks**.

The evaluation (**AO2**) contains a restricted range of points all of which are superficial, worth **2 out of 6 marks** (this may be a little bit mean but 3 marks seems overly generous; the content is closer to the bottom band 'just discernible' – see mark scheme on page 9).

Total = **8 out of 12 marks**, a **Grade B** answer.

Answer 2

AO1

The first paragraph describes Milgram's first study – procedures and findings.

The second paragraph describes the findings from subsequent studies.

Milgram (1963) used male volunteers in a series of lab experiments to study the impact of orders from an authority figure. These were designed to investigate the effect on obedience of various situational manipulations. Milgram found that 65% of participants followed the experimenter's orders and gave the maximum shock level to a learner in a simulated learning task. He found that this level of obedience decreased when the learner was visible to the participant and could also be heard, and decreased when the authority figure was not in the same room as the participant and gave their orders over the phone.

Obedience levels (the percentage of participants who continued to the maximum 450 volts) increased to their highest level when two obedient confederates appeared happy to give shocks, with almost all participants continuing to the full 450 volts. However, obedience rates decreased dramatically when two confederates working alongside the participant refused to continue giving shocks. In this condition, only 10% of participants continued to the full 450 volts.

Milgram was criticised for deception, in that he deceived his participants by telling them the true purpose was to test the effects of punishment on learning (rather than obedience). Baumrind accused Milgram of putting his participants under considerable stress, therefore he did not protect them from psychological harm. However, Milgram claimed that his participants were not harmed and employed a psychiatrist to interview them looking for any signs of lasting harm. He found none. In his defence, Milgram claimed the participants suffered only from 'momentary excitement'.

Mandel (1998) argued that Milgram's studies of obedience lack real world validity. Milgram had claimed that his research had explained the actions of many Nazi war criminals who had defended themselves by claiming they had only been obeying orders. However, Mandel points out that these claims are not supported by actual events, and uses the example of Reserve Police Battalion 101 to illustrate that situational factors such as physical proximity to the victim or an absent authority figure made no difference to obedience rates for these killers.

(341 words)

AO2

A number of critical points are presented and elaborated. First is the criticism of Milgram's ethics and second is Milgram's defence.

A third critical point is made and elaborated in considerable depth.

Examiner's comments | The description (**AO1**) is reasonably detailed, showing sound knowledge and understanding, **6 out of 6 marks**.

The evaluation (**AO2**) covers a relatively narrow range of points but they are provided in great depth, so is awarded the full **6 out of 6 marks**.

Total = **12 out of 12 marks**, a clear **A grade** answer.

Explanations of why people obey

Question 1 (a) Outline **two** explanations of why people obey. *(3 marks + 3 marks)*
(b) Give **one** criticism for one of the explanations outlined in **(a)**. *(3 marks)*

Chris's answer

(a) People obey because authority figures have the power to punish them. For example, if a policeman gives an order to move on and somebody ignores it, they can be arrested. Therefore it is the fear of punishment that makes people obey. People also obey because they have been socialised from a young age. We learn to obey parents and teachers without questioning them, and so when we are older we have a tendency to obey anyone in authority, particularly if they are in a uniform.

(b) Not everybody obeys authority. Some people are socialised differently, and are anti-authority. Their early experiences make them more hostile to authority, so obedience is not an automatic response in all people.

Chloe's answer

(a) Agentic shift – When people receive an order from someone in authority, Milgram claimed they shift from an autonomous state, in which they feel responsible for their own actions, to an agentic state, in which they act as an agent for carrying out the orders of someone else.

Gradual commitment – Milgram found that by agreeing to a small request (15 volts) people found it harder to resist the experimenter's instruction to give increasingly higher levels of shock. Stopping was made even more difficult for them because each step towards the final 450 volts was small (15 volt increments) so the transition was very gradual.

(b) The idea of gradual commitment has been shown to have real world relevance. Lifton (1986) studied Nazi doctors working at Auschwitz and found that their commitment was also gradual, beginning with sterilisations of people considered mentally defective, and then obeying more and more extreme orders ending in carrying out medical experiments where the subjects died.

Examiner's comments

(a) Chloe has presented a very clear and coherent answer, basing her explanations on key psychological terms, so **full marks**. Chris's answer is less well presented but nonetheless he does have two explanations and each of them has been explained in reasonable detail so he also scores **full marks**.

(b) Chris's criticism is not actually a criticism, so **0 marks**. Chloe has got the right idea – providing research support for the explanation, so the **full 3 marks**.

Question 2 Milgram investigated obedience, finding quite high levels of obedience in some situations but not others. Describe **two** factors that explain high levels of obedience. *(4 marks)*

When Milgram carried out his study in Yale University, he got high levels of obedience, but when he moved it to a run-down warehouse, the levels of obedience dropped.

Some people are more likely to obey than others. There are some personality types that are more obedient, so they are more likely to obey personality types that are less obedient.

One factor that would explain high levels of obedience is whether the authority figure is physically close or not. Milgram found that participants found it easier to disobey when the authority figure gave their orders over the phone rather than when they were in the same room.

Another factor is the presence of others who either obey or resist obedience. Milgram found that when the participant was joined by confederates who were willing to continue with the shocks, most also continued to 450 volts. When the confederates defied the authority and refused to continue, then so did the participant.

In his first answer Chris has not identified the factor (prestige) but his second answer is spot on, so **3 out of 4 marks**. Chloe has sensibly started each answer by saying 'The factor is…' to ensure she has answered the question, so **full marks**.

Question 3 A number of the participants in Milgram's study refused to continue giving shocks but most of the participants did continue. Outline **one or more** explanations of why most of the participants did obey. *(6 marks)*

Most of the participants obeyed to the full 450 volts because they found it difficult to resist the authority figure. For some of these it was because the study took place in a university, for others it was because the experimenter used prods such as 'you must continue'. Some people find it difficult to resist an authority figure, so as these were just ordinary working men, they would find it very difficult not to do what they were told by someone in a university, particularly as they were in a white coat, so looked more official.

When people receive an order from someone in authority, Milgram claimed they shift from an autonomous state, in which they feel responsible for their own actions, to an agentic state, in which they act as an agent for carrying out the orders of someone else. In Milgram's study, although many of the participants were uneasy about continuing to deliver electric shocks, when the experimenter assured them that he would take responsibility for any consequences, many of the participants were then more likely to continue. This can be explained in terms of agentic shift, as participants were more concerned about the consequences of their actions when in the autonomous state, but this concern decreased when they moved into the agentic state, and carried out the orders of the experimenter.

Both candidates have answered the question appropriately – applying their knowledge of explanations to the specific situation. Chloe's answer has plenty of detail for the **full 6 marks**. Chris's answer is good too but less detailed and somewhat repetitive, so **3 out of 6 marks**.

RESEARCH METHODS QUESTION

(a) Validity is an important issue in psychological research. In the context of Milgram's study, explain why validity is important. *(6 marks)*

Chris's answer

There are different types of validity. For example, internal validity is whether a study has really studied what it set out to research. To achieve this, the experiment should accurately mirror real life. This is called mundane realism, and this is important because without it, a study like Milgram's would not tell us anything about real behaviour.

Chloe's answer

It is important that an experiment has experimental realism, i.e. participants should believe in the experimental set up and so, as a result, should act naturally. This is a measure of a study's internal validity. In Milgram's study it was important that participants believed the deception, and that they were really giving electric shocks, otherwise the data obtained would be worthless. It is also important that a research finding can be generalised beyond the research situation. Milgram, for example, claimed that his findings could be used to explain many of the Nazi atrocities committed in World War II (i.e. 'only obeying orders').

Examiner's comments

Both candidates have taken a useful approach which is to start by explaining an aspect of validity and then linking this concept to the context of Milgram's study. Chloe's answer covers several aspects of validity and is generally more detailed, for **full marks**. Chris's response doesn't quite answer the question and would receive **3 out of 6 marks**.

(b) Milgram designed his study so that it was valid. However, others have criticised the validity of the study. Outline **one** factor that enhanced the validity of the study and **one** way in which the study lacked validity. *(3 marks + 3 marks)*

One thing that enhanced its validity was when Milgram took the study to a run-down warehouse rather than in a laboratory in the university. This made it more realistic.

Milgram's study lacked ecological validity because it was carried out in an artificial laboratory rather than in the real world.

One factor that enhanced the validity of the study was using a professional actor to play the part of the learner. His behaviour made it more plausible that he was a genuine participant who was really in pain when receiving the shocks, therefore the participant was more likely to believe the deception.

One way in which the study lacked external validity was in the application of its main findings. For example, Milgram generalised the findings out to an explanation of Nazi war crimes, yet Mandel (1998) claims that there is no evidence that the psychological processes (e.g. agentic shift) were the same in the two situations.

Chris has misunderstood the study in the run-down office – this was not to improve validity but to compare the effects of prestige, so **0 marks**. Chris's second answer is the usual 'knee jerk' response about lab experiments and would get **1 out of 3 marks**. Chloe's answers are worth **full marks**.

Extended writing question

Outline and evaluate research relating to obedience. *(12 marks)*

EXAM ADVICE

This question, unlike the extended writing question on page 97, asks for research generally rather than just research studies – which means that theories, explanations and/or studies are creditworthy.

AO1

The first paragraph contains a slightly limited description of Milgram's study. It also contains explanations which are creditworthy when the question asks for 'research' (research = studies and/or explanation).

Milgram (1963) studied the effect of situational variables on obedience. A higher percentage of participants obeyed (gave a maximum shock level) when the authority figure was in the same room and the learner in a different room. Obedience levels dropped when the learner was in the same room. The most influential variation was the presence of confederates, with obedient confederates producing very high levels of obedience and disobedient confederates producing very low levels of obedience in the participant. Milgram found that the main explanation of why people obey is agentic shift, as people shift from an autonomous state where they take responsibility for their actions to an agentic state, where they carry out the orders of someone else.

This is challenged by Mandel, who argues that most real-life examples of atrocities that have been attributed to obedience have occurred over a much longer period of time and are unlikely to be the product of a simple switch from autonomous to agentic state. Milgram's study has been challenged as lacking internal validity (i.e. participants did not believe they were giving real electric shocks) and external validity (i.e. the findings do not apply to real-life contexts outside the laboratory). Mandel claimed that close physical proximity to the victim made no difference to the actions of killers such as Reserve Police Battalion 101. Milgram's study was criticised as being unethical, particularly exposing participants to great emotional stress. However, Milgram claimed that checks showed no lasting damage that could be attributed to participation in the study.

(254 words)

AO2

An evaluation of Milgram's explanation by Mandel is presented in depth.

Further challenges relate to internal and external validity, with detailed elaboration for external validity.

A final critical point is developed relating to ethical issues and including Milgram's defence.

Examiner's comments

The description (**AO1**) is appropriate but limited in terms of breadth covered, this makes it closer to 'basic' (the 3–2 mark band) rather than 'reasonably detailed' (the top band – see mark scheme on page 9), so **4 out of 6 marks**.

The evaluation (**AO2**) represents a relatively broad range of points in some depth – although not all points are fully elaborated, so **5 out of 6 marks** again because the content is closer to the band above.

Total = **9 out of 12 marks**, a **Grade A** answer.

Extended writing question

Outline and evaluate explanations of why people obey. *(12 marks)*

AO1

The beginning of this paragraph concerns Milgram's explanations for obedience, in reasonable detail.

When people receive an order from someone in authority, Milgram claimed they shift from an autonomous state, in which they feel responsible for their own actions, to an agentic state, in which they act as an agent for carrying out the orders of someone else. This process is known as agentic shift. Milgram also claimed that this same process was operating in his lab and in the actions of Nazi war criminals who had been 'only obeying orders'. Mandel (1998) argues that this comparison is inappropriate as evidence from the study of Reserve Battalion 101 (Browning, 1992) and suggests that obedience due to agentic shift was not the main cause of the atrocities carried out by this group of men, who had been indoctrinated in anti-Semitic discrimination against Jews over the course of many years.

In the second paragraph a second explanation, linked to Milgram's study, is given.

In Milgram's study the learner was in a different room to the teacher, and so was neither heard nor seen by the teacher. This acted as a psychological 'buffer', preventing the teacher seeing the consequences of their actions, and therefore making it easier for them to obey the commands of the experimenter. When these buffers were removed, with the learner brought into the same room as the teacher, obedience was less likely. However, when tested in the real world, the idea of physical proximity having an inhibitory effect on obedience is not really supported. In the study of Reserve Police Battalion 101, close physical proximity to their victims made no difference to their willingness to kill when ordered to do so.

A third explanation is described again in reasonable detail.

Milgram also suggested gradual commitment as an explanation of obedience. He found that, by agreeing to a small request (15 volts), people found it harder to resist the experimenter's instruction to give increasingly higher levels of shock. Stopping was made even more difficult for them because each step towards the final 450 volts was small (15 volt increments) so the transition was very gradual. This gradual commitment of the participant made it easier for the authority figure to manipulate the participant, and more difficult for the participant to resist them. The idea of gradual commitment has relevance in the real world. Lifton (1986) studied Nazi doctors working at Auschwitz and found that their commitment was also gradual, beginning with sterilisations of people considered mentally defective, and then obeying more and more extreme orders, terminating in carrying out medical experiments where the subjects died.

(399 words)

AO2

Mandel's criticism is presented in reasonable depth.

The same evidence from Reserve Police Battalion 101 is used to effectively evaluate the second explanation.

A positive criticism of this third explanation is given with reference to a research study.

Examiner's comments

The description (**AO1**) is appropriate and reasonably detailed. There is both breadth of research covered and depth in terms of specific detail, so **6 out of 6 marks**.

The evaluation (**AO2**) represents a narrow range but in depth (i.e. elaborated) making it effective, so **6 out of 6 marks**.

Total = **12 out of 12 marks**, full marks!

Explanations of independent behaviour

Question 1. The following statements all relate to factors that reduce or increase obedience. Tick the three factors that reduce obedience. *(3 marks)*

☑ Being in face-to-face contact with victim.
☐ Presence of an authority figure.
☐ Gradual increase in requests.
☑ Presence of disobedient peers.
☑ Having strong moral convictions.

FULL MARKS!

Question 2 Conformity and obedience are two forms of social influence. Research has investigated the factors that lead to conformity and obedience, but the same factors may explain why people sometimes are able to resist social influence.
Outline **two** factors that increase the likelihood that people will resist social influence. *(2 marks + 2 marks)*

Billy's answer

The presence of allies has been shown to increase the ability of an individual to resist both conformity and obedience.

Zimbardo argues that by developing a 'heroic imagination', people are able to resist an unjust authority or pressure to conform in the future.

Dawn's answer

People can resist social influence by refusing to do what they are told, despite what the consequences might be. They can resist conformity by developing a non-conformist personality which will help them stand against the crowd.

Examiner's comments

Billy's answer demonstrates psychological knowledge and understanding, therefore **full marks**. Dawn's answers are reasonable but the lack of psychology in her answer would mean **0 marks**.

Question 3 Outline what research has shown about how people resist pressures to conform. *(6 marks)*

Asch discovered that people would conform if they believed the costs of conformity were not particularly great. However, in tasks with a more moral dimension, people were more likely to resist because the personal costs would be greater. Asch found that the presence of an ally who also stands against the majority makes the participant more confident in their own opinion and more confident to reject the view of the majority. Asch's work also showed that many of the participants who remained independent in their judgements (i.e. giving the right answer rather than agreeing with the majority's wrong answer) were less concerned with social norms than were those who conformed.

Asch found that people were able to resist pressures to conform in individualist cultures compared to collectivist cultures. Although a lot of people went along with the majority, more people resisted it and stuck with their original decisions, which shows they were able to resist the pressure to conform. Also, minorities stand against the majority in order to get their point across. The suffragettes resisted the majority who didn't want them to have the vote, despite what happened to them as a result.

Both answers are based on psychological research. Billy sticks with research on conformity (majority influence) but Dawn veers off topic onto minority influence (and suffragettes) which is not relevant to conformity and therefore only gets **3 out of 6 marks**.

Billy's answer is worth the **full 6 marks** as he has included a good range of research details.

Question 4 Outline what research has shown about how people resist pressures to obey authority. *(6 marks)*

Milgram found that resistance increased in the presence of disobedient confederates. They were able to provide social support and so made it more likely that the individual felt able to resist pressures to obey. In a replication of Milgram's study (Rosenhan, 1969) individuals who resisted the pressure to obey tended to base their decisions on more advanced moral principles than those who obeyed, and who tended to reason at a less mature level of morality. Zimbardo believes that a key factor in being able to resist unjust authority is through the development of a heroic imagination. This is a way of thinking that makes it more likely that someone will feel able to resist pressures to obey in later situations that the individual will face.

Milgram found that when the teacher could see the victim, they were less likely to obey the authority figure. This means that we should try to see the victim and think about the consequences of our actions. Milgram also found that people were more able to resist the authority figure when they were out of the room. When other people refused to give any more electric shocks, participants refused to carry on. He also found that when he moved the experiment to some run-down offices only half the participants went all the way to 450 volts, which shows that status is important in obedience.

Both candidates have done well to focus just on the findings/conclusions of research, as required in the question. It is easy to forget and start writing about procedural details. Billy's answer contains plenty of detail for the **full 6 marks**. Dawn has selected appropriate evidence but failed to twist it around as evidence of resistance rather than obedience, which makes her answer basic, **3 out of 6 marks**.

Question 5 Tanya has recently moved with her family and started at a new school. She wants to fit in and be liked by everyone but the other girls are all particularly unkind. They pick on some of their classmates and often are badly behaved in lessons.
(a) Identify **one** factor that explains how people resist the pressure to conform. *(1 mark)*
(b) Outline advice that you might give to Tanya, based on your knowledge of psychology. *(3 marks)*

(a) Finding an ally who also stands against the majority.

(b) By finding an ally, another girl who also doesn't want to join in with the bad behaviour of the majority, Tanya will gain more confidence that what she is doing by not joining in is the right thing to do, and will have more confidence about resisting any pressure from the majority for her to conform.

(a) Socialisation. Some people are brought up as non-conformists.

(b) I would tell her to go along with the other girls in public. This will make it more likely that they will accept her and they will then leave her alone. She doesn't have to change her mind in private though.

(a) Both answers gain **1 mark**.

(b) Billy has used his answer to (a) to inform his answer for (b), which is both detailed and informed, so **full marks**. Dawn's answer for (a) doesn't lend itself so nicely to (b). Her advice isn't appropriate because it means Tanya is still conforming (complying), so **0 marks**.

Question 6 Outline what research has shown about the effects of locus of control on independent behaviour. *(6 marks)*

Research has shown that people who are high in internality believe that they are in control of their own behaviour. For example, if someone fails a driving test, a high internal will blame themselves, but a high external will blame the weather, the examiner, bad luck, etc. People who are high in externality believe their behaviour is generally caused by factors outside their control, such as the actions of other people or bad luck. For someone to be more independent in their behaviour, research has shown that they are more likely to have an internal locus of control than an external locus of control.

Twenge et al. (2004) carried out a meta-analysis of studies conducted in young people in the USA. They found that between 1960 and 2002 people had become progressively more external. They put this down to factors such as increasing unemployment and divorce rates that led people to see many aspects of their lives as being out of their control.

Other research has investigated whether people who take more responsibility for their actions (i.e. those high in internal locus of control) are more successful at work.

A study by Linz and Semykina (2005) found no relationship between locus of control and earnings for males, but found that among females, internals earned significantly more than externals.

Barbie again goes all out with a detailed answer, including names and dates as well – there is no need for dates, you certainly won't be penalised if you don't memorise them but they do provide 'detail' to your answer (see pages 10 and 11).

Some of the information presented in her answer is not related to findings/conclusions but there is more than enough for the **full 6 marks**.

Ken's answer isn't linked to specific research – he has written more generally about locus of control and hasn't shaped it to explain independent behaviour, so his answer is described as 'basic', **2 out of 6 marks**.

Extended writing question

Discuss explanations of how people resist pressures to conform. *(12 marks)*

In exam questions like this one and the one below, students who just describe and evaluate studies like Asch or Milgram would get almost no credit. They see the word 'conformity' or 'obedience' and fail to read the whole question. You must *use* this research to explain *resistance*.

If you throw away 10 marks this will reduce your overall grade drastically, so take great care.

AO1

There are four reasonably detailed descriptions of different explanations.

Notice how each time the explanation has been clearly linked to resisting conformity – even though they are explanations of conformity too.

Also notice how each explanation is presented in a separate paragraph, which helps an examiner read this answer.

Asch discovered that people would conform if they believed the costs of conformity were not particularly great. In Asch's study, the significance of a line matching task was not high, so participants were happy to conform just to save face. However, in tasks with a more moral dimension (e.g. joining the rest of the group in cheating), people were more likely to resist because the personal costs would be greater.

Asch found that the presence of an ally who also stands against the majority makes the participant more confident in their own opinion and more confident to reject the view of the majority. This was the case even when the other person gave a different wrong answer, which suggests that breaking the unanimity of the group was the important factor.

Asch's work also showed that many of the participants who remained independent in their judgements (i.e. giving the right answer rather than agreeing with the majority's wrong answer) were less concerned with social norms than were those who conformed.

McKelvey and Kerr (1988) carried out an experiment similar to Asch's and found there was significantly less evidence of conformity among groups of friends compared to groups of strangers. Because friends know and accept each other, there may be less normative pressure in some situations and therefore they feel more confident about resisting any pressures to conform.

(227 words)

AO2

This research study could have been presented as evaluation but hasn't been introduced in that way, so it's not AO2.

Examiner's comments

The description (**AO1**) is appropriate and reasonably detailed, demonstrating sound knowledge and understanding, so **6 out of 6 marks**.

There is no evaluation (**AO2**), **0 out of 6 marks**.

Total = **6 out of 12 marks**, a **Grade D**.
Using the research evidence as evaluation might have added another 2 marks and turned this into a Grade B answer, which shows how important even a little bit of evaluation is.

Extended writing question

'Some people behave more independently than others. One explanation is in terms of locus of control.'
Discuss research into locus of control. *(12 marks)*

AO1

In this essay a definition of the terms is only marginally creditworthy insofar as there is some theory here.

A reasonably detailed description of an appropriate study.

A further study is described. The sentence beginning 'however' does not count as evaluation as it is a continued description of the study.

The final sentence is more description than evaluation.

Locus of control refers to people's perception of the amount of personal control they have over what happens to them. Those with an internal locus of control see themselves as having a great deal of control and those with an external locus of control judge much of their behaviour as being caused by external forces.

Twenge et al. (2004) carried out a meta-analysis of studies conducted in young people in the USA. They found that between the years of 1960 and 2002, people had become progressively more external. They put this down to factors in their lives such as increasing unemployment and divorce rates that led people to see many aspects of their lives as being out of their control. Twenge et al. claimed that the implications of this finding are worrying for future generations, because externality is associated with poor school achievement and an increase in depression.

Other research has investigated whether people who take more responsibility for their actions (i.e. those high in internal locus of control) are more successful at work. A study by Linz and Semykina (2005) found no relationship between locus of control and earnings for males. However, there was a clear gender difference in this finding with female internals earning significantly more than externals, showing that the relationship between locus of control and success is not a universal one.

The application of locus of control to external events suggests that the concept has considerable external validity. For example, the power to resist coercion and to determine their own destiny comes from an individual's internal locus of control. In contrast, those more likely to be coerced show an external locus of control. Zimbardo (2007) claims that whistleblowers such as Joe Darby, who brought prisoner abuses at Abu Ghraib to public attention, refused coercion from others to keep quiet, and so displayed the characteristics of an internal locus of control. An internal locus of control encourages people to think independently and critically about the forces that attempt to influence them and to distinguish good from bad and fact from propaganda.

(344 words)

AO2

The implications of the study can be credited as evaluation, with some elaboration.

The final part of the paragraph again deals with implications ('showing that…').

Considering applications of this research is again evaluation.

Examiner's comments

The description (**AO1**) is appropriate but slightly limited, so **5 out of 6 marks**.

The evaluation (**AO2**) represents a relatively narrow range but in some depth (see mark scheme on page 9) – although not all points are fully elaborated and thus lack effectiveness, so **5 out of 6 marks** – a slightly generous mark.

Total = **10 out of 12 marks**, a **Grade A** answer.

Understanding social change

Question 1 Explain what is meant by 'social change'. *(2 marks)*

Ceyhun's answer

This is when a society or a significant section of society adopts a new way of thinking or acting, which then becomes the norm.

Nadine's answer

Social change is all about when societies change and people change the way they behave, e.g. from not recycling to recycling.

Examiner's comments

Both answers deserve the **full 2 marks**. Appropriate examples are a good way of providing detail.

Question 2 Describe how social influence research has helped us to understand social change. *(6 marks)*

Research into minority influence has implications for social change. Being exposed to the views of a deviant minority (such as the suffragettes) draws the majority's attention to the views they are expressing. If the minority are consistent in these views over time, then the majority takes them more seriously. The suffragettes were consistent in their arguments for votes for women over many years, through lobbying and education. The impact of the minority position is increased if the minority is seen to suffer for their views (the augmentation principle). In the case of the suffragettes, many were imprisoned and went on hunger strike, so people started to take them seriously. Once a few politicians started to accept the views of the suffragettes, this led to a snowball effect as more and more people defected to the minority position, and wide scale social change then occurred.

There are two main types of social influence that are important in social change. The first of these is minority influence. This is where a minority changes the views of a majority. An example of a minority changing the minds of a majority is the story of the suffragettes. The suffragettes were a minority who demanded votes for women. They eventually changed the views of the majority and now society has changed so that women have the vote. Another way in which social influence research can lead to social change is through obedience. There are lots of examples of obedience in history that have contributed to social change. For example, the Nazis wanted to rid Europe of Jews, causing social change. In order to do this they had to get people to obey them. Milgram's research told us how they might have achieved this, i.e. people have a natural tendency to obey people in authority.

Both answers are spot on, weaving psychological research with real-life events as required in the question – and making it clear that these events were examples of social change. **Full marks** for both Ceyhun and Nadine. This question usually poses difficulty for students, but the key is to have just one or two examples of social change and be able to use these as examples of psychological processes such as minority influence and obedience to authority.

Question 3 Social attitudes are changing all the time although the process is very slow. One current example is attitudes towards the environment and the damage humans are doing to it. In Britain the first 'green' MP was elected in 2010 which demonstrates how much attitudes have changed.

Using your knowledge of minority influence, explain how this social change has occurred. *(4 marks)*

'Green' campaigners as a minority first brought environmental issues to the majority's attention. These views were expressed consistently over time, through media campaigning and through protests, increasing their impact on the majority. To begin with, campaigners suffered a great deal of antagonism from the majority, so people started to take them seriously because of the augmentation principle, that people who suffer for the views must really believe in them. Gradually more and more people started taking an interest in environmental issues, until through the snowball effect this became the majority position.

There used to be just three main political parties, labour, conservative and the liberal democrats. People weren't interested in environmental issues, so green politics was not really popular. Now people are far more interested in conserving energy and recycling, so green issues (e.g. saving the planet through reducing our carbon footprint) are more important in politics. As these become more popular, and most people in a road start recycling, others conform in order to be accepted as being 'green'. The same would be true of electing a 'green' MP. People are led to believe that the candidate is representing the views of the majority, so they vote for him.

Both are excellent, informed answers – but Nadine's answer makes little reference to psychological research – a very common error – good knowledge but minimal psychology. **Full marks for Ceyhun and just 2 out of 4 marks for Nadine.**

RESEARCH METHODS QUESTION

A psychologist plans to investigate whether certain types of people are more conformist than others. The table on the right displays some of the results.

Participant type	% of participants who conformed
Young (under 10 years)	45%
Older (over 40 years)	23%
Females	32%
Males	28%

(a) Describe a method that the psychologist could use to assess how conformist each participant is. *(3 marks)*

Ceyhun's answer

The psychologist could carry out a controlled observation. He could design a task (e.g. an Asch type conformity task) and arrange for a group of confederates to sometimes give the wrong answer and see if the participants would give the same wrong answer as that given by the majority.

Nadine's answer

Asch studied conformity by showing participants three lines and then a standard line. He measured how conformist people were by seeing if they gave the same wrong answer as the majority or whether they gave the right answer.

Examiner's comments

It is perfectly creditworthy to answer this question by describing what Asch did. Ceyhun's answer is detailed and worth the **full 3 marks**. Nadine's answer lacks clarity so would gain **2 out of 3 marks**.

(b) Give **one** criticism of the method you described in **(a)**. *(3 marks)*

A problem with this method is the possibility of demand characteristics, which may be greater for some age groups than others. For example, the older participants might guess what the experimenter is doing and so go along with the group because they believe it is their 'role'. This means that their behaviour is not natural so the results are misleading.

This would be a fairly trivial task, and it is possible that people would not take it that seriously, or maybe children would take it more seriously than the adults and this might account for the age differences in conformity.

Both candidates have given an answer in the context of the age-related conformity study – which is not necessary but a good way of providing extra detail. Each of them has identified a criticism, explained it in context and explained why it would be a problem (see the three-point rule on page 10), so **full marks**.

(c) What conclusions could you draw from the table about conformity? *(4 marks)*

First of all the table indicates that there are age differences in conformity, with young people being more conformist possibly because they are more uncertain and thus more easily influenced by the behaviour of others. Second, there appears to be a gender difference but this is less pronounced. Women were more conformist but only just. It may be that the task was gender biased and one where the women felt less certain and therefore were more likely to conform.

The data in the table shows two things. It shows that there is an age difference with young participants being more conformist than older participants. It also shows a gender difference that women were more conformist than men. Psychological research has shown a similar tendency.

Nadine has provided a description of the findings and failed to tell us what conclusions we might draw from this, so just **2 out of 4 marks**. Her reference to psychological research is not creditworthy here. A detailed response from Ceyhun for the **full 4 marks**.

Extended writing question

Discuss how social influence research has contributed to an understanding of social change.

(12 marks)

AO1

A reasonably detailed description of two examples of the implications for social change of social influence research – in fact, the same answer as given on the facing page which received 6 marks.

Here is a further example of social change with an attempt to link it to social influence research – but without success.

The suffragettes were an example of social change brought about by social influence. They fought to get votes for women by taking part in a practice called civil disobedience. By chaining themselves to railings and refusing to eat when arrested, they eventually managed to make people sit up and take notice of what they were about. One suffragette even threw herself in front of the king's horse and died, just to get the suffragettes' point across. Milgram found that some people could become social heroes by standing against laws that were wrong. The suffragette who threw herself in front of the king's horse would be an example of a social hero. Milgram also found that it was easier to resist authority if there were other people who resisted as well. This is what happened with the 'women's lib' movement more recently, women regarded other women as 'sisters' who were fighting for the same cause.

Another example where social influence has been used to bring about social change is in the story of Rosa Parks. She was a black woman who refused to give up her seat on a bus when a white woman got on. Her actions got her arrested and sparked the civil rights movement in America. Some psychologists believe that governments only have power if people obey, so if people don't obey, they lose that power. In Milgram's study there was one participant who obeyed until he was given a direct order and told he had no choice, he then refused. That is what happened to Rosa Parks and this led to social change.

(266 words)

AO2

This was a wasted paragraph. Just one line of evaluation would have been valuable in lifting the final mark. It is always a great mistake to leave out evaluation.

Examiner's comments

The description (**AO1**) in the first paragraph is sufficient on its own for **6 out of 6 marks**. The second paragraph is also description.

There is no evaluation (**AO2**), **0 out of 6 marks**.

Total = **6 out of 12 marks**, a **Grade D** answer.

Extended writing question

'Research on minority influence has helped us to understand many of the significant examples of social change.'

Discuss the role of minority influence in social change.

(12 marks)

AO1

A detailed description of one example of the implications for social change of social influence research. Again, the same answer as given on the facing page which received 6 marks.

A further description of this implication of social influence research.

Research into minority influence has helped us to understand the processes involved in social change. Being exposed to the views of a deviant minority (such as the suffragettes) draws the majority's attention to the views they are expressing. If the minority are consistent in these views over time, then the majority takes them more seriously. The suffragettes were consistent in their arguments for votes for women over many years, through lobbying and education. The impact of the minority position is increased if the minority is seen to suffer for their views (the augmentation principle). In the case of the suffragettes, many were imprisoned and went on hunger strike, so people started to take them seriously. Once a few politicians started to accept the views of the suffragettes, this led to a snowball effect as more and more people defected to the minority position, and wide scale social change then occurred.

The external validity of minority influence as an explanation of social change was demonstrated by an analysis of Gandhi's 'salt march' in the 1930s. Research has claimed that the power of a minority's position is strengthened if they are seen as suffering for their beliefs. The influence of Gandhi and his followers was strengthened because of their willingness to suffer physical attacks without retaliation. In fact, Gandhi appeared aware of this form of influence because he would not allow women to join the march because he believed this would inhibit the British from attacking the marchers.

The importance of using research into social influence to understand social change is that people can use this understanding to bring about social change. For example, if you want to change people's attitudes about the use of animals in research, you would demonstrate consistency and also a willingness to suffer. However, injuring other people will mean that public sympathies may lie with the victims rather than the animal rights movement. It is better, like Gandhi, to remain above violence and then people will listen to you.

(326 words)

AO2

In this answer the second example is used as a form of evaluation, confirming the first example. However it lacks effectiveness as it becomes more of a description.

A comment on how such insight was used.

This is a valiant attempt to provide further evaluation in the form of applying the knowledge gained from psychology. There could have been more credit if the paragraph started with a sentence clearly making it AO2, such as 'One practical application of …'.

Examiner's comments

The description (**AO1**) is appropriate and reasonably detailed, so **6 out of 6 marks**.

The evaluation (**AO2**) represents a restricted range of points, which are not always effective. However there has been an attempt to offer evaluation – and this is a very difficult topic to evaluate, so a generous **4 out of 6 marks**.

Total = **10 out of 12 marks**, a **Grade A** answer.

Extra questions for you

Some further examples of questions requiring you to apply your knowledge to novel situations.

Question 1 Dion's family moves around a lot so he has to change schools frequently. This has made the process of making friends quite difficult for him. At his latest school he begins hanging around with a group of other boys who seem to like him. However, it soon becomes obvious that they are more interested in messing about than in academic work. Although he really wants to work, he finds himself joining in with their activities, and finds himself in trouble with the school authorities.

(a) Identify the type of conformity that Dion is displaying. *(1 mark)*

(b) Explain why he is conforming to the other boys' behaviour. *(3 marks)*

(c) Outline **two** ways in which Dion might resist the pressure to conform to their deviant behaviour. *(2 marks + 2 marks)*

Question 2 Davina is training to be a teacher. She and her fellow student teachers spend one class discussing the issue of disobedient students.

Outline **two** methods that the student teachers might use to prevent disobedience in class. Refer to psychological research in your answer. *(6 marks)*

Question 3 In the Second World War there were a number of Resistance movements that were dedicated to protecting people whose lives were threatened by the Nazis. Many people did not join such resistance movements in the war but some did.

Using your knowledge of psychology, describe personality characteristics that might be typical of those people who did join a resistance movement. *(6 marks)*

Question 4 Molly has been teaching psychology for two years, and has discovered that her students love nothing better than finding out as much as they can about themselves. As a result, she frequently gives them personality tests to complete and they discuss the results in class. As they are studying independent behaviour, she decides to give the students a locus of control questionnaire and correlate their scores with their academic success. She asks each student to complete the questionnaire and calculate their GCSE score (6 points for an A*, 5 points for an A and so on). Their scores are collected, collated and then discussed by the class.

(a) Based on your knowledge of locus of control, what would you expect Molly to find about the relationship between locus of control and academic performance? *(2 marks)*

(b) Using research evidence, explain your answer to (a). *(3 marks)*

(c) Explain **one** methodological problem with Molly's investigation. *(3 marks)*

(d) Identify **one** potential ethical problem with this investigation and consider how this might be overcome. *(3 marks)*

Question 5 It is estimated that there are four million vegetarians in the UK – about 7% of the population – although among younger people that figure rises to 12%. It is also estimated that approximately 5,000 more people each week are choosing to become vegetarian.

Using your knowledge of research into social influence, explain how this example of social change might be taking place. *(6 marks)*

Question 6 In the UK most people do not do as much exercise as they should. Recent research shows that exercise is good for mental and physical health, therefore the Government has decided to launch a campaign to change people's attitudes towards exercise so that a majority rather than a minority of people become daily exercisers.

Using your knowledge of social influence research, suggest two techniques that the government might use to change social attitudes towards exercising. *(3 marks + 3 marks)*

RESEARCH METHODS QUESTION

Question 1 Some psychology students decided to assess how conformist and obedient people are. They did this by designing a questionnaire. Each question described a situation related to conformity or obedience. Participants had to indicate whether or not they would conform/obey. For each participant a score could be calculated as to how conformist they were and how obedient they were. The scattergram on the right shows the results of their study.

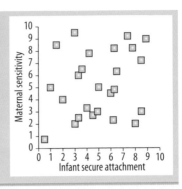

(a) Explain what each dot on the scattergram represents. *(2 marks)*

(b) Describe the correlation shown in the scattergram. *(2 marks)*

(c) What conclusion could you draw from the scattergram? *(2 marks)*

(d) Outline **one** strength and **one** limitation of using correlations in conformity research. *(6 marks)*

(e) Describe the aims of this study. *(3 marks)*

 **RESEARCH METHODS QUESTION**

Question 2

(a) Research on obedience is often conducted in a laboratory. Outline **one** strength of conducting research into conformity in a laboratory. *(2 marks)*

(b) Some studies that are conducted in a laboratory are experiments, whereas other studies are non-experimental. Explain the difference between experiments and studies that are not experiments. *(4 marks)*

(c) An alternative way to conduct research is a field experiment. Explain why a field experiment might be preferable to a laboratory experiment. *(3 marks)*

(d) There is a third kind of experiment, called a natural experiment. Outline the key features of a natural experiment. *(3 marks)*

RESEARCH METHODS QUESTION

Question 3

(a) How have psychologists investigated locus of control? *(6 marks)*

(b) (i) Explain **one** possible problem with the validity of this study. *(2 marks)*

 (ii) Explain how a researcher might deal with this problem of validity. *(2 marks)*

(c) Identify **one** ethical issue that might arise in this study and explain how it would be dealt with. *(3 marks)*

SPECIFICATION BREAKDOWN

Specification content

Comment

Defining and explaining psychological abnormality

- Definitions of abnormality, including deviation from social norms, failure to function adequately and deviation from ideal mental health.

- Limitations associated with these definitions of psychological abnormality.

- The biological approach to psychopathology.

- Psychological approaches to psychopathology, including the psychodynamic, behavioural and cognitive approaches.

This specification begins with the question 'what is abnormality?' – how can we define what we mean when we say a person's behaviour is abnormal? The specification points to three possible ways of defining abnormality. You need to be able to outline these as well as being able to discuss their limitations.

There are four 'approaches to psychopathology' – one biological and three psychological. 'Psychopathology' refers to *explanations* of abnormality. It is easy to get confused between definitions and explanations but it is an important distinction to understand – a definition sets out the criteria used to decide when a behaviour is abnormal, for example in what way is depression or schizophrenia abnormal? An explanation provides an account of why a person might have developed an abnormal behaviour, for example trying to understand why a particular person became depressed or schizophrenic.

Treating abnormality

- Biological therapies, including drugs and ECT.

- Psychological therapies, including psychoanalysis, systematic desensitisation and Cognitive Behavioural Therapy.

Psychologists' greatest concern is in trying to discover effective methods of treating abnormality. These are linked to the approaches to psychopathology – if abnormality is caused by biological factors, then treatments should be biological, such as using drugs or ECT. On the other hand, if the causes of abnormality are psychological then psychological treatments are likely to be effective.

The specification lists three psychological treatments which are each linked to the psychological approaches to psychopathology – psychoanalysis is a psychodynamic approach, systematic desensitisation is a behavioural approach and Cognitive Behavioural Therapy is a cognitive approach.

Chapter 5

INDIVIDUAL DIFFERENCES are the aspects of each of us that distinguish us from others, such as our personality and intelligence. Each of us also differs in the extent to which we are 'normal'. For the most part deviation from normal is not a problem, but in some circumstances it is – but how do we know when abnormality is unacceptable?

CHAPTER CONTENTS

Individual differences: psychopathology (abnormality)

Definitions of abnormality

Question 1 Which of the following statements apply to the 'deviation from social norms' definition of abnormality? Tick the two correct boxes. *(2 marks)*

☐ Not being able to cope with day-to-day living.　　☐ Lack of self-esteem.

☐ Experiencing personal distress.　　☑ Behaviour which is antisocial or undesirable.

☑ Behaving in the same way as other members of your society.

FULL MARKS!

Question 2 (a) Explain what is meant by 'deviation from social norms'. *(3 marks)*
(b) Outline **one** limitation of this definition. *(3 marks)*

Bruce's answer

(a) People who consistently behave in a way that breaks unwritten social rules concerning decency, politeness, sexual behaviour, etc. are considered antisocial by other members of society, therefore they (and their behaviour) are considered 'abnormal'.

(b) A limitation of this definition is that it does not take into consideration the context or degree of the behaviour when determining abnormality. Some behaviours are socially deviant in one context but not in another, and there is no clear line between behaviour that is 'abnormal' and what is merely 'eccentric'.

Yazzy's answer

(a) This is when people break laws that society has made about how they should behave. An example would be talking to yourself in public. This would be considered undesirable.

(b) A limitation of this definition is that it doesn't take cultural differences into consideration. For example, in some cultures it might be considered perfectly normal for people to talk to themselves in public so this sort of behaviour would not therefore be considered abnormal in that culture.

Examiner's comments

(a) Good answer from Bruce, worth the **full 3 marks**. Yazzy's answer isn't quite as good. First of all people aren't breaking 'laws' and second, the example needs further explanation to be illustrative, so **1 out of 3 marks**.

(b) Both limitations are appropriate but again Yazzy's lacks information – her final sentence is a repetition of what has already been said. Nevertheless she has named a limitation and given some elaboration, so **2 out of 3 marks**. Full marks for Bruce for a good amount of elaboration.

Question 3 (a) Abnormality can be defined in terms of the deviation from mental health model. Give two examples of behaviours that are used to judge mental healthiness. *(2 marks)*
(b) Explain how the concept of mental health can be used to define abnormality. *(3 marks)*

(a) Whether a person possesses a positive sense of self-esteem and a strong sense of identity; whether they have an accurate perception of reality.

(b) Jahoda identified a number of characteristics that a mentally healthy person should possess (e.g. being able to deal with stressful events). The absence of these criteria means that an individual has deviated from 'ideal' mental health, which indicates an abnormality and therefore a possible mental disorder.

(a) Two behaviours that are used to judge mental healthiness are happiness, whether somebody is happy or depressed, and also personality, whether somebody has a neurotic personality, which would be an indication of abnormality.

(b) Mental health is used as a way to define abnormal behaviour because it means you have an idea of what mental health is. As I said above things like happiness or lack of depression define mental health.

(a) Yazzy's answer doesn't demonstrate any familiarity with the deviation from mental heath model, so **0 marks**, whereas Bruce has given two clear answers for **2 out of 2 marks**.

(b) Yazzy's answer again suggests she doesn't really know anything about this model, so **0 marks**. Bruce's answer describes the model (a list of characteristics) but more importantly explains how the criteria are used, so the **full 3 marks** for sufficient detail.

Question 4 (a) Give **one** example of a behaviour that illustrates the 'failure to function adequately' definition of abnormality. *(1 mark)*
(b) Outline **one** limitation of this definition. *(3 marks)*

(a) Not being able to leave the house without checking all the locks several times.

(b) Some behaviours that appear to indicate failure to function adequately may actually be adaptive for the individual. For example, someone who displays the symptoms of depression may cause other people to be helpful and supportive towards them. This helps them to deal more effectively with the stressor.

(a) Not being able to make friends easily.

(b) A limitation of the 'failure to function adequately' definition is cultural relativism, because different cultures have different ideas of what it means to function 'adequately'. People in the UK would consider many people who live in slums in Brazil as abnormal because they are not living 'adequately' by UK standards.

(a) Bruce's answer is good (**1 mark**) and Yazzy's is just about acceptable, although 'easily' isn't really relevant. She would just about receive **1 mark**.

(b) Both limitations are appropriate and Bruce's elaboration is sufficient for the **full 3 marks**. Yazzy's example is not appropriate because it is not related to mental health, so only **1 out of 3 marks** (but it is a strong 1 mark, making up for the weak mark in (a)).

Question 5 Eva left home when she was 16 and tried to get a job without success. She had no money from home so she couldn't pay rent and ended up sleeping in the street. She was able to get some money from begging but has used this to buy drugs rather than food.

(a) Outline **one** definition of abnormality. *(2 marks)*
(b) Use this to explain why Eva's behaviour is abnormal. *(3 marks)*

(a) Mentally healthy people should be able to operate within certain acceptable limits. If any aspects of their behaviour interfere with this (e.g. not being able to eat in front of other people), they are considered abnormal.

(b) Eva is unable to operate within acceptable limits. By sleeping rough and begging rather than working, she is showing that she is unable to deal with the everyday pressures of living. She uses what money she has to buy drugs. Her drug habit and begging interferes with her ability to live a 'normal' life.

(a) Deviation from social norms

(b) Eva is deviating from a number of social norms. These include begging, sleeping rough and taking drugs. All of these would be considered deviant behaviours, so Eva would be considered abnormal.

(a) Yazzy receives **1 out of 2 marks** as she has just named the definition and provided no further detail. Bruce hasn't named a specific definition but has provided an informed description (of failure to function adequately), so **2 out of 2 marks**.

(b) Both Bruce and Yazzy have clearly used their definitions to explain why Eva's behaviour might be regarded as abnormal, so the **full 3 marks** for each answer.

Extended writing question

Outline and evaluate one or more definitions of abnormality.

Answer 1

AO1

There is a penalty for using side headings like this, but also some advantages. The poor style will mean lower marks for presentation, however the headings make your answer clearer to the examiner. Detail is more important and this definition lacks detail.

The second definition is also brief and the 'happiness' criteria is not appropriate. Self-esteem could have been explained.

The third definition is again lacking detail.

Deviation from social norms

People who break rules in society are considered abnormal. For example, people who talk out loud when nobody else is around, or people who urinate in public would be considered abnormal.

Evaluation

• Whether something is abnormal depends on the context of the behaviour.
• Whether something is abnormal depends on the culture, behaviour that is abnormal in one culture may not be in another.

Deviation from ideal mental health

Six criteria of positive mental health — include having a positive self-esteem and feeling happy about life in general. People who don't have positive self-esteem and who are depressed rather than happy are considered abnormal.

Evaluation

• Unrealistic for people to achieve all six criteria so everybody abnormal to some degree.
• Cultural differences in what is considered ideal mental health.

Failure to function adequately

People who can't look after themselves or do things that everybody else takes for granted (e.g. keeping clean, holding down a job) are considered to be abnormal.

Evaluation

• Could be racist because some people are considered abnormal because their behaviour is different to that of the majority group.
• Unethical to study people who are mentally ill just to prove a point.

(195 words)

AO2

Bullet points also are not good style but again might make your answer more readable – more important is the issue of elaboration. Here we have two criticisms, both of which are superficial (lack elaboration and effectiveness).

Again, two limitations which are superficial.

One superficial limitation and one that is irrelevant.

Examiner's comments

The descriptions (**AO1**) lack detail but a range of definitions have been provided – you could achieve full marks with one reasonably detailed explanation or several in less detail. Here we have several which are all lacking detail, and the style of presentation is basic, so **3 out of 6 marks** for breadth.

The evaluation (**AO2**) is superficial. Again, there is a good range but a lack of depth and the unsophisticated style only achieves **3 out of 6 marks**.

Total = 6 out of 12 marks, a **Grade D**.

Answer 2

AO1

A reasonably detailed description of one definition.

A second definition is described in reasonable detail.

A third definition is described in reasonable detail.

Social norms are unwritten standards of acceptable behaviour that are set by the social group, and monitored by its members. These standards include rules about decency, politeness, sexual behaviour, etc. The 'deviation from social norms' definition says that people who consistently behave in a way that breaks these unwritten social rules are considered socially deviant by the majority of group members. Therefore they (and their behaviour) are considered 'abnormal'.

This does not take into consideration the context or degree of the behaviour when determining abnormality. Some behaviours are socially deviant in one context but not in another, with no clear line between behaviour that is 'abnormal' and what is merely 'eccentric'. This definition fails to consider cultural differences in what is 'abnormal'. Some behaviours are considered socially deviant in one culture but not in another. This means that it is difficult to have universal standards of what might be considered 'abnormal' behaviour.

The 'failure to function adequately' definition states that mentally healthy people are able to operate within certain acceptable limits. This definition presents abnormality in terms of an individual's ability to cope. If any aspects of their behaviour interfere with this ability to cope (e.g. not being able to eat in front of other people), they might be considered abnormal and would seek, or be told to seek, treatment.

Some behaviours that indicate failure to function adequately may actually be adaptive for the individual. For example, someone who displays the symptoms of depression may cause other people to be helpful and supportive towards them. This helps them to deal more effectively with the stressor and would be considered adaptive rather than abnormal. Definitions of what is considered to be adequate functioning may also differ from culture to culture, which is likely to result in different diagnoses when these standards are applied to people from different cultures.

In the 'deviation from ideal mental health' definition, Jahoda identified six characteristics that a mentally healthy person should possess (e.g. being able to deal with stressful events). The absence of any of these means they have deviated from 'ideal' mental health, indicating an abnormality and a possible mental disorder.

A problem is that it is unusual to find anybody who satisfies all six characteristics of positive mental health. Consequently, everybody would be considered abnormal to some degree. Therefore judging abnormality in terms of the absence of any of these criteria would be unrealistic.

(400 words)

AO2

Two limitations are identified and both are well elaborated making them effective.

A further two limitations are given, each well elaborated. Notice how they often follow the three-point rule (see page 10).

A final elaborated criticism.

Examiner's comments

The description (**AO1**) is reasonably detailed and shows sound knowledge and understanding in its breadth. Possibly just two definitions would have been sufficient for full marks but three definitions is clearly worth **6 out of 6 marks**.

The evaluation (**AO2**) consists of a broad range of criticisms all in reasonable depth or better, so **6 out of 6 marks**.

Total = 12 out of 12 marks, a **Grade A**.

The biological approach to psychopathology

Question 1 Two of the following statements apply to the biological approach to psychopathology. Tick the **two** correct boxes. *(2 marks)*

☑ Abnormality can be explained in terms of the physical processes of the body.

☐ The unconscious mind affects behaviour.

☐ Irrational thinking causes abnormal behaviour.

☑ Research has shown that mental disorders may be inherited.

☐ Abnormal behaviour is learned in the same way that all behaviour is learned.

FULL MARKS!

Question 2 Outline the biological approach to psychopathology. *(6 marks)*

Tristan's answer

The biological approach claims that it is our biology that goes wrong when we develop psychopathology. This can be due to brain damage, caused by accident or disease such as what happened to Phineas Gage who went mad after an accident working on the railway. Some psychopathology (such as schizophrenia) can be caused by not having enough or having too much or a specific chemical in the brain. There is even evidence that some commercially available drugs can cause psychopathology. For example, the drug Tamiflu has been found to cause hallucinations and delusions. This has caused some people to jump from windows or to run out in front of traffic. Other people taking this drug have even committed suicide because of the hallucinations and delusions they experience.

Isolde's answer

Mental disorders are thought to be the consequence of some change, illness or dysfunction in the body that results in psychopathological behaviour. Genetic explanations claim that psychopathology is the result of genetic inheritance. By studying the incidence of a particular disorder within individuals of known genetic similarity, researchers can assess the likelihood that genetic inheritance is a causal factor. Abnormalities in the structure of the brain (e.g. enlarged ventricles in schizophrenia) and altered brain chemistry (e.g. low levels of serotonin in depression) are also associated with the development of psychopathology. Finally, some research has suggested that an individual's exposure to certain viruses while still in the womb may contribute to the development of disorders such as schizophrenia.

Examiner's comments

Isolde's answer has the edge on Tristan's because she has used psychological terminology (e.g. 'serotonin' instead of 'specific chemicals in the brain'). Both answers are detailed and display a high level of knowledge and understanding. The **full 6 marks** for Isolde and **5 out of 6 marks** for Tristan for slightly less detail and being slightly off the point with some of his examples.

Question 3 Explain **one** limitation of the biological approach to psychopathology. *(3 marks)*

A limitation of the biological approach is that it is only one explanation of psychopathology. It does not recognise that psychopathology might also be learned (the behavioural approach) or might be caused by the way people think irrationally about problems (the cognitive approach).

Szasz (1972) claimed that, unlike physical illnesses, most mental disorders do not have a physical basis, therefore should not be thought of or treated in the same way. He claimed that the concept of 'mental illness' is used as a form of social control within society – to control, through drugs or surgery, the behaviour of those who society cannot accept as they are.

Isolde's answer is clearly worth the **full marks** as she has identified a limitation and provided further elaboration. Tristan has also given a limitation – but one that is rather general (the same is true for all approaches to psychopathology). However, he saves the day by explaining what in particular the biological approach is lacking, so he also gets **full marks**.

Question 4 Harriet has recently had a baby and has been experiencing feelings of worthlessness and depression since giving birth. Both her sister and mother also suffered from such feelings of depression after they gave birth.

Use the biological approach to psychopathology to explain why Harriet might be feeling depressed. *(4 marks)*

Harriet is probably suffering from post-natal depression (also known as the baby blues) which is caused by changes in hormone levels which trigger the feelings of depression. Lots of women get this after they give birth. It can last for a few days and then disappear. Women with post-natal depression cry a lot, and, like Harriet, can feel worthless.

There are two possible reasons why Harriet feels depressed since giving birth. Because both her mother and sister also felt depressed after giving birth, it is possible that this form of depression has been passed on through the genes, from mother to daughters. Second, It is possible that there has been a change in these women's brain chemistry since giving birth, perhaps lowering their serotonin levels, and it is this altered brain chemistry that has led to the depression.

Isolde has used her knowledge of psychology (genes and brain chemistry) to provide an educated answer to this question and one worth the **full 4 marks**. Tristan knows about post-natal depression so has been able to put together an answer more specific to this. However, he hasn't referred much to the biological approach (except to mention hormones) and has ignored the clues in the stem, so **1 out of 4 marks**.

RESEARCH METHODS QUESTION

Outline how psychologists have investigated the biological approach to psychopathology. *(3 marks)*

Tristan's answer

Psychologists have investigated the biological approach using the case study method. They study people who are brain damaged and look for any signs of abnormal behaviour which might be caused by the brain damage. An example of a case study in the biological approach is the case study of Phineas Gage.

Isolde's answer

Researchers can measure the extent to which two individuals of known genetic similarity (e.g. identical twins) are alike in terms of a particular mental disorder (such as schizophrenia). If individuals of closer genetic similarity are also more similar in terms of the disorder, this suggests a strong genetic influence for that disorder.

Examiner's comments

Both our candidates have followed the three-point rule (see page 10) – they have identified their method and provided two further points of elaboration. A little more detail on why Phineas Gage is an example would have been good but there is enough in both answers for the **full 3 marks**.

Answer 1

AO1

> The first sentence hasn't been totally supported by the examples – it is still not clear how biology differs from psychology – and the examples don't demonstrate a clear understanding of biology. Finally, there is really no need for two examples of the same thing.

> A limited/basic explanation of genes as an example of the biological approach.

The biological approach claims that all psychopathology is biological rather than psychological. For example, it could be caused by brain damage. Research with KF (who was brain damaged after a motorbike accident) found that his memory was damaged and he had other problems as well. A very famous case was a man called Phineas Gage. He was working on the railway and a spike went through his head when he hit it because of the explosive charge underneath it. Although Phineas Gage seemed okay after the accident, he later became foul-mouthed and showed other changes in his behaviour which might be seen as abnormal.

Genetics is another explanation of psychopathology. Characteristics can be passed on from parents to their children. This is called the nature–nurture debate, and psychologists have shown that some psychopathological behaviours are caused by nature (genes) rather than nurture (environment).

A problem with the biological approach is that it is very difficult to test these ideas scientifically. For example, it is possible that there were other reasons for Phineas Gage's behaviour beyond the brain damage he suffered when the spike went through his head. For example, he might have changed his personality because people were treating him like a freak. We can't replicate this study because it would be unethical to drive a spike into someone's head. Also, the nurture side of the nature–nurture debate claims that psychopathological behaviours are caused by the environment rather than genetics. There are also alternative explanations which are not biological, for example the cognitive approach claims that psychopathology is caused by the way people think about problems not their biology.

In this answer I have outlined the biological approach to psychopathology and illustrated it with different examples. I then went on to evaluate the biological approach, pointing out some of the problems with it and offering an alternative way of explaining psychopathology.

(313 words)

AO2

> This is a fair criticism of the Phineas Gage case study.

> A second criticism which is reasonably effective.

> A summary such as this does not count as analysis and receives no credit.

Examiner's comments

The description (**AO1**) covers two features of the biological approach, each with limited detail, so **4 out of 6 marks**.

The evaluation (**AO2**) is restricted in range although slightly better than superficial (see mark scheme on page 9), but it doesn't quite rate 4 out of 6 marks – **3 out of 6 marks**.

Total = **7 out of 12 marks**, a **Grade C**.

Answer 2

AO1

> This first paragraph begins with a general introductory sentence and then presents the genetic explanation in considerable detail.

> A second example of the biological approach (structural abnormalities) is described in detail. In this case examples have been used well to amplify the explanation.

> A third example of the biological approach (viruses) is described in detail.

Mental disorders are thought to be the consequence of some change, illness or dysfunction in the body that results in psychopathological behaviour. Genetic explanations claim that psychopathology is the result of genetic inheritance. By studying the incidence of a particular disorder within individuals of known genetic similarity, researchers can assess the likelihood that genetic inheritance is a causal factor. For example, research has shown that identical twins are more alike for schizophrenia than non-identical twins, suggesting a strong genetic influence for this disorder. However, the influence of genetics as measured by such studies is rarely more than 50%, suggesting that disorders such as schizophrenia are not simply brain diseases but are also linked to other factors such as social adversity. It is possible that what is inherited is the vulnerability for a disorder which only develops under certain stressful conditions (the diathesis-stress model).

Abnormalities in the structure of the brain can cause psychopathological behaviour. For example, some people with schizophrenia have enlarged ventricles, indicating shrinkage of the brain tissue around the ventricles. Altered brain chemistry (e.g. low levels of serotonin in depression) is also associated with the development of psychopathology. However, research has yet to establish a clear cause and effect relationship between these factors and psychopathological behaviour. For example, some researchers claim that rather than enlarged ventricles being the cause of schizophrenia, they are a consequence of the anti-psychotic medication used in its treatment.

Finally, some research has suggested that an individual's exposure to certain viruses while still in the womb may contribute to the development of disorders. For example, foetal exposure to a particular strain of the influenza virus has been suggested as a causal factor in the development of schizophrenia. However, it is unlikely that viral infections act in isolation, but rather that genetic and other factors increase an individual's susceptibility to the influence of viral infection.

Szasz (1972) claimed that unlike physical illnesses, most mental disorders do not have a physical basis, therefore should not be thought of or treated in the same way. He claims that the concept of 'mental illness' is used as a form of social control within society to control, through drugs or surgery, the behaviour of those who society cannot accept as they are.

(373 words)

AO2

> This paragraph ends with a critical comment about the possibility that this alone could explain abnormality. There is some elaboration.

> An effective critical point, well elaborated.

Examiner's comments

The description (**AO1**) is excellent; sound knowledge and understanding, highly detailed – worth more than **6 out of 6 marks**. Overall this answer is lengthier than expected in the time available (300 words would be reasonable in the 15–20 minutes available for a 12 mark question).

The evaluation (**AO2**) is very restricted. Even though there is some elaboration, the range is too narrow for more than **3 out of 6 marks**.

Total = **9 out of 12 marks**, a **Grade A** (just).

Psychological approaches to psychopathology

Question 1 Identify and outline **two** psychological approaches to psychopathology. *(3 marks + 3 marks)*

Aron's answer

The psychodynamic approach is based on Freud's theory. Freud believed that there were three parts of the personality, the id, ego and superego. These three parts are in conflict with each other, and psychopathology is when this conflict goes wrong. There are also defence mechanisms like repression and projection which can be overused.

The behavioural approach is based on classical conditioning, operant conditioning and social learning. An individual learns their behaviour through one of these types of learning, and if they learn the wrong thing this becomes psychopathological.

Holly's answer

The behavioural approach sees all abnormal behaviours as being learned as a result of experiences in the person's life. These experiences can lead to abnormal behaviours being reinforced, but can be adaptive for the individual (e.g. avoiding a feared situation). This approach focuses on behaviour, and not on internal states or underlying biology.

The cognitive approach assumes that a person's thoughts and expectations direct their behaviour. Psychopathology is the result of faulty thinking, where irrational beliefs (e.g. the belief that they are being watched) lead to negative consequences for the individual (e.g. feelings of anxiety).

Examiner's comments

Aron demonstrates good knowledge of two psychological approaches – but he has failed to apply these to psychopathology so he will only receive **1 out of 3 marks** for each answer. Holly has done better for her first answer on the behavioural approach, which is clearly linked to psychopathology (**3 out of 3 marks**), but less well on the cognitive approach (**2 out of 3 marks**).

Question 2 Explain the difference between the psychological and biological approaches to psychopathology. *(4 marks)*

The biological approach to psychopathology explains abnormality in terms of brain damage, brain chemistry (e.g. depression is caused by low levels of serotonin) and genetics (e.g. schizophrenia appears to run in families). The psychological approach explains psychopathology in terms of irrational thought processes of the person or because of learning the wrong sort of behaviours so that they cause problems for the individual in their life.

Biological approaches to psychopathology see abnormality being caused by physical factors, such as brain disease, altered brain chemistry or genetics, whereas psychological explanations explain abnormal behaviour in terms of non-physical factors, such as the person's learning history or as the product of their faulty and irrational thinking. Biological approaches see the development of abnormal behaviour as being outside the individual's control, but some psychological explanations, such as the cognitive approach, see the individual as responsible for their own thinking and therefore their own behaviour.

Aron has failed to answer the question – and instead just described the biological approach and then the psychological approach, so **1 out of 4 marks**. Holly's excellent answer first of all contrasts the approaches in terms of physical versus non-physical factors and second, in terms of control – so the **full 4 marks**. One difference with a little more elaboration would also score full marks.

Question 3 (a) Outline the psychodynamic approach to psychopathology. *(6 marks)*
(b) Explain **one** limitation to this approach. *(3 marks)*

(a) Freud said that there are three parts of personality. The id operates on the pleasure principle, and requires instant gratification, i.e. 'I must have it, and I must have it now'. The superego is the conscience, and is a sort of internalised model of the parents. It demands behaviour that is morally right. The ego operates on the reality principle, and tries to deal with the conflict between id and superego. The ego tries to protect itself by using ego defence mechanisms such as repression and projection. If the id is allowed to dominate, the person can be very aggressive and selfish, but if the superego is dominant, the person can feel guilty all the time.

(b) A limitation is that Freud based most of his theory on case studies of neurotic women. These are difficult to generalise out to other people so we don't know if his theory applies to normal people as well. Also he based much of his theory on sex, and ignored other aspects of a person's behaviour such as cognition. These are also important in determining psychopathological behaviour.

(a) Freud's psychoanalytic approach suggests that psychopathological disorders such as depression are not physical in origin, but are the result of unresolved conflicts (e.g. conflict between id, ego and superego) or repressed memories of early trauma. The unconscious mind influences behaviour through the influence of traumatic memories that have been repressed into the unconscious. Traumatic memories are usually repressed into the unconscious in childhood because the ego is not yet mature enough to deal with them. Later trauma (e.g. divorce) may then trigger repressed memories of an earlier trauma, causing it to be re-experienced. Individuals are distressed because they don't understand why they are behaving in such an abnormal way.

(b) Most of the concepts of this approach (e.g. ego, unconscious) are abstract and don't refer to any physical structures within the body therefore cannot be seen or measured in a scientific way. This also means that processes such as repression and conflicts such as the conflict between id, ego and superego operate at an unconscious level, therefore there is no way to know for certain that they are really taking place.

(a) Again, Holly has clearly focused on the approach as it is applied to psychopathology and provides plenty of detail for the **full 6 marks**. Aron is still forgetting to direct his answer towards psychopathology, but there are elements of his answer that are relevant (e.g. ego defence), so **2 out of 6 marks**.

(b) Aron has made the mistake of presenting more than one limitation but only the best one will be creditworthy – his first one has some elaboration, so **2 out of 3 marks**. Aron would have gained more marks by writing a little bit extra about the first limitation. Holly's limitation is well explained, so the **full 3 marks**.

Question 4 Evaluate the psychodynamic approach to psychopathology. *(6 marks)*

A major problem for this approach is that it can't be proved or disproved, therefore there is no evidence to support it. This means that it cannot be regarded as a scientific theory. Another problem is that Freud was accused of being sexist but it is probably more to do with when he was writing, in Victorian times, and society was sexist at that time. Finally, Freud's theory is supported by the success of psychoanalysis as a form of therapy, but critics have claimed that people don't get better and some actually get worse. One study found that psychoanalysis was no different in terms of improvement than people who had no treatment at all. This means that if the therapy doesn't work, the theory is not a good one.

Most of the concepts of this approach (e.g. ego, unconscious) are abstract and don't refer to any physical structures within the body. Similarly, major processes such as repression and the conflict between id, ego and superego are also abstract and so cannot be seen or measured in a scientific way. However, although the theory is difficult to prove or disprove scientifically because of this, there is still experimental support for many of Freud's claims. Fisher and Greenberg (1996) reviewed 2,500 experimental studies, finding, for example, support for Freud's ideas on the origins of depression. Freud has been criticised for being sexist in claiming that women were more prone to mental disorders. However, his claim does receive support from research which shows that gender differences do occur in the rates of common mental disorders such as depression and anxiety.

Aron has claimed that there is no evidence to support the approach – this is always a foolish claim to make because there is usually some evidence for almost everything. Aron has provided two further evaluative points and given some elaboration for each which are relevant to psychopathology, so **4 out of 6 marks** (just). If he had named the source of the research (as Holly has) the answer would gain more credit. Holly's answer is actually not much better because in places it is not made relevant to psychopathology, so **5 out of 6 marks**.

Question 5 (a) Outline the behavioural approach to psychopathology. *(6 marks)*

(b) Explain **one** limitation to this approach. *(3 marks)*

(a) This approach claims that all behaviour is learned, and it doesn't matter whether it is normal or abnormal, it is learned in the same way. The first way in which abnormal behaviour is learned is through classical conditioning. If the UCS and CS are presented together, eventually the CS produces the CR, which could be psychopathological behaviour. The second way is operant conditioning. Behaviour that is reinforced is more likely to be repeated, so if abnormal behaviour is reinforced it is repeated. Finally there is social learning, where people see other people rewarded for their behaviour and then imitate it.

(b) A limitation of this approach is that it ignores other possible explanations of psychopathology. For example, the biological approach does not explain psychopathology in terms of learning but explains it in terms of physical changes in the body. This is a better explanation because it is more scientific.

(a) The behavioural approach sees all abnormal behaviours as being learned (through conditioning or through social learning) as a result of experiences in the person's life. If behaviour leads to a desired outcome then that behaviour is likely to be repeated. This can lead to some behaviours being acquired that are maladaptive (e.g. developing a school phobia) simply because they lead to something desirable for the individual or the avoidance of something undesirable. For example, for a school phobic, not going to school lowers their anxiety, which makes them feel better, so this behaviour is reinforced. This approach focuses only on behaviour, and not on internal states or underlying biology. The behaviour is the external manifestation of the anxiety felt by the individual, and treatments focus on changing this behaviour rather than tackling the underlying reasons for it.

(b) Because this approach focuses only on the symptoms of a disorder, treatment does not address its underlying causes. This means that the behavioural approach is a limited approach because, although the symptoms of a disorder are behavioural, the causes of these symptoms may be cognitive, emotional, or even biological. As a result, this means that changing one behaviour may simply result in symptoms re-emerging at some future date.

(a) Aron has made the same mistake again, simply explaining the behaviourist approach and making no reference to psychopathology. He might just get **3 out of 6 marks** because he has mentioned 'abnormal'. Holly's answer is superior – not because she has added the word 'abnormal' and 'maladaptive' occasionally but because she has also given appropriate examples, so **6 out of 6 marks**.

(b) Aron's limitation is fair but his defence of it is a little thin on detail – his comparison with the biological approach is not very effective and the last sentence is irrelevant, so only **1 out of 3 marks** (perhaps a bit mean but 2 out of 3 marks is too generous). Holly's answer is well elaborated and firmly set in the context of psychopathology for the **full 3 marks**.

Question 6 Evaluate the behavioural approach to psychopathology. *(6 marks)*

A criticism of this approach is that it only focuses on behaviour rather than on any underlying causes. For example, a person may be afraid of snakes for all sorts of reasons, but the behavioural approach ignores this. Another limitation is that it claims that all abnormal behaviours are bad for the individual, but this is not necessarily true. For example, if somebody has panic attacks, they may get more attention from other people, which they find rewarding. This means that some abnormal behaviours are actually helpful and allow the person to cope much better with whatever is causing the abnormal behaviours in the first place.

A strength of this approach is that its claims can be tested scientifically. However, research has not always supported these claims. For example, explaining the acquisition of phobias (e.g. a fear of snakes) in terms of conditioning or social learning does not tell us why many people have such a fear, yet cannot recall any incident in their past which might have led to such learning taking place. The behavioural approach focuses only on the symptoms of a disorder, therefore treatment does not address its underlying causes. This means that the behavioural approach is a limited approach because, although the symptoms of a disorder are behavioural, the causes of these symptoms may be cognitive, emotional, or even biological. As a result, this means that changing one behaviour may simply result in symptoms re-emerging at some future date.

Aron has provided two appropriate and elaborated criticisms – the first one is less elaborated than the second, so **5 out of 6 marks**. Holly has considered strengths as well as limitations, which doesn't gain any more credit but it is nice to see! She too has only dealt with two criticisms but given greater elaboration, so **6 out of 6 marks**.

Question 7 Outline the cognitive approach to psychopathology. *(6 marks)*

- Behaviour is caused by faulty thinking.
- This causes problems if it interferes with a person's ability to live life normally.
- The person is seen as controlling their own thoughts.
- A is the activating event, i.e. something in the person's environment.
- B is the belief, which can be rational or irrational.
- C is the consequence, which can be healthy or unhealthy depending on the belief.

The cognitive approach assumes that a person's thoughts and expectations direct their behaviour. Psychopathology is the result of distortions in an individual's thought processes, which in turn cause them to behave maladaptively. If this maladaptive behaviour goes against social norms, or interferes with their ability to lead a normal life, it becomes psychopathological. In the ABC model, A is an activating event (e.g. seeing a man outside the house) that may set into motion irrational thought processes, such as the irrational belief (B) that they are being watched. This may lead to negative consequences (C) for the individual. Following an activating event, rational beliefs would lead to healthy emotions and adaptive behaviours, but irrational beliefs lead to unhealthy emotions (e.g. feelings of anxiety or paranoia) and maladaptive behaviours.

Aron has used bullet points in his answer which is not a problem as long as the points contain detail and demonstrate knowledge and understanding. The final three bullet points cover Ellis' ABC model but this has not been made clear so makes no sense and are not really creditworthy. The first three points are focused on psychopathology, so **3 out of 6 marks**.

Holly's answer provides more detail and perhaps importantly provides an introduction to the ABC model so it doesn't come out of the blue, **full 6 marks**.

Question 8 Bridget's mother died when she was a little girl. She nevertheless had a reasonably happy childhood. However, she recently lost her job and her boyfriend left her. Suddenly she feels extremely depressed and for the first time really feels she misses her mother.

Use the psychodynamic approach to psychopathology to explain why Bridget has only now started grieving for her mother. *(4 marks)*

This can be explained in terms of defence mechanisms. Bridget has repressed memories of her mother dying when she was a little girl. This memory still continues to affect her though, and would make her tearful for no apparent reason. Another defence mechanism is regression, which is when adults respond to stress by returning to a time when they were young. Because Bridget has recently had two more losses, which has made her anxious and unable to cope, she has regressed to childhood, which has uncovered the memory of her mother dying.

Freud's psychoanalytic approach suggests that psychopathological disorders such as depression are the result of repressed memories of early trauma. Traumatic memories such as the death of Bridget's mother are repressed into the unconscious in childhood because the ego is not yet mature enough to deal with them. Later trauma, in this case the loss of a job and the break up of her relationship, can then trigger repressed memories of the earlier trauma, causing it to be re-experienced and causing her to begin grieving for her lost parent.

When you read Holly's answer it helps to make better sense of Aron's answer. Both answers are clearly informed by a knowledge of the psychodynamic approach and for 4 marks are sufficiently related to the question stem and to psychological knowledge to be worth **full marks**.

Question 9 Charlie is terrified of dogs and thinks this is probably because he was bitten when he was a young boy.

 (a) Use the behavioural approach to psychopathology to explain why Charlie is terrified of dogs. *(4 marks)*

 (b) Use the cognitive approach to psychopathology to explain why Charlie is terrified of dogs. *(4 marks)*

(a) Charlie was bitten by a dog when he was young. Being bitten is a punishment and so whatever behaviour preceded the punishment will become less frequent. In this case he would have approached the dog and this would be the behaviour that would be punished. This would stop him approaching dogs in the future, which would explain why he is now terrified of dogs.

(b) The cognitive approach sees psychopathology as being caused by faulty thinking. In this case, Charlie has become terrified of dogs because when he was a young boy he was bitten by one. This makes him think that all dogs are dangerous and that they will bite him, which is an irrational way of thinking.

(a) The behavioural approach sees all abnormal behaviours as being learned as a result of experiences in the person's life. These experiences can lead to abnormal behaviours being reinforced, but can be adaptive for the individual. As a child he had a traumatic incident involving a dog, and he is now conditioned to feel terror whenever a dog is nearby. By developing a phobia of dogs, he is more likely to avoid them, which lowers his levels of anxiety, and makes him feel better.

(b) The cognitive approach assumes that a person's thoughts and expectations direct their behaviour. Psychopathology is the result of faulty or distorted thinking, where irrational beliefs lead to negative consequences for the individual. Because he had a traumatic experience with a dog as a child, this now guides his thought processes concerning dogs. Any dog now acts as an activating event, which leads Charlie to believe he will be attacked again (an irrational belief), and as a consequence he experiences a negative and maladaptive emotion — terror.

(a) Holly's answer looks better and certainly contains a lot more sophisticated psychology which has been applied to Charlie's phobia. However, Aron's answer contains enough psychology and has been appropriately related to the dog phobia, so both answers get **full marks**.

(b) Holly has again provided a wealth of irrelevant extra detail – there is no need to give a description of the psychology in this depth. She receives **full marks** but may have wasted valuable exam time. Aron's answer is perhaps a little short on detail so a rather mean **3 out of 4 marks**.

RESEARCH METHODS QUESTION One way to investigate explanations of psychopathology is to use the case study method.

(a) Explain what is meant by the 'case study method'. *(3 marks)*

Aron's answer	Holly's answer	Examiner's comments
The case study method is where psychologists study one person and try to find as much as they can about that person rather than studying a whole group of people and then coming up with general laws of behaviour that apply to all of them.	This is a detailed study of a single individual or group or event. It involves the use of several different techniques, e.g. observation, interviews and psychometric tests, to build up a thorough profile of the person or group in question.	Both answers are good but Aron's is a little limited because he sees case studies as being about one person whereas they can be about a group, events or even institutions. So **2 out of 3 marks** for Aron and **full marks** for Holly.

(b) Outline **one** strength and **one** limitation of the case study method. *(2 marks + 2 marks)*

It is a good way of finding out lots of information about a single individual. It is an expensive method because it is very time-consuming for the researcher.	Strength – It is useful as a way of investigating unusual types of psychopathological behaviour where only individual cases are available. Limitation – Because individual cases tend to be a product of unique circumstances, it is difficult to generalise out from the study of just one individual to the general population.	Aron's answers lack elaboration – for example, why is it time-consuming? So just **1 out of 2 marks** for each. Holly's answers are worth the **full 2 marks**.

Extended writing question

Outline and evaluate the psychodynamic approach to psychopathology. *(12 marks)*

AO1

A basic outline of the psychodynamic approach which is reasonably related to psychopathology rather than just being a straightforward account of Freud's theory of personality.

The psychodynamic approach sees abnormal behaviour as being caused by underlying psychological forces that the individual is largely unaware of. These are often the result of traumatic experiences from childhood or the conflict between id, ego and superego. A well-adjusted person develops a strong ego that allows both the id and superego expression at appropriate times. However, if this conflict between id and superego is not managed effectively by the ego, problems occur. Traumatic early experiences are repressed into the unconscious mind because the ego is not sufficiently well developed to cope with the emotional disturbances they create. These experiences can eventually re-emerge in later psychological problems. Freud believed that everybody suffered from these conflicts so we are all abnormal to some degree.

Some critics of the psychodynamic approach claim that people who undergo psychodynamic therapy (e.g. psychoanalysis) do little better in terms of improvement than those people who do not have any form of therapy over the same period of time. Another problem with this model is that it is very difficult to test scientifically, although there have been some studies that supported its claims. Freud carried out a number of case studies to support his theory (e.g. The Wolf Man and Anna O), but the problem with case studies is that they are difficult to generalise to other people, so have limited scientific value. There have been some more recent studies, which have tested the validity of the psychodynamic approach, and there has been some support for the psychodynamic explanation of the origins of depression being due to loss in childhood.

(263 words)

AO2

Three critical points are examined. The second one (testing the model scientifically) is effective and well supported with references to specific case studies. The other critical points are less well elaborated.

Examiner's comments The description (**AO1**) is appropriate, but a little bit on the short side (i.e. limited) so **4 out of 6 marks**.

The evaluation (**AO2**) is relatively narrow in range and restricted in depth, so **4 out of 6 marks**.

Total = **8 out of 12 marks**, a **Grade B**.

Extended writing question

Outline and evaluate the behavioural approach to psychopathology.

(12 marks)

AO1

The first paragraph provides a fairly detailed outline of the behavioural approach, the same as given on the previous spread, which got 6 marks. This shows how essays can be constructed by putting elements together. You could see them as 2 x 6-mark chunks (or sometimes 4 x 3-mark chunks).

However, when it comes to the extended writing question, answers to 6-mark questions don't necessarily translate into half of a 12-mark question. So you need to remember to add that bit more.

The behavioural approach sees all abnormal behaviours as being learned (through conditioning or through social learning) as a result of experiences in the person's life. If behaviour leads to a desired outcome then that behaviour is likely to be repeated. This can lead to some behaviours being acquired that are maladaptive (e.g. developing a school phobia) simply because they lead to something desirable for the individual or the avoidance of something undesirable. For example, for a school phobic, not going to school lowers their anxiety, which makes them feel better, so this behaviour is reinforced. This approach focuses only on behaviour, and not on internal states or underlying biology. The behaviour is the external manifestation of the anxiety felt by the individual, and treatments focus on changing this behaviour rather than tackling the underlying reasons for it.

A strength of this approach is that its claims can be tested scientifically. However, research has not always supported these claims. For example, explaining the acquisition of phobias (e.g. a fear of snakes) in terms of conditioning or social learning does not tell us why many people have such a fear, yet cannot recall any incident in their past which might have led to such learning taking place. The behavioural approach focuses only on the symptoms of a disorder, therefore treatment does not address its underlying causes. This means that the behavioural approach is a limited approach because, although the symptoms of a disorder are behavioural, the causes of these symptoms may be cognitive, emotional or even biological. As a result, this means that changing one behaviour may simply result in symptoms re-emerging at some future date.

(274 words)

AO2

This paragraph received 6 marks as an evaluation on the previous spread – a narrow range of points but in considerable depth.

Examiner's comments

The description (**AO1**) is **5 out of 6 marks**.

The evaluation (**AO2**) is **5 out of 6 marks** because the range is too narrow.

Total = 10 out of 12 marks.

Overall this is a very short answer and even though the separate components scored 6 + 6 marks on the short answer questions this is not sufficient for full marks on an extended writing question. Nevertheless it is a **Grade A** answer.

Extended writing question

Outline and evaluate the cognitive approach to psychopathology.

(12 marks)

AO1

Again this first paragraph, an outline of the cognitive approach, is the same as the 6-mark answer given on the previous spread – with the addition of one sentence on the end.

The cognitive approach assumes that a person's thoughts and expectations direct their behaviour. Psychopathology is the result of distortions in an individual's thought processes, which in turn cause them to behave maladatively. These include distortions in cognitive processes, the way in which we process information. For example, anxious people process information differently from people who are less anxious. Cognitive products are the conclusions that people reach as a consequence. In the ABC model, A is an activating event (e.g. seeing a man outside the house) that may set into motion irrational thought processes, such as the irrational belief (B) that they are being watched. This may lead to negative consequences for the individual. Following an activating event, rational beliefs would lead to healthy emotions and adaptive behaviours, but irrational beliefs lead to unhealthy emotions (e.g. feelings of anxiety or paranoia) and maladaptive behaviours. If a maladaptive behaviour goes against social norms (i.e. causes the person to act in a way that is considered deviant by others), or interferes with their ability to lead a normal life, it becomes psychopathological.

Part of the success of this approach has been that it has led to successful therapies for treating psychopathological behaviours. For example, a study by Thase et al. (2007) compared cognitive therapy with drug treatments for depression. Both therapies were equally effective, but the cognitive therapy was better tolerated by patients, who were therefore more likely to continue with their treatment.

However, by focusing only on cognitive factors in determining psychopathology, this approach ignores the role of situational factors such as life stressors and poverty. A cognitive therapist would only attempt to change the way a person thinks about stressors rather than changing the stressors themselves. This means that for many people they would still have to endure the same stressful live events, and so the anxiety or depression would persist. There is a problem of determining cause and effect with this approach. It is possible that distorted thinking has caused a mental disorder such as depression, but it is also possible that the mental disorder causes the distorted thinking. This happens in depression, with individuals developing a distorted and self-defeating way of looking at the world.

(366 words)

AO2

In this paragraph one critical point (a positive one) is dealt with in depth (i.e. it is elaborated) and this makes it effective.

The first three sentences deal with a further critical point and discuss this in depth.

A final critical point is made about cause and effect.

Examiner's comments

The description (**AO1**) is reasonably detailed and shows evidence of sound knowledge and understanding, **6 out of 6 marks**.

The evaluation (**AO2**) includes a range of points – not a broad range – but they are in considerable depth so **6 out of 6 marks**.

Total = 12 out of 12 marks, a **Grade A**.

Biological therapies

EXAM ADVICE

The specification names two biological therapies: drugs and ECT.

This means that questions could be set on biological therapies in general, or on any one of the named biological therapies.

Question 1 The following statements all relate to criticisms of biological therapies used in treating psychopathology.

A Easy to use.

B Tackles the symptoms rather than the problem.

C Could be particularly suitable for severe depression.

D No real understanding of how the method works.

In the table below, write write which statement applies to explanations. *(4 marks)*

Chemotherapy (drugs)	A, B
ECT	C, D

FULL MARKS!

Question 2 (a) Identify **one** drug therapy used to treat abnormal behaviour. *(1 mark)*

(b) Explain how this method works in treating abnormal behaviour. *(4 marks)*

(c) Describe **one** limitation of using drug therapy to treat abnormal behaviour. *(3 marks)*

Domo's answer

(a) Antipsychotic drugs.

(b) These are used in the treatment of schizophrenia. They work by blocking the transmission of the neurotransmitter dopamine at the synapse because schizophrenia is thought to be caused by too much dopamine activity. This has the effect of reducing many of the symptoms of this disorder.

(c) One limitation of drug therapies is that drugs only offer temporary relief from the symptoms of the disorder rather than offering a cure. As soon as a patient stops taking the drug, which may happen because of the side effects associated with many drug therapies, the symptoms return.

Fiona's answer

(a) One drug therapy used to treat abnormal behaviour is antidepressant drugs such as the SSRIs (selective serotonin reuptake inhibitors) such as Prozac. These are used to treat depression.

(b) SSRIs work by increasing the amount of serotonin in the synapse. They do this by stopping the serotonin being taken back into the pre-synaptic cell after it has acted on the post-synaptic cell. They only affect serotonin, not other neurotransmitters.

(c) A limitation is that there are side effects. There is a claim in the US that SSRIs can cause people to commit suicide, and this has led to court cases against the makers of SSRIs.

Examiner's comments

(a) Domo's answer is sufficient for **1 mark**, so clearly Fiona also gets **1 mark**.

(b) Both answers are detailed insofar as they use the 'technical' psychological terms, thus displaying sound knowledge and understanding, so **full marks** for both candidates.

(c) Both candidates have identified an appropriate limitation and offered some further elaboration. Fiona's final point about court cases is not fully relevant, so only **2 out of 3 marks**, where Domo gets **full marks**.

Question 3 Evaluate the use of drugs in treating abnormality. *(6 marks)*

A strength of drug treatments is that they tend to be effective, particularly when tested against placebos.

However, for the treatment of disorders such as schizophrenia, drug treatment alone is less effective than drugs plus psychological therapy.

Drugs have the added advantage of being easy to use compared to psychological therapies because they require little effort from the patient, who is therefore more motivated to continue treatment, compared with the more time-consuming psychological therapies.

A limitation of drug therapies is that drugs only offer temporary relief from the symptoms of the disorder rather than offering a cure. As soon as the patient stops taking the drug, which may happen because of the side effects associated with many drug therapies, the symptoms return.

Drugs only treat the symptoms not the cause, so don't cure the problem a person is suffering from. A better alternative would be to use psychological treatments such as psychoanalysis, which do address the cause of a problem by retrieving it from the unconscious.

Another problem with drug treatments is that there are side effects. These side effects can be so disturbing that people stop taking their medication, and in the USA there was a multi-million pound court case because a person with schizophrenia sued the drug makers because of the side effects that the drug gave them. They sued them based on the Human Rights Bill.

A strength of drug treatments is that they are cheap and easy to use.

Another strength is that research has showed that they work better than a placebo.

Domo has used the same limitation as in (c) above as part of his evaluation, which is fine – evaluation consists of a set of critical points. Domo identifies and elaborates two other critical points and so this answer is worth the **full 6 marks**.

Fiona has also 'reused' her limitation from (c) and gone on to elaborate this further – but the elaboration (about the court case) isn't relevant to explaining why this is a limitation. In addition to the point about side effects, three further critical points are made but only one of these has been elaborated, so there is a broad range of critical points but not always in depth, **5 out of 6 marks**.

Question 4 ECT is used in the treatment of abnormality. Outline what is involved when ECT treatment is used. *(4 marks)*

ECT is used for severely depressed patients who don't respond to other forms of treatment. A patient is first given a muscle relaxant, then a small amount of electric current is passed through the brain for about half a second.

This is enough to produce a seizure, which affects the whole brain.

A course of treatment usually requires between 3 and 15 treatments depending on the severity of the depression.

ECT involves giving someone an electric shock of about 200 volts through electrodes in their brain and then this shock has a beneficial effect on their symptoms of depression. The person is also given an anaesthetic so they don't break any bones during treatment. A problem for ECT is that it can lead to memory loss after treatment. It is used for people who are suicidal.

Fiona's answer contains more detail than Domo's (e.g. she cites 200 volts) but she finishes her answer with an irrelevant point about problems – the question asked for techniques only (so the point about beneficial effects is also irrelevant).

Overall Domo's answer is actually more 'detailed' because of the breadth of points covered. Domo receives the **full 4 marks** and Fiona's answer gets **2 out of 4 marks**.

Question 5 Evaluate the use of ECT in treating abnormality. *(6 marks)*

ECT appears to be effective in relieving the symptoms of severe depression. Comer (2002) states that about 70% improve after treatment, although critics claim that most of these had relapsed six months after receiving ECT, suggesting that any improvements were only temporary. However, because ECT is often used in cases where there is a risk of suicide, this temporary improvement can be life saving.

It is possible that for some people, the improvement associated with ECT is due to the extra attention and hope that ECT offers. Studies that have compared the use of sham ECT with real ECT have found that although the real ECT patients were more likely to recover, some sham patients also recovered, supporting this suggestion.

A problem with ECT is the possibility of side effects, including impaired memory and cardiovascular problems, and in about one-third of patients, an increase in fear and anxiety.

A problem for ECT is that it is only good for people with severe depression and does not really make a difference if people have other disorders, such as schizophrenia, even though it was first developed as a treatment for schizophrenia.

Bev Callard, an actress who plays Liz McDonald in Coronation Street was given ECT when she was severely depressed and she claims it probably saved her life, but she was worried about some of its side effects such as memory loss, particularly as an actress she would then have problems learning her lines.

There is evidence that people who go through ECT do suffer memory loss. Many of the negative effects of ECT treatment are irreversible, therefore it has also been criticised as being inhumane, particularly when people are given ECT against their wishes. It has also been criticised as being a bit like kicking a television set when it isn't working, because as yet we don't know why it works.

Domo's use of paragraphs has made the task of marking easier for the examiner because he has separated out three clear evaluative points – although the first two are related. These first two points are well elaborated – following the three-point rule described on page 10. The final point is not as well elaborated but overall the answer is worth **6 out of 6 marks**. The use of names and dates is not required for full marks but it does add quality to an answer.

Fiona's use of an everyday example (of Bev Callard) is not entirely appropriate (it tends towards the anecdotal) but she has tied it in well, linking memory loss to learning lines. Altogether there are again three critical points – the last two are not well elaborated and the first one has anecdotal elements; a fairly narrow range lacking depth, so **4 out of 6 marks**.

Question 6 ECT is used to treat patients suffering from severe disorders such as depression. One hospital decides that it would be useful to prepare a brief guide for relatives of patients receiving ECT so they can understand the treatment better and so that they are aware of the strengths and limitations.
What information could you put in this leaflet? *(6 marks)*

What is ECT?

ECT stands for electroconvulsive therapy. It is used in cases of severe depression, where patients have not responded to psychotherapy or drug medication.

What happens in ECT?

Two electrodes are placed on the scalp, one on the side of the head and one on the forehead.

Patients are given a short-acting sedative so they are unconscious when the shock is applied, and a nerve-blocking drug, which temporarily paralyses the limbs.

A small amount of electric current is passed through the head for half a second. This produces a seizure in the brain, which lasts about one minute.

What are the risks?

Although ECT is relatively harmless, some patients report slight memory loss or an increase in anxiety after treatment.

I would put information about what happens during ECT. It would mention the fact that electrodes are put on the head and then an electric shock is given. It would also mention that patients are given a drug first so that they don't feel the shock and also that they are given another drug so that they don't thrash around and break bones during the brain seizure. I would also mention some of the studies that have shown that ECT is effective as a treatment of depression. For example, Comer (2002) states that 70% of patients get better after ECT. I would also warn patients about some of the side effects, this is necessary for informed consent. I would let patients know their rights to refuse treatment if they don't want to go through with it.

Domo's answer is nicely set out and very informative. The drawback is he has omitted any strengths e.g. effectiveness, so **5 out of 6 marks**.

Fiona has included evidence about strengths but overall her answer is quite inappropriate as an answer to this question – she has not produced clear information for relatives and patients and some of the information that has been included ('breaking bones' and 'brain seizure') would scare people and be unlikely to be included in such a pamphlet. Fiona has omitted to mention any limitations, but she has included some key pieces of information, such as electrodes, effectiveness and informed consent, so **3 out of 6 marks**.

Question 7 Sonia has been experiencing panic attacks recently. For no reason she suddenly feels an overwhelming sense of panic.
Drugs can be used to successfully treat panic attacks so Sonia visits her GP to see if he will prescribe the drugs.
Her GP isn't sure whether drugs will be suitable for Sonia and outlines the strengths and limitations of drug treatments.
(a) Outline **one or more** strengths of drug treatments that the GP might explain to Sonia. *(4 marks)*
(b) Outline **one or more** limitations of drug treatments that the GP might explain to Sonia. *(4 marks)*

(a) Drug treatments work, significantly reducing the feelings of panic, although their effectiveness is increased when combined with psychological therapies.

They are also easy to use, requiring little effort from the patient, therefore patients are more motivated to continue with their treatment, which in turn makes it more likely they will experience an improvement in their condition.

(b) Most drugs have side effects, for example, SSRIs can cause nausea, and in very rare cases, feelings of suicide. This is one of the main reasons that drug treatments fail, as people choose to stop taking their medication because of the side effects.

Drugs also only tackle the symptoms of panic, steps must be taken to address the possible causes of these attacks as well otherwise the underlying anxiety may simply resurface with different symptoms.

(a) He could explain to Sonia that drugs are the best way to treat panic attacks. If he prescribed BZs, they would make her feel less anxious and so better able to cope with whatever was causing her to panic. He could tell her that lots of musicians take BZs to help them overcome stage fright, so they would certainly help her.

(b) He should warn her about the possible side effects of the drugs she might take. For example, she should only take BZs for a short period of time because they can become addictive. She needs to find other ways to sort out her panic attacks rather than just relying on the BZs.

(a) Domo has outlined two strengths and provided additional details for each so the **full 4 marks**. Fiona hasn't really given any strengths except to say that drugs are best – there is no explanation of why they are popular or best, so **1 out of 4 marks**.

(b) Again, Domo has outlined two criticisms and provided additional elaboration for each, so the **full 4 marks**. Fiona has identified just one limitation and given some elaboration. The final sentence isn't a limitation, so **2 out of 4 marks** (a generous mark).

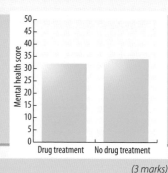

RESEARCH METHODS QUESTION

Research on the effectiveness of any drug treatment is often conducted by giving one group of participants the drug while a second group receive a 'sugar pill' (a placebo) – they think they are receiving an active drug but it doesn't actually contain anything. After a period of time the two groups are compared to see whether there is a difference in their recovery.

Recovery can be assessed in terms of the improvement in a patient's score on a mental health questionnaire (maximum score of 50) after the study is completed. A high score indicates healthiness. The bar chart shows the results of one such study.

(a) Describe **one** ethical issue with this kind of research.

(3 marks)

Domo's answer

An ethical issue is that for patients with a mental disorder who could be helped with an active drug, they are deprived of treatment by being given a placebo with no active ingredient. This goes against the duty of care that psychologists have for their participants, and so would be regarded as unethical.

Fiona's answer

An ethical issue is lack of informed consent, if ECT is given without the person's full consent as it sometimes is (e.g. when it is given after sectioning someone under the Mental Health Act).

Examiner's comments

Domo is spot on with his ethical issue and well explained too, so **3 out of 3 marks**. Fiona identifies informed consent, which is an issue – but not in the way described. From the point of view of the researcher the consent that is required would be to take part in the study. The patients would be receiving ECT as part of their treatment and the responsibility for informed consent for treatment lies with the doctor. So **1 out of 3 marks** for Fiona.

(b) Describe the conclusions you could draw from the graph.

(4 marks)

There are two main conclusions that can be drawn from this graph. First, the difference in improvement in mental health scores between the active drug treatment and the placebo treatment is very small, indicating that the drug treatment was not significantly more effective than the placebo. Second, both groups showed improvements, suggesting that even a placebo (with no side effects) could be used to bring about improvement for people suffering from this condition.

I could draw two conclusions.

1) The drug group does better than the placebo group.

2) Neither group achieves a perfect mental health score (which is 50), so neither the drug nor the placebo work that well.

Domo has identified two findings and given the conclusions that can be drawn from these, **4 out of 4 marks**.

The problem with Fiona's answer is that finding 1 doesn't link to a conclusion – which she has managed to do for finding 2. Therefore **3 out of 4 marks**.

Extended writing question

Outline and evaluate biological treatments of abnormality.

(12 marks)

AO1

Most of the first paragraph is a reasonably detailed description of the action of two kinds of drugs relating these specifically to the treatment of abnormality.

This is a reasonably detailed account of ECT, fairly similar to the 4-mark account given on the previous spread – another example of using building blocks in an essay.

Drugs are used in the treatment of abnormal behaviours such as anxiety, depression and schizophrenia. Unlike psychological treatments, which address the cause of abnormal behaviour, drugs only deal with the symptoms. Anti-depressant drugs are used to relieve the low mood associated with depression by increasing the action of neurotransmitters such as serotonin. Anti-psychotic drugs are used in the treatment of schizophrenia. They work by blocking the transmission of the neurotransmitter dopamine at the synapse, which has the effect of reducing many of the symptoms of this disorder, including hallucinations and delusions.

A strength of drug treatments is that, compared to psychological treatments, they work quickly and require little effort on the part of the patient, who is therefore more motivated to continue treatment compared with the more time-consuming psychological therapies. Although drug treatments are generally effective for disorders such as depression and schizophrenia, drug treatment on its own is less effective than drugs plus psychological therapy. A limitation of drug therapies is that drugs only offer temporary relief from the symptoms of the disorder rather than offering a cure. As soon as a patient stops taking the drug, which may happen because of the side effects associated with many drug therapies, the symptoms return.

ECT is used for severely depressed patients who don't respond to other forms of treatment. A patient is first given a muscle relaxant, then a small amount of electric current is passed through the brain for about half a second. This is enough to produce a seizure, which affects the whole brain, and is thought to help different parts of the brain communicate better with each other, which is why it has a beneficial effect on reducing depressive symptoms.

ECT appears to be effective in relieving the symptoms of severe depression. Comer (2002) states that about 70% improve after treatment, although critics claim that most of these had relapsed six months after receiving ECT, suggesting that any improvements were only temporary. However, studies that have compared the use of sham ECT with real ECT have found that although the real ECT patients were more likely to recover, some sham patients also recovered, supporting this suggestion. A problem with ECT is the possibility of side effects, including impaired memory and cardiovascular problems, and in about one third of patients, an increase in fear and anxiety.

(389 words)

AO2

The comparison with psychological treatments counts as a brief piece of AO2.

This evaluative paragraph contains four critical points – with some elaboration (depth).

Three critical points are covered all in some depth.

Examiner's comments The description (**AO1**) covers two examples of biological treatments each in reasonable detail, but ECT is slightly limited, so a slightly mean **5 out of 6 marks**.

The evaluation (**AO2**) covers a broad range of points, effectively presented in some depth, so **6 out of 6 marks**.

Total = **11 out of 12 marks**.

Discuss the use of drugs to treat abnormality.

(12 marks)

AO1

A basic description of anti-anxiety drugs.

The second paragraph contains a basic description of drugs used to treat depression.

A more detailed description of antipsychotic drugs is given here.

Drugs are used to treat many different types of abnormality, such as anxiety, depression and schizophrenia. For example, drugs used to treat anxiety include beta-blockers and BZs. These work by calming the person down and reducing anxiety. Research has supported the effectiveness of these drugs when used in the treatment of anxiety, particularly when compared to patients who are just treated with a placebo. There are problems with these drugs though, because they can become addictive.

Drugs are also used in the treatment of depression. These include SSRIs, which stands for selective serotonin reuptake inhibitors. They work by stopping the reuptake of serotonin, which reduces the symptoms of depression. Research has shown that when treated with SSRIs, people are likely to feel less depressed than when treated with a placebo. However, one of the problems with SSRIs is that they can make some people suicidal, although there is evidence that with old people they can actually protect them against suicidal thoughts.

The final use of drugs is to treat schizophrenia. These are called antipsychotics. It is believed that schizophrenia is due to an excess of the neurotransmitter dopamine. Antipsychotic drugs work by sitting in the receptors for dopamine so they can't fire. By blocking dopamine it means that the cells can't be stimulated and so the symptoms of schizophrenia are reduced. A problem with antipsychotic drugs is that they don't work for all schizophrenics. They also have side effects, and some of these are almost as disturbing as the symptoms of the disorder, so people stop taking their medication.

(259 words)

AO2

Two somewhat superficial critical points are made about effectiveness and addiction.

A further two somewhat superficial points. The elaboration provided does not actually add much information – so lacks effectiveness.

A further two superficial points.

Examiner's comments

The description (**AO1**) varies from reasonably detailed to basic. Overall the range of drug treatments covered partly compensates for the lack of detail but not enough to even be tempted by the top band (see mark scheme on page 9), so **4 out of 6 marks**.

The evaluation (**AO2**) is generally superficial and is not always effective, but a broad range has been covered, so **4 out of 6 marks**.

Total = **8 out of 12 marks**, a **Grade B**.

Describe and evaluate the use of ECT to treat abnormality.

(12 marks)

AO1

This description of ECT is more detailed than the answer that received 4 marks on the previous spread – this contains more general information as well as more specific details (e.g. '0.6 amps') – both of which add up to more detail.

ECT is used for severely depressed patients who don't respond to other forms of treatment. Electrodes are placed on the head prior to sending a small amount of electric current through the head to induce a brain seizure. Before the shock is administered, the patient is given a short-acting drug that makes them unconscious during the electric shock, which lasts about half a second, and the following seizure, which lasts about one minute. The electrical current, about 0.6 amps is enough to produce the seizure, which affects the whole brain. A course of ECT usually requires treatment three times a week and a patient normally requires between 3 and 15 treatments depending on the severity of the depression.

ECT appears to be effective in relieving the symptoms of severe depression. Comer (2002) states that about 70% improve after treatment, although critics claim that most of these had relapsed six months after receiving ECT, suggesting that any improvements were temporary only. However, because ECT is often used in cases where there is a risk of suicide, this temporary improvement can be life saving. It is possible that for some people, the improvement associated with ECT is due to the extra attention and hope that ECT offers.

There is still some doubt about how ECT works, although it is known to affect the action of neurotransmitters. It is believed that the seizure caused by ECT works to release neurotransmitters, which deliver messages from one part of the brain to another, and so recovery from depression may be due to improved communication between the different parts of the brain. However, studies that have compared the use of sham ECT with real ECT have found that although the real ECT patients were more likely to recover, some sham patients also recovered, supporting this suggestion. A problem with ECT is the possibility of side effects, including impaired memory and cardiovascular problems, and in about one third of patients, an increase in fear and anxiety.

(329 words)

AO2

Several critical points are linked together here – so could be described as three points with little elaboration or one point in considerable depth and highly effective.

Again the first part of this paragraph could count as two separate points or one highly effective point.

There is a final point about side effects, given in some depth.

Examiner's comments

The description (**AO1**) is reasonably detailed and shows evidence of sound knowledge and understanding, so **6 out of 6 marks**.

The evaluation (**AO2**) includes a reasonable range of points, many of which are in considerable depth. The answer could be interpreted differently and seen as a broad range in less depth, either way **6 out of 6 marks**.

Total = **12 out of 12 marks**.

Remember, though, that these full mark answers are not perfect, nor are they 'model' answers – they just show you the tricks that enable you to get a **Grade A**.

Psychological therapies

Question 1 The following statements relate to different psychological therapies. Select the two statements that relate to systematic desensitisation. *(2 marks)*

☐ The therapist interprets the patient's thoughts.

☐ Irrational thoughts are turned into rational ones.

☑ The patient is taught to relax.

☑ It is a form of counterconditioning.

☐ The aim is to make unconscious feelings conscious.

Question 2 Outline **two** techniques used in psychoanalysis. *(6 marks)*

Liam's answer

The therapist lies the patient down on a couch and asks them to say whatever comes into their head. This is a way of finding out what is in their unconscious mind without the patient really thinking about it (and censoring what is said).

Another way is to analyse the patient's dreams, because when people dream they don't have the ego acting like a watchdog, so if they dream about flying, for example, they might really desire sexual adventure. This is another way of the psychoanalyst finding out what is going on in their unconscious mind. Once they know this they can start helping them to deal with the underlying problem.

Jade's answer

In free association, the person undergoing psychoanalysis expresses their thoughts exactly as they occur to them. It is a spontaneous association of thoughts and emotions and is not directed by the therapist. This is intended to reveal areas of conflict in the unconscious that are causing the current problem and bring them into consciousness, where the therapist can help interpret them for the patient who can be helped to cope with them.

The psychoanalyst listens for clues from the patient's free association and draws tentative conclusions about the possible cause of their problems. The patient may offer resistance to these interpretations, or may display transference, where they recreate emotions associated with the cause of their problem (e.g. childhood abuse) and transfer these onto the therapist, who uses this information to determine how close they are to the real conflict.

Examiner's comments

Jade's answer shows an excellent level of detail, more than enough for the **full 6 marks**. Liam is a bit casual in his comments and his answer lacks the sharp psychological terminology, such as 'spontaneous association'. However he has included some important information, such as 'censoring'. Much of what he has written for the second technique is not relevant, such as 'This is another way…' and 'Once they know…'. He would receive **4 out of 6 marks**.

Question 3 Psychoanalysis is not one of the most popular therapies. Explain why it is less likely to be used than other psychological therapies for abnormality. *(6 marks)*

It is less likely to be used today because there are not as many psychoanalysts around today as there were in Freud's day when psychoanalysis was far more popular.

Also psychoanalysis is not as fashionable as it used to be in the 1960s, when 'going to see your analyst' was what most Americans liked to do.

There has also been a lot of controversy over false memories that are 'discovered' during therapy. For example, in 2001, a jury awarded an American woman $5 million in damages after deciding that therapists had planted false memories of childhood sexual abuse by her parents and brothers.

A final reason why it is less used today is that research has shown that compared to other therapies it is very expensive and not particularly effective.

A study of 450 patients undergoing psychoanalysis found that the longer the treatment, the better the outcome. This suggests that psychoanalysis is only really suitable for patients who can invest the considerable cost and time that it would involve, particularly as drug treatments are much more time- and cost-effective treatments for abnormality. Research has also suggested that only certain types of patient are likely to benefit from psychoanalysis. The term YAVIS has been used to describe these, for example, Y = young, people who still have the energy required to change, and V = verbally skilled enough to be able to describe their inner feelings. Finally, Eysenck (1986) claims that the outcome for patients undergoing psychoanalysis is not sufficiently better than simply leaving them with no treatment for the same period. This casts doubt over the validity of psychoanalysis as a treatment for abnormality.

The first two sentences of Liam's answer are not creditworthy – he is just saying that the therapy isn't popular – we want to know why. He does say that repressed memory therapy might be a reason and, right at the end, also says its expensiveness and lack of effectiveness may be explanations but no details are given to support this. Altogether it makes his answer at best 'superficial' and a lot is irrelevant, so **2 out of 6 marks**.

Jade's answer has plenty of detail, including names and dates, but not all of it actually answers the question. The first and final points have been linked to the question of popularity but the issue of 'YAVIS' hasn't, so **5 out of 6 marks** for some lack of effectiveness.

Question 4 Outline what is involved in systematic desensitisation. *(6 marks)*

This was invented by a man called Wolpe. He locked a girl who was afraid of cars into a car and drove her around for hours until she was no longer afraid of cars. In systematic desensitisation, the therapist starts by asking the patient what it is that causes them anxiety, what they could cope with, and what would terrify them. If it is a spider then they present a spider to them very gradually, for example, starting with a cartoon spider, then a small dead spider 10 feet away, a dead spider close up and so on. Eventually they have a large live spider actually on their arm. At each stage, the patient has to get used to the spider before going on to the next stage. Eventually the patient should be able to have a spider on them without being afraid.

This is based on the principles of classical conditioning and is used as a treatment for the anxiety experienced during phobias. In this treatment, the patient is gradually exposed to the feared stimulus (e.g. a spider) while they are in a relaxed state. Because the responses of fear and relaxation are incompatible, the feelings of fear gradually subside. The therapist and the patient construct a desensitisation hierarchy, which is a series of imagined scenes involving the feared object, each one causing slightly more anxiety than the previous one. Once the patient has learned to relax at one level in the desensitisation hierarchy they are ready to move on to the next level, and eventually they are able to master the fear that previously accompanied the presentation of the feared object.

Liam has failed to focus on the question and instead has written all he knows about systematic desensitisation – but fortunately much of it is relevant to the question of 'how' SD is done. He has used the example of a spider effectively to illustrate the steps but says little about relaxation techniques, so **4 out of 6 marks**.

Jade's answer may look better (lots of specific detail) but much of it is focused on explanations (such as classical conditioning and incompatible responses) instead of just saying how it is done, so she too receives **4 out of 6 marks**.

Question 5 Kelly has a phobia of balloons, which makes it difficult for her to go to parties. She decides to seek treatment for her phobia and her doctor recommends systematic desensitisation.

What information could her doctor give her to help her decide whether this therapy would be suitable? *(6 marks)*

The doctor would tell her what is involved. If she has a phobia of balloons, the doctor would start by presenting her with her a deflated balloon some distance away. If Kelly was okay with that, the doctor could move the deflated balloon a bit closer, then half inflate it and so on. Eventually, if she didn't get too anxious with each of these stages, the doctor could surround her with fully inflated balloons and she would be cured of her phobia. This would be suitable for her because it is a fairly quick and effective way of getting rid of a phobia like the one Kelly is suffering from.

Her doctor should tell her that she will be asked to imagine being in the presence of balloons while she is in a relaxed state. Because the responses of fear and relaxation are incompatible, the feelings of fear towards balloons will then gradually subside. Kelly and her doctor will construct a desensitisation hierarchy, a series of imagined scenes involving balloons each one causing slightly more anxiety than the previous one. The benefits of this type of therapy are that it is relatively quick and has been used effectively with a range of different phobias. However he/she should warn her that her fear of balloons could be symptomatic of some more deep-seated fear, and that dealing with the fear of balloons using this technique rather than addressing the underlying cause of the problem may simply result in symptoms reappearing some time in the future.

Liam has given a fairly competent description of systematic desensitisation but hasn't given Kelly any advice (as required in the question), so **3 out of 6 marks**. Jade has included all aspects of systematic desensitisation and discussed these in the context of balloon therapy. She has also mentioned benefits and limitations, as required, so the **full 6 marks**.

> **EXAM ADVICE**
> Note that neither candidate has made the mistake of thinking that stress inoculation therapy would be relevant here – both have focused on abnormality not stress.

Question 6 Explain what is involved in Cognitive Behavioural Therapy. *(6 marks)*

Cognitive Behavioural Therapy is based on the principle that a person's thoughts and attitudes determine their behaviour, therefore therapy is all about changing these if they are inappropriate, and by changing the person's thoughts about an object or event, this will also change their behaviour. This is why it is called 'cognitive behavioural' therapy, because it involves changing cognitions and behaviour. If an activating event like a snarling dog causes an irrational belief (such as the belief that the dog will attack), then this leads to fear and running away (the consequence). What the therapist needs to change is the belief, so the person no longer believes that the dog will attack them, so they no longer feel the need to run away.

CBT attempts to change both the faulty thinking and the maladaptive behaviour, and as a result, help people become better adjusted and less anxious about life. During therapy, the patient is encouraged to dispute any self-defeating beliefs. This is achieved by challenging some of the irrational beliefs held by the individual. For example, in empirical disputing, they may be challenged to provide proof that their belief is accurate. In pragmatic disputing they may be challenged to explain how having a particular irrational belief is likely to help them. As a result of this approach, individuals are then able to move on to more rational interpretations of events, and their behaviour changes as a consequence to become more healthy and adaptive.

It is important to note the words 'what is involved' in this question. This means that a general overview of the therapy will not suffice, and an outline of what actually goes on in the therapy is required. Jade's answer is excellent, she briefly sets the scene by giving the aims of therapy, and then proceeds to describe what is typically involved in a therapeutic session. The answer is clearly worth the **full 6 marks**. Liam's answer includes some of the general principles of CBT, but doesn't really get to grips with the practical (i.e. 'what is involved') side of the therapy. As a result he would only receive **3 out of 6 marks**.

Question 7 The principles of Cognitive Behavioural Therapy are used by many GPs when discussing medical problems with their patients. For example, when a patient visits their doctor complaining that they have difficulty sleeping and feel tired all the time, the GP might put Cognitive Behavioural Therapy into action.

(a) Describe how the GP might apply the principles of Cognitive Behavioural Therapy when treating a person with sleep problems. *(4 marks)*
(b) Outline **one** problem the GP might face in trying to use Cognitive Behavioural Therapy in this situation. *(3 marks)*

(a) The GP could talk to them about their sleep problems and try to change the way they think about sleep, for example, some people take all their worries to bed with them, and this stops them sleeping. The doctor could try to reassure them so they worried less. The bed can also act as an activating event, so that when the person goes to bed they have irrational fears. They could perhaps overcome this by associating the bed with pleasant things, then they would not worry so much when in bed, and would sleep more easily.

(b) The main problem is that there may be other things that are wrong and which might be causing the sleep problems. These can't be solved just by using CBT. For example, the patients may have insomnia, or drink too much coffee before going to bed, which keeps them awake. There are many causes of sleep problems.

(a) CBT can be used to help a person identify the attitudes and beliefs that stop them sleeping. For example, some people worry about not sleeping and it is the worry of not sleeping that keeps the person awake. The patient can be challenged by asking them how this attitude (i.e. that they won't sleep) helps them (pragmatic disputing) and whether lying there worrying about not sleeping makes any sense (logical disputing). They can be taught to overcome these negative thoughts and replace them with more positive attitudes and beliefs that cause them to behave in a way that is more conducive to sleep.
(b) A problem the GP may face is that CBT is not suitable for everybody and may not always be what people want. For example, the individual may find it difficult to put these principles into practice and may be unable to break the habit of confining their 'worry time' to when they are in bed, with the result that they continue to experience sleeplessness.

(a) Again, Jade's answer is much more competent and detailed but Liam's has enough psychology and enough engagement with the question to also be awarded the **full 4 marks**.

(b) Both candidates have provided sufficient elaboration of their criticism for the **full 3 out of 3 marks**. In each case they have identified the problem and made two further points to explain in what way this is a problem and why this would be a problem (the three-point rule, see page 10).

Question 8 Explain the difference between biological and psychological therapies. *(4 marks)*

Biological therapies try to change our biology, e.g. by using drugs, whereas psychological therapies try to change our psychology, for example by using CBT to change the way we think or systematic desensitisation to change the way we behave.

Biological therapies are based on the assumption that abnormal behaviour is physical in origin (e.g. altered brain chemistry), therefore the most appropriate form of treatment must also be physical, addressing this underlying physical cause. Psychological therapies, on the other hand, are based on the belief that although the symptoms of a disorder may be physical, this does not mean that the causes are. Therefore any treatment should be based more on the individual's psychological make-up. Dealing with the symptoms alone (as in biological therapies) will not deal with the underlying psychological processes that cause the abnormal behaviour.

Liam has attempted to identify a difference by using the word 'whereas' but the key strength of his answer is that he has identified a <u>dimension</u> for comparison – what it is that is changed. However, his answer has little elaboration, so just **2 out of 4 marks**. Jade has provided much more detail which makes it more difficult to see if she has actually made any comparison – she has considered the different assumptions of each approach and the implications of these assumptions for treatment but these comparisons might have been more explicit, so **3 out of 4 marks**.

RESEARCH METHODS QUESTION

When psychologists try to assess the effectiveness of different psychological therapies they often compare recovery rates after the use of different therapies. One study looked at 10,000 patient histories and found that 80% of those patients receiving psychoanalysis had recovered, whereas only 65% of those using other psychological methods had recovered.

(a) Outline **one** conclusion you could draw from this study. *(2 marks)*

Liam's answer

Psychoanalysis is better than other psychological therapies, with 80% getting better with psychoanalysis and only 65% getting better with other therapies.

Jade's answer

The conclusion would be that psychoanalysis is more effective, in terms of recovery rates for patients, than other psychological therapies.

Examiner's comments

For 2 marks both answers are sufficient to get **full marks** as they each draw a conclusion and link this to findings.

(b) (i) Explain what is meant by 'validity'. *(2 marks)*
   (ii) In the study described above, outline **one** factor that might affect its validity. *(3 marks)*

(a) Validity means whether something truly measures what it is trying to measure.

(b) It is possible that some of the studies were not carried out effectively, for example, some might have suffered from low internal validity, for example they may have failed to control certain factors that would have made a difference (e.g. whether the patients knew they were in a study, in which case they may have tried harder to make a recovery, and less hard if they knew they were in a placebo condition).

(a) It means how far the results of a study are legitimate given what the study was attempting to find out.

(b) The different outcomes may be influenced by the type of disorder being studied as well as the severity of the disorder being treated. For example, psychoanalysis tends to be used for less serious neurotic illnesses than some other psychological therapies, therefore this might account for its better outcome rates.

(a) Both definitions of validity are appropriate, so **full marks**. Liam's answer relates specifically to internal validity but that's OK.

(b) Again, both answers deserve **full marks**. Liam and Jade have dealt with different issues and given sufficient elaboration for 3 marks.

Extended writing question

Outline and evaluate the use of psychoanalysis to treat abnormality. *(12 marks)*

AO1

A brief and basic statement of what psychoanalysis is.

A reasonably detailed outline of how psychoanalysis is conducted, covering free association, therapist interpretation and transference.

AO2

Psychoanalysis is based on the belief that behaviour is influenced by unconscious desires and fears that are the result of repressed memories or unresolved conflicts from childhood. During therapy, the psychoanalyst tries to bring these desires and fears into the conscious mind and to help the individual deal with them.

In free association, the person undergoing psychoanalysis expresses their thoughts exactly as they occur to them. It is a spontaneous association of thoughts and emotions and is not directed by the therapist. This is intended to reveal areas of conflict in the unconscious that are causing the current problem and bring them into consciousness, where the therapist can help interpret them for the patient who can be helped to cope with them. The psychoanalyst listens for clues from the patient's free association and draws tentative conclusions about the possible cause of their problems. The patient may offer resistance to these interpretations, or may display transference, where they recreate emotions associated with the cause of their problem (e.g. childhood abuse) and transfer these onto the therapist, who uses this information to determine how close they are to the real conflict.

A study of 450 patients undergoing psychoanalysis found that the psychodynamic therapies such as psychoanalysis were more effective over the long term than the short term, and the longer the treatment, the better the outcome. This suggests that psychoanalysis is only really suitable for patients who can invest the considerable cost and time that it would involve, particularly as drug treatments are much more time- and cost-effective for abnormality.

A second criticism that can be made is that only certain types of patient are likely to benefit from psychoanalysis. The term YAVIS has been used to describe these, for example, Y = young people who still have the energy required to change, and V = verbally skilled enough to be able to describe their inner feelings.

Finally, Eysenck (1986) claims that the outcome for patients undergoing psychoanalysis is not sufficiently better than simply leaving them with no treatment for the same period. This casts doubt over the validity of psychoanalysis as a treatment for abnormality. Eysenck also suggests that the success of behavioural therapies makes psychoanalysis less valid as a useful treatment of abnormal behaviour.

(372 words)

An effectively constructed positive criticism.

A second criticism which perhaps could be more effective – why does this matter?

In the final paragraph two further criticisms are made in limited depth.

Examiner's comments

The description (**AO1**) is reasonably detailed with an appropriate selection of material, **6 out of 6 marks**.

The evaluation (**AO2**) includes a broad range of points most in limited depth, so **5 out of 6** marks because we are not tempted by the band below ('restricted and superficial' – see mark scheme on page 9).

Total = **11 out of 12 marks**, clearly a **Grade A**.

Extended writing question

Outline and evaluate the use of systematic desensitisation to treat abnormality.

(12 marks)

AO1

A reasonably detailed and accurate outline of systematic desensitisation. It is relatively short but contains all the key details.

Systematic desensitisation is a behavioural treatment based on the principles of classical conditioning. It is used as a treatment for the anxiety experienced by patients suffering from phobias. The patient is first taught relaxation skills, and then gradually exposed to the feared stimulus while they are in a relaxed state. Because fear and relaxation are incompatible, the feelings of fear gradually subside. The therapist and the patient construct a desensitisation hierarchy, a series of imagined scenes involving the feared object, each one causing slightly more anxiety than the previous one. Once the patient has learned to relax at one level in the desensitisation hierarchy they are ready to move on to the next level, and eventually they are able to master the anxiety they feel in the presence of the feared object.

Systematic desensitisation is a relatively quick form of treatment and requires less effort on the patient's part compared to other psychological treatments. This means that patients are more likely to persevere with their treatment. It has also been shown to be effective for a range of different anxiety disorders, including fear of flying.

A problem with systematic desensitisation is that it only deals with the symptoms of a disorder, although it may eliminate the symptoms, the cause of the problem is not dealt with. As a treatment of phobias, it is less effective in the treatment of those phobias that were linked to survival among our ancestors (e.g. fear of the dark).

(244 words)

AO2

Two strengths of the approach are identified with some elaboration.

Two limitations are identified and given some elaboration making them only somewhat effective.

Examiner's comments

The description (**AO1**) is reasonably detailed and shows evidence of sound knowledge and understanding. However, it is limited in terms of breadth, so **5 out of 6 marks**.

The evaluation (**AO2**) includes a reasonable range of points but is limited in depth and effectiveness, thus **4 out of 6 marks** because, comparatively speaking, the range is not broad but it is better than 'restricted' and the depth is better than 'superficial' (criteria which would have led us to award 3 out of 6 marks – see mark scheme on page 9).

Total = **9 out of 12 marks**, a **Grade A** answer (but only just).

Extended writing question

Outline and evaluate the use of Cognitive Behavioural Therapy to treat psychopathology.

(12 marks)

AO1

This 'building block' description is the same as given in answer to a 6-mark question asking for a description of Cognitive Behavioural Therapy (see previous spread) – accurate, detailed and shows sound knowledge and understanding.

However, as pointed out on page 115, you often need to write a bit more to gain 6 marks in an extended writing questions.

Cognitive Behavioural Therapy is based on the assumption that many problems are the product of irrational thinking and the behaviours that occur as a consequence. It attempts to change both the faulty thinking and the maladaptive behaviour, and as a result, help people become better adjusted and less anxious about life. During therapy, the patient is encouraged to dispute any self-defeating beliefs. This is achieved by challenging some of the irrational beliefs held by the individual. For example, in empirical disputing, they may be challenged to provide proof that their belief is accurate. In pragmatic disputing they may be challenged to explain how having a particular irrational belief is likely to help them. As a result of this approach, individuals are then able to move on to more rational interpretations of events, and their behaviour changes as a consequence to become more healthy and adaptive.

Engels et al. (1993) carried out a meta-analysis of studies of rational-emotive behavioural therapy. In this form of CBT, the patient is taught to understand how many of their problems are the result of their irrational thinking and the consequences of thinking in this way. They found that this form of therapy was effective for people suffering from a number of different disorders.

Some studies have shown that CBT is not only useful for people suffering from psychopathology, but also for students suffering from examination anxiety. It may not be possible to help everybody suffering from anxiety, because sometimes anxiety is not irrational for the individual, but is very real, particularly for people who have a bullying boss at work or who are in an abusive relationship at home. Their anxiety cannot be reduced just by making them think differently about their problems. When they return to work or to the bullying relationship, their anxiety returns. This limits the usefulness of CBT.

(307 words)

AO2

A reasonably elaborated point on the effectiveness of the therapy. There is a sentence of description in the middle.

A second point which has been thoroughly explained.

Examiner's comments

The description (**AO1**) is reasonably detailed and shows evidence of sound knowledge and understanding, **5 out of 6 marks**.

The evaluation (**AO2**) includes a very narrow range of points only one of which has been well elaborated, so overall this is worth **3 out of 6 marks** as it is not good enough for a narrow range in depth.

Total = **8 out of 12 marks, Grade B.**

Extra questions for you

Some further examples of questions requiring you to apply your knowledge to novel situations.

Question 1 Liang's behaviour is beginning to worry his parents. He seems unable to deal with even the most minor problems in his life, and is constantly putting himself down. His parents think his behaviour is possibly a sign of abnormality.

    (a) Identify and explain the definition of abnormality that best accounts for Liang's behaviour. *(3 marks)*

    (b) Outline **one** limitation of this definition in this particular situation. *(3 marks)*

Question 2 Some people find it very difficult talking to other people. Although many of us are shy from time to time, in some people this can become pathological. Ewan is one such person. In his case he becomes exceptionally nervous when faced with a member of the opposite sex.

    (a) Identify and explain the definition of abnormality that best explains Ewan's behaviour. *(3 marks)*

    (b) Outline **one** limitation of this definition in this particular situation. *(3 marks)*

    (c) Explain Ewan's behaviour from the perspective of two different approaches to psychopathology. *(3 marks + 3 marks)*

    (d) Ewan is sceptical about these explanations. Give one limitation of each of these two explanations of his behaviour. *(2 marks + 2 marks)*

Question 3 Obsessive compulsive disorder is an increasingly common psychological illness. People with this condition are compelled to repeat certain actions over and over again, for example washing their hands until they become red and raw or checking and rechecking that they have locked the door when they leave home.

    (a) Identify and explain the definition of abnormality that best explains why obsessive compulsive disorder is abnormal. *(3 marks)*

    b) Use **one** psychological approach to psychopathology to explain why obsessive compulsive disorder might develop in some individuals. *(3 marks)*

Question 4 Ewan is referred for therapy to treat his extreme anxiety in the presence of members of the opposite sex. His GP decides Cognitive Behavioural Therapy would be most appropriate for Ewan.

    (a) Outline what would be involved in Cognitive Behavioural Therapy as a treatment for Ewan's behaviour. *(3 marks)*

    (b) Explain why you think this therapy might be appropriate. *(3 marks)*

    (c) Outline **one** reason why you feel Cognitive Behavioural Therapy might not be effective in treating Ewan's condition. *(3 marks)*

Question 5 Katerina is 30 years old. She has become very sad and depressed over the last five years. She is concerned that her mother did not want her as a child and this is affecting their relationship now.

Use the psychodynamic approach to psychopathology to explain why events in Katerina's past may be causing her to become depressed now. *(4 marks)*

Question 6 Katerina has been undergoing psychoanalysis for over three years to deal with her depression.

    (a) Outline **two** techniques that her psychoanalyst might use during their psychoanalytic sessions. *(4 marks)*

    (a) Outline **one** strength of using psychoanalysis to treat Katerina's problems. *(4 marks)*

Question 7 Katerina is not noticing a great deal of improvement in her depressive symptoms. She goes to see her GP, who prescribes drugs to help deal with these symptoms.

    (a) Outline what would be involved in drug therapy for treating Katerina. *(3 marks)*

    (b) Outline **two** strengths of a biological approach to Katerina's problems. *(2 marks + 2 marks)*

    (c) Outline **two** limitations of a biological approach to Katerina's problems. *(2 marks + 2 marks)*

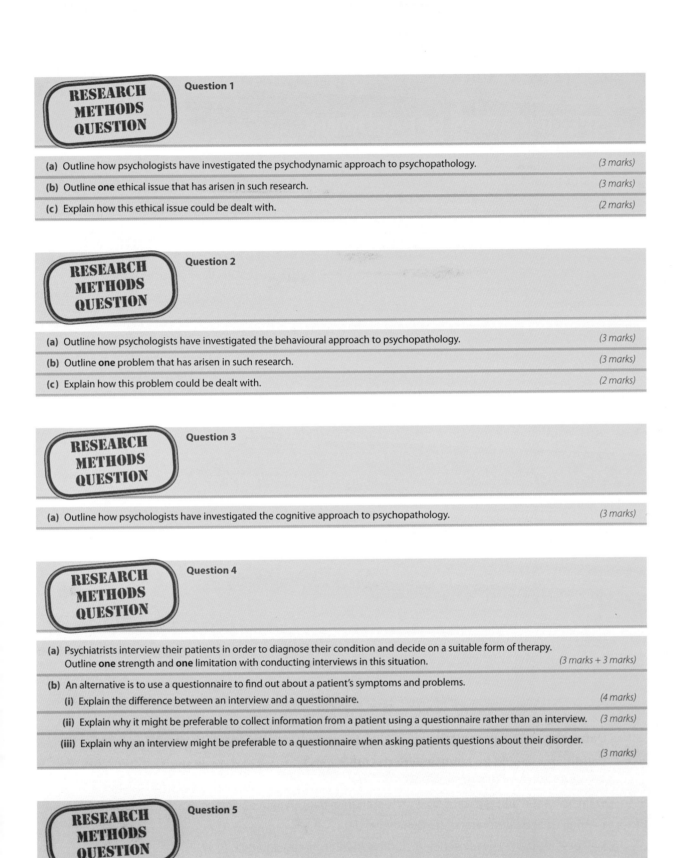

RESEARCH METHODS QUESTION — **Question 1**

(a) Outline how psychologists have investigated the psychodynamic approach to psychopathology. *(3 marks)*

(b) Outline **one** ethical issue that has arisen in such research. *(3 marks)*

(c) Explain how this ethical issue could be dealt with. *(2 marks)*

RESEARCH METHODS QUESTION — **Question 2**

(a) Outline how psychologists have investigated the behavioural approach to psychopathology. *(3 marks)*

(b) Outline **one** problem that has arisen in such research. *(3 marks)*

(c) Explain how this problem could be dealt with. *(2 marks)*

RESEARCH METHODS QUESTION — **Question 3**

(a) Outline how psychologists have investigated the cognitive approach to psychopathology. *(3 marks)*

RESEARCH METHODS QUESTION — **Question 4**

(a) Psychiatrists interview their patients in order to diagnose their condition and decide on a suitable form of therapy. Outline **one** strength and **one** limitation with conducting interviews in this situation. *(3 marks + 3 marks)*

(b) An alternative is to use a questionnaire to find out about a patient's symptoms and problems.
   (i) Explain the difference between an interview and a questionnaire. *(4 marks)*

   (ii) Explain why it might be preferable to collect information from a patient using a questionnaire rather than an interview. *(3 marks)*

   (iii) Explain why an interview might be preferable to a questionnaire when asking patients questions about their disorder. *(3 marks)*

RESEARCH METHODS QUESTION — **Question 5**

(a) Outline **one** study that has investigated the effectiveness of drugs as a means of treating abnormality. *(6 marks)*

(b) Explain **one** possible problem with the validity of this study and say how it might be dealt with. *(4 marks)*

(c) Identify **one** ethical issue that might arise in this study and explain how it would be dealt with. *(3 marks)*

SPECIFICATION BREAKDOWN

Specification content

Methods and techniques

Candidates will be expected to demonstrate knowledge and understanding of the following research methods, their strengths and limitations:

- Experimental method including laboratory, field and natural experiments.
- Studies using a correlational analysis.
- Observational techniques.
- Self-report techniques, including questionnaire and interview.
- Case studies.

Investigation design

Candidates should be familiar with the following features of investigation design:

- Aims.
- Hypotheses including directional and non-directional.
- Experimental design (independent groups, repeated measures and matched pairs).
- Design of naturalistic observations, including the development and use of behavioural categories.
- Design of questionnaires and interviews.
- Operationalisation of variables, including independent and dependant variables.
- Pilot studies.
- Control of extraneous variables.
- Reliability and validity.
- Awareness of the BPS Code of Ethics.
- Ethical issues and ways in which psychologists deal with them.
- Selection of participants and sampling techniques, including random, opportunity and volunteer sampling.
- Demand characteristics and investigator effects.

Data analysis and presentation

Candidates should be familiar with the following features of data analysis, presentation and interpretation:

- Presentation and interpretation of quantitative data, including graphs, scattergrams and tables.
- Analysis and interpretation of qualitative data.
- Measures of central tendency, including median, mean and mode.
- Measures of dispersion, including ranges and standard deviation.
- Analysis and interpretation of correlational data. Positive and negative correlations and the interpretation of correlation coefficients.
- Presentation of qualitative data.
- The processes involved in content analysis.

Appendix

Research Methods

Comment

Psychologists (and scientists) use many different research methods and techniques when conducting research. The specification focuses on the most common of these as listed on the left. You will be asked questions on these, and about their strengths and limitations of these methods/techniques.

In order to test any explanation of behaviour, a scientist needs to state research aims and (usually) a hypothesis.

The next step is to design the study – the design of the study will differ depending on the method/technique that is selected. The specification requires that you are able to design experiments, naturalistic observations, and self-report techniques (questionnaires and interviews).

There are some issues common to most kinds of methods/techniques: operationalisation, use of pilot studies, control of extraneous variables, reliability and validity, consideration of ethical issues and how to deal with them, selection of participants, and understanding of the factors that influence participants (most notably demand characteristics and investigator effects).

Exam questions will be set which assess your ability to deal with all of these issues, for example asking you to explain what a pilot study is or to explain how you would conduct a pilot study or why you would conduct one.

A key part of any research is the analysis of data – presenting the results and working out what they mean. The data may be presented graphically and/or in terms of measures of central tendency
(e.g. mean) and dispersion (e.g. range).

If your results are numerical then they are described as 'quantitative'. Sometimes psychologists collect data which is 'qualitative', for example collecting data about people's individual thoughts and feelings. Content analysis is a means of dealing with qualitative data by putting complex behaviours into categories.

There is no research methods chapter in this book because the questions on research methods are embedded in the other chapters in the same way as they are embedded in the exam.

There is no section in the exam called 'Research Methods'. In Unit 1 there are just two sections called:
Cognitive psychology and Research methods.
Developmental psychology and Research methods.

In Unit 2 there are also research methods questions scattered through each section but not as many as in Unit 1. In fact, to be precise there are 24 marks' worth of research methods questions in Unit 1 and 12 marks' worth in Unit 2.

Research methods concepts are an integral part of the study of all areas of psychology, so it makes sense to embed the questions in this way.

All that remains is to wish you GOOD LUCK in your exams – except you don't need luck because by now you should be well prepared for anything that comes up. KEEP YOUR EYE ON THE BALL and remember, YOU DO KNOW THE ANSWER TO THE QUESTION, you just need to think clearly and make sure you SELECT the APPROPRIATE bits to use in any question. Simply writing down everything you know about a topic seldom attracts credit… remember, often LESS IS MORE.

Mike and Cara

References

You should refer to *Psychology A2: The Complete Companion*, where you will find the full references for studies cited in this book. We have added some extra references below that are included in this book, but were not covered in the main textbook.

Allport, G.W. and Postman, L. (1947) *The Psychology of Rumor.* New York: Henry Holt.

Baddeley, A.D., Lewis, V.J. and Vallar, G. (1984) Exploring the articulatory loop. *Quarterly Journal of Experimental Psychology, 36,* 233–252.

Baker, M., Gruber, J. and Milligan, K. (2008) Universal child care, maternal labor supply, and family well-being. *Journal of Political Economy, 116*(4).

Bernstein, D.M., Laney, C., Morris, E.K. and Loftus, E.F. (2005) False beliefs about fattening foods can have healthy consequences. *Proceedings of the National Academy of Sciences, 102,* 13724–13731.

Browning, C. (1992) *Ordinary Men: Reserve Police Battalion 101 and the Final Solution in Poland.* New York: HarperCollins.

Buzan, T. (2006) *The Buzan Study Skills Handbook.* London: BBC Active.

Calder, J. (2006) Chunking as a cognitive strategy: teaching students how to learn more in less time. *Teaching Tools and Techniques.*

Fisher, R.P., Geiselman, R.E. and Amador, M. (1989) Field test of the cognitive interview: Enhancing the recollection of actual victims and witnesses of crime. *Journal of Applied Psychology, 74,* 722–727.

Flin, R., Boon, J., Bull, R. and Knox, A. (1992) The effects of a five month delay on children's and adults' eyewitness memory. *British Journal of Psychology, 83,* 323–336.

Fontana, J.L., Scruggs, T.E. and Mastropieri, M.A. (2007) Mnemonic strategy instruction in inclusive secondary social studies classes. *Remedial and Special Education, 28,* 345–355, doi: 10.1177/07419325070280060401 (accessed January 2011).

Friedman, M. and Rosenman, R.H. (1960) Overt behavior pattern in coronary artery disease: Detection of overt pattern behavior A in patients with coronary artery disease by a new psycho-physiological procedure. *The Journal of the American Medical Association, 173,* 1320–1325.

Garandeau, C.F. and Cillessen, A.H.N. (2006) From indirect aggression to invisible aggression: a conceptual view on bullying and peer group manipulation. *Aggression and Violent Behavior, 11,* 612–625.

Hart, S., Field, T., Jones, N. and Lundy, B. (1998) Depressed mothers' interaction styles influence infants' toy exploration and affect in a teaching situation. *Infant Behavior and Development, 21,* 447.

Hull, J.G., VanTreuren, R.R. and Virnelli, S. (1987) Hardiness and health: A critique and alternative approach. *Journal of Personality and Social Psychology, 53,* 518–530.

Hurst, M.W., Jenkins, C.D. and Rose, R.M. (1978) The assessment of life change stress: A comparative and methodological inquiry. *Psychosomatic Medicine, 40,* 126–141.

Johnson, C. and Scott, B. (1976) *Eyewitness testimony and suspect identification as a function of arousal, sex of witness, and scheduling of interrogation.* Paper presented at the American Psychological Association Annual Meeting, Washington, DC.

Karpel, M.E., Hoyer, W.J. and Toglia, M.P. (2001) Accuracy and qualities of real and suggested memories: nonspecific age differences. *Journals of Gerontology Series Psychological Sciences and Social Sciences, 56,* 103–110.

Kebbell, M., Milne, R. and Wagstaff, G. (1999) The cognitive interview: a survey of its forensic effectiveness. *Psychology, Crime, and Law, 5,* 101–115.

Kobasa, S.C. (1979) Stressful life events, personality, and health: An inquiry into hardiness. *Journal of Personality and Social Psychology, 37*(1), 1–11.

Kobasa, S.C. and Maddi, S.R. (1977) Existential personality theory. In R. Corsini (ed.) *Current personality theories.* Ithaca, IL: Peacock.

Kunz-Ebrecht, S.R, Kirschbaum, C. and Steptoe, A. (2004) Work stress, socioeconomic status and neuroendocrine activation over the working day. *Social Science and Medicine, 58,* 1523–1530.

Lancer, K. (2000) *Hardiness and Olympic women's synchronized swim team.* Paper presentation at University of Nevada, Los Vegas.

Larner, M. *et al.* (1989) The peer relations of children reared in day care centers or home settings: a longitudinal analysis. *Paper presented at the Biennial Meeting of the Society for Research on Child Development,* 21st, Kansas City, MO.

Loftus, E.F. (1975) Leading questions and the eyewitness report. *Cognitive Psychology, 7,* 560–572.

Loftus, E.F. and Pickrell, J.E. (1995) The formation of false memories. *Psychiatric Annals, 25,* 720–725.

Maddi, S.R. (2002) The story of hardiness: Twenty years of theorising, research, and practice. *Consulting Psychology Journal, 54,* 173–185.

McKelvey, W. and Kerr, N.H. (1988) Differences in conformity among friends and strangers. *Psychological Reports, 62,* 759–762.

Melhuish, E.C. (NESS Research Team) (2005) Early Impacts of SureStart Local Programmes on Children and Families. *SureStart Report 13.* London: DfES

Perfect, T.J., Wagstaff, G.F., Moore, D., Andrews, B., Cleveland, V., Newcombe, S., Brisbane, K.A. and Brown, L. (2008) How can we help witnesses to remember more? It's an (eyes) open and shut case. *Law and Human Behaviour, 32*(4), 314–324.

Rosenhan, D. (1969) Some origins of concerns for others. In P. H. Mussen, J. Langer, and M. Covington (eds) *Trends and Issues in Developmental Psychology.* New York: Holt, Rinehart and Winston, pp.134–153.

Tollenaar, M.S., Elzinga, B.M., Spinhoven, P. and Everaerd, W.A.M. (2008) The effects of cortisol increase on long-term memory retrieval during and after acute psychosocial stress. *Acta Psychologica, 127,* 542–552.